THE RUNNING SKY

Tim Dee

The Running Sky

A Birdwatching Life

JONATHAN CAPE
LONDON

Published by Jonathan Cape

4 6 8 10 9 7 5 3

Copyright © Tim Dee 2009

Tim Dee has asserted his right under the Copyright,
Designs and Patents Act 1988 to be identified as the author of this work

The author and the publisher have made every effort to trace the holders of copyright
in quotations. Any inadvertent omissions or errors may be corrected in future editions.

First published in Great Britain in 2009 by
Jonathan Cape
Random House, 20 Vauxhall Bridge Road,
London SW1V 2SA

www.rbooks.co.uk

Addresses for companies within The Random House Group Limited can be found at:
www.randomhouse.co.uk/offices.htm

The Random House Group Limited Reg. No. 954009

A CIP catalogue record for this book is available from the British Library

ISBN 9780224081986

The Random House Group Limited supports The Forest Stewardship
Council (FSC), the leading international forest certification organisation.
All our titles that are printed on Greenpeace approved FSC certified paper carry the
FSC logo. Our paper procurement policy can be found at:
www.rbooks.co.uk/environment

Typeset in Jenson by Palimpsest Book Production Limited,
Grangemouth, Stirlingshire

Printed and bound in Great Britain by
CPI Mackays, Chatham, Kent ME5 8TD

Contents

Introduction – Flying 1

June 6

July 22

August 44

September 53

October 75

November 102

December 120

January 137

February 157

March 169

April 186

May 206

Afterword – Singing 229

Notes and References 234

Acknowledgements 253

For my parents and for my children.

If hands could free you, heart,
Where would you fly?
Far, beyond every part
Of earth this running sky
Makes desolate?

Philip Larkin

Introduction – Flying

> ... these were the first words
> We spread to lure the birds that nested in our day ...
>
> Louis MacNeice

The first bird I can remember watching flew through the garden of the house where I was born.

It was summer. I had just had my third birthday. I was pulling my red wooden train on its string; the train driver with his blue cap swayed a little, because the grass beneath was bumpy. We were in the back part of the big garden of the house – it was called Acresfield – on the outskirts of Liverpool. I steered carefully because we were going along a thin strip between furrows of turned soil where the old man who lived in the flat above us grew his vegetables. I concentrated to make sure that the train followed me and the driver – he had a column of blue painted wood instead of legs – didn't wobble too much, topple over and roll from the train.

I heard shouting and I looked towards the noise: far across the wide lawn beyond the vegetable patch, the old man was leaning out of an open window and waving his arms like a bear. A year or so later when I met Mr McGregor in *The Tale of Peter Rabbit* I knew him already. The man at the window seemed too far away to be real, and though his voice must have been loud and angry, it grew thin and fell towards the lawn. But he was shouting at me and I didn't like it. It was too much. I had to drop the string, abandon the train and driver, and flee.

I looked up for my mother, who was somewhere in the garden, and headed for the greenhouse at the edge of the vegetable patch. The path bulged around a water butt; I followed it and kept going towards a wide black space of dark, the opening of the garden shed. From behind me, over my head as I moved towards the dark, came a bird. It pulled up into the dusty black rectangle of the open doorway and disappeared inside. It was showing me the way. I followed it.

In the sunshine, the space seemed to be hung with a black curtain. I walked through it; the air cooled and the noises dimmed. The throat-catching smell of warm creosote came. Everything was still. My eyes liked the bandage of the dark. Then, with a suddenness that made me gasp, the swallow was there and gone, diving back into the bright. It called once as it left, its buzzing twitter like an electrical spark. I looked up through the murk and saw on a crossbeam a little mud pie with tiny sticks of straw poking from it. I forgot my train and the shouting.

That afternoon my father took me back to the shed so I could peer into the nest. Again, as we stepped into the dark, the swallow slipped over us; it was so close I could feel the air rub against me. On my father's shoulders I raised my arms towards the nest, slowing and softening my reach as I felt for the bumpy balls of mud and the prickly stems. There were no young birds, or even any eggs yet. I couldn't see into the cup, but let my fingers creep over its rim, feeling the smoothed lip and the feathers lining the tiny bowl. It was warm.

Some days later, I went to the shed but found it empty. On the hard ribbed concrete floor was a square mess of baby swallow, a miniature hooked beak, downy balding feathers, raised but useless open wings, dead half-meat beneath thin bat-skin.

I remember just these two scenes – one of calm and one of horror. I didn't see the birds fledge any young; I had no concept of their departure. But I became a birdwatcher that summer. The swallows, their flight, their music, their stopped moments perched on wires or incubating their eggs, their nest – all this was somehow laid deep inside me, like iron in my blood, so that no swallow after Acresfield has been my first, but all swallows since have joined that bird appearing above me and flying on ahead.

I have watched more than forty swallow springs and forty swallow autumns since that pair and their nest in the shed. All that time, I have lived my life under birds and I cannot remember a single birdless day. I have felt birds' rhythms answering mine, like a heartbeat or a stride, like a cuckoo's *cuckoo*. Birds come and go, they fly and land, they sing and call, they breed and die. Now, and then again. Locally they can get lost, sicken, go wrong or be late, but birds fit the world, they are apt and at home in it. What they do and how they do it, the same over and over, gives their lives alongside ours an expression or a pattern in the air, that can seem like art or ritual, as if they are deeper in the world than us, more joined to it, as we might dream it only. We have broken from nature, fallen from the earth, put ourselves beyond it, but nature, ever forgiving, comes towards us, makes repairs to the damage we have done. The swallow returns and builds a nest. Birds begin and end beyond us, out of reach and outside our thought, and we see them doing things apparently without feeling or thinking, but – and because of this – they make us think and feel.

I try to do both in these pages. This book is written from a life with birds but follows a single year of them, from one summer to the next; it begins with nests and eggs and chicks on the sea cliffs of Shetland, and it ends, a year later, with nests, eggs and chicks in the holes of an oak wood on Exmoor. I wrote it over such a year but I put into it many summers, many swallows.

I saw everything that happens in the chapters that follow – there are common birds as well as rarities and spectacles and remote terrain – but most of what is really my birdwatching isn't spelt out here, though it lies at the heart of this book. It is a birdwatching best explained by invoking the birds I am hardly aware of watching – the birds that are all around me, seen but not really noticed, there only in the corner of my eye, the pigeons and sparrows of the city. My day lists of birds usually stop with those species plus a gull or two. In some senses this book is about trying to make myself look at the pigeons, to go beyond simply noting them, to look at these birds (and so all birds) and see them as if for the first time but with eyes informed by years of seeing, to capture life looking at life.

As a teenager I was hard-core and obsessed, but I am not a professional bird-man now. I am not very sharp in the field. I misidentify birds and get bored and eat my packed lunch at half past ten in the morning. I do not want to fly, I am scared of heights, my palms sweat before every take-off. I am allergic to feathers too, and sleep under polyester rather than goose down. In other words, my birds are mostly the same as everyone else's, my basic birdwatching no different from that of most watchers of birds. But I fell in with birds early and I fell in deeply, and ever since then I have kept a kind of company that has taken me beyond birdwatching, back somehow to the pigeons and sparrows and that swallow at Acresfield, forward somehow to impossibly shared lives.

Here at the fountain's sliding foot,
Or at some fruit-tree's mossy root,
Casting the body's vest aside,
My soul into the boughs does glide:
There like a bird it sits, and sings,
Then whets, and combs its silver wings;
And, till prepared for longer flight,
Waves in its plumes the various light.

Andrew Marvell

June

I will sing of the white birds
In the blue waters of heaven,
The clouds that are spray to its sea.

Ezra Pound

The seagull has no English.

David Thomson

I t is hard to sleep under a northern summer night. At midsummer in Shetland rain galloped on the roof. Outside, arctic terns and blackbirds kept up their noises through the early hours, a troubling mix of scream and serenade, harangue and consolation. I woke again and again to a pared-back half-light – like a prisoner's memory of day – my broken sleep crowded with thoughts of an impossible project.

I had the task of launching into the sky all the seabirds from all the cliffs of Shetland: the shags and razorbills from the boulders at the sea edge, the guillemots and kittiwakes from the open faces of rock, the gannets from their shanty towns along ridge backs and fault lines, the fulmars from the tussocked *neuks* below the cliff lip, and the puffins from their burrows in the turf on the top. It was hopeless: no sooner had I flushed one wheel of puffins over the edge than a gannet banked close to its nest and landed; kittiwakes dusted off in a cloud of bleached white, but guillemots flickered back, chocolate and cream; razorbills came, shags went.

Watching a seabird colony from a Shetland cliff top is not so different from my Shetland dream, except the birds resolve what my sleep couldn't. Looking down and out to sea from the cliff edge at Hermaness or the Noup of Noss, you find yourself dizzyingly, exhilaratingly, in the middle of a performance. Through every summer and for as long as the devastated seas can feed them, the wheels and flights of birds from their cliff places out over the sea and back again will continue. No one could get there before it started, and everyone will leave before it ends.

Without colliding, without even appearing to adjust their flying to avoid one another, thousands of birds are perpetually in flight. There are clouds of birds, there are wheels of birds, birds alone joining groups, other bird parties breaking up, birds landing, birds taking off, a line of shags heading out to sea, a line of guillemots rising to a cliff ledge, a carousel of puffins that collects and deposits participants on each, always anti-clockwise, rotation, gannets singly and in tiers, beating away from the cliff, fulmars spreadeagled on landing attempts and forced back into the air by irate neighbours. My eyes cannot stay on any one bird for more than a second or two; always another comes between me and the bird I am watching, always another flies behind it. I reach for words: it is a city, a metropolis, a theatre, a cloud of gnats, Brownian motion, heaven, hell, space dust, bright stars in a dazzling universe – but nothing will do to describe the colony. The only true account would be the thing itself. And it would have to include time, space and sound. The colony is above me, below me, perched and in flight, far out, close to, huddled and singular, in burrows and beneath the waves. It begins with noise and smell, and ends with light and quiet.

I heard, and gagged on, the gannets at Hermaness before I

could see them. Low cloud smeared the rocks at Muckle Flugga and the nearer stacks. The thousands of nesting birds on them were hidden, but the rain from the north brought their fishy whiff in gobbets of stink, along with their homely rubbery conversation. Shafts of sunlight broke up the rain for moments and I saw patches of open sea beyond the shrouded stacks. In every patch at every moment there was a gannet dive. I have watched them plunge into the sea thousands of times before. Again and again they do the same thing to catch their food, but each dive shines. Nature's repetitions are never boring. Every time it is like witnessing a fresh marvel in a new world: their visible decision-making, with its corrective twisting and corkscrewing, the rapid origami of themselves, and then their brilliant white match strikes, fizzing into the water at 60 mph to leave puffs of lit sea spray. It is hard not to blink and hold your breath as they go in. Against the hubbub of wind and rain and puffin coo and gannet vibrato, it was impossible to hear them break through the sea, but the splash they make looks exactly like a sound and I found myself adding it to the ruckus.

From the cliff top I could see how the bubbling blue turbulence made by the brilliance of their dives traps the shape the gannet forms underwater. The diver pulls away and surfaces with or without a fish, but the cast of its plunge seethes like a tight net of ice just below the point where the gannet went in. It is rare for a bird to leave evidence, even fleetingly, of how it has moved through the world. It reminded me of the X-ray print a collared dove left of itself on a window at home in Bristol when I was a boy. The dove misjudged its flight from the bird table and briefly crashed into the glass. A ghost trace of its raised wings was printed onto the pane by the oil and dust of its feathers. It looked religious and medical: an annunciation and the scan of a single flap. The dove continued to come to the bird table and for weeks, it and its flight print could be seen together, one through the other. The ghost lasted all summer, visible only when the sun was low, uncollectable, not even photographable, and I was sorry when the first heavy rain of autumn washed it away.

The rain at Hermaness had thinned. I could see further. The gannets pulled up to the surface of the sea after their dives with a bucking torpedo energy. Every one I watched had to break out of a caul of water that their dive had thrown around them. They were hatching from the sea. I followed one bird dive and surface and take off, running along the sea to get airborne. I tried to track it back to the stacks but lost it in the mind-wiping swirl of birds.

To see vast numbers of birds in silent movement is beautifully strange. In this crowd of so many moving things, the eye leaps constantly from individuals to the whole event. These are not flocks but countless single birds caught in a storm of life. Individuals fly fast but the ensemble seems to be moving at dream speed. The rush of the single bird somehow slows in the crowd. I cannot focus for long on a puffin with its hurrying wings in the wheeling cloud; instead I see a tumbleweed of birds rolling out from their grassed lawns and terraces over a gulf of air, a slow-motion collective rotation. Its drift reminds me of the paper mobiles suspended over my infant children's beds that were blown above them through the night by their sleeping breath.

The noise of the cliff and the sea's moan down below is also silenced by these flights. On the ledges, I can see the auks jabbering and the gannets fretting. Nearer to me, fulmars *ack ack* and puffins are busy with their matronly growls. But the flying wheels and lines of birds move with a filtered quiet. They are silent in flight. I can hear only the whicker of the nearest puffins' wings.

The gannet at sea and the gannet on its nest are hard to

9

grasp as the same bird. In the air they move like great white flying shelves. They never touch one another. But they must pair and breed and live within a beak-jab of others in a teeming midden glued to a dripping rock. They squabble and moan. Their nests are huge bleached thatches built up over years, each merging into another, all held together with string and other irresistible rubbish the birds have collected at sea. They look like the nests of sea-storks; guillemots, like house sparrows sheltering beneath storks' nests in Spain, breed underneath the gannet's eaves. Who would call the gannet the scrap merchant of the ocean or its binman? But it is. A shag's nest, for all its putrid reek, is a far more organic affair. One gannet's nest has a blue plastic carrier bag carefully woven into its seaweed heart; another has a length of blue marine rope hanging down like a bell pull, and gannet neighbours occasionally lean across and tug it, as part of the continuing neighbourhood battles over living space and furniture.

The sharp angles of the gannets' wings and beaks do half their territorial fighting. Their non-song does the rest. At sea, singing, talking, arguing, speaking of any kind has very little place in bird life. A gannet's face is silent. But on its nest it finds some half-aggressive half-soothing noise in its throat, an elasticated gurgle which works for love song and battle hymn.

Bonxies, or great skuas, which breed over the moor behind the cliffs at Hermaness and on Noss, have an even more comically bathetic voice. 'Bunksie' means thickset in Norse and perfectly suggests their cunning – their business is the piratical harrying of other birds – and the heft of the meaty ballast they seem to carry. They are dog-food brown, the size of a fat buzzard. In the air they are heavyweight bullies who behave like doormen to their own club, but on the ground they look dim and lumpen, and there is something of a leftover dodo about them. Some call with a baby-gargle *gu gu gu gu gu gu gu gu*; others manage a caveman *ug ug ug ug ug ug ug*.

I spotted three bonxies coming in off the sea at Hermaness. As they reached the beginnings of their breeding moor of bog, they raised their wings simultaneously into deep Vs and held them up for a few seconds. Then they came closer and they let off an *ug ug*, and I thought of the sea-world they had come from and the land-world they had returned to.

We want birds to be wild and free, but we bring our ideas of them indoors – into our houses or into our minds – and we domesticate them there. Defining the skua calls as baby talk and seeing their wings as heraldic was not enough. In my grand-mother's house, in the shadow of a chocolate factory at Keynsham outside Bristol, three ceramic drake mallards lived in permanent flight up the wall of the front room, their raised wings like those of the bonxies. But what could be less wild than those china ducks? To see a gannet stealing string from a neighbour, or a bonxie clucking at its babies? To know the seasonally grounded lives of these great maritime heroes, that they must land and coddle their eggs and sweet-talk their young, ought to stretch our mind. The bonxie isn't just the oceanic corsair, the gannet not just the fisher king. 'Wild' does not describe nearly enough about the lives of these or any birds.

Puffins confound us too. They come stooping out of their burrows like badgers and stroll at a post-prandial pace through the shivering pink thrift of their front gardens. On the cliff top they seem at a kind of leisure. For a few sun-driven days of the year they are happy to walk with grass stems in their rainbow beaks. They dig tunnels, garden their lawns, take up flower arranging and live like northern bowerbirds. They dance and croon and preen and kiss their lovers. They gurn at their rivals and joust with their multicoloured bills. It is hard not to laugh.

Then the puffins fly out over the cliff edge, joining a rippling flex of themselves, and are taken utterly from the world we think we share with them. At every moment some slip from the turf and are shaken out over the great arena of air and sea, forming and yet always joining a spiral of puffins that rolls along the cliff. Sometimes a bonxie or a great black-backed gull drifts close to their burrows and a mass panic ensues; at other times, as some puffins land, new birds simply go. Their launches are briefly clumsy: a miniature badger is taking off. But once they are drawn up into their torqued spiral, their flight is superb. On any one wheel, all the available puffins are lifted and spun centrifugally in a continuous circuit three hundred feet across and a hundred feet deep. There are maybe four hundred birds all rotating in the same direction. What function these spirals have is hard to know – the strategic befuddlement of predators perhaps, but it could just as well be a way of reducing collisions on departure, or practice for their whirring-parrot flight, or – dare I say it – simply fun.

I sat on the cliff top at Noss watching the endless, soothing helix of puffins. By turn I resisted and succumbed to mapping the birds' world onto mine. The puffin on the grass at its nest is where we live; the puffin in the air is where we dream. We see the standing bird as substantial; it has two feet like us on the ground. The flying bird, by contrast, is transitory and adventuring. Flight thrills us because it suggests the weightlessness we cannot achieve but also the freedom of mind that we can. I was scribbling this in my notebook until a splash of egg yolk-yellow puffin shit from a passing wheel-rider put a dribbling full stop to my thoughts. It is still there now, like the Shetland sun pressed into my page.

I rested my eyes and watched the sea and then, suddenly yet dreamily slow, great fins came breaking through the water about half a mile off the Noup. A family party of five killer whales was crossing the mouth of the wide bay where the seabirds crowded. Their blows – the outbreath of their lungs – caught in a sparkle of sunshine. They brought up the wet of the deep on their backs and showed it to the sky and the auks and the gannets and me. Then they rolled forward like dark planets bowled under the sea. I tried to follow them beneath the water, trying to feel their rhythm, the whale road, so that I could predict when and where they would surface next. I got it wrong every time.

I walked back around the cliff edge, chasing the whales, stopping to look when their fins came cartwheeling. The day seemed brighter still. The sea rose in the sunlight and smelt and sang. The whales went quietly through it, intent only on their swim. I felt like a bystander behind a stage, glimpsing the backs of the main act; or as if I was beneath a huge loom where the great skin of the sea was being stretched over my head, the whales passing from one side of it to the other; or like my five-year-old self, woken in the night, sitting in my pyjamas, unseen at the top of the stairs, with my parents and their friends partying below me, laughing and drinking and dancing.

I was watching the sea, waiting for the whales, when something blurry and close crossed busily in front of me. I lowered my binoculars. A tiny earth-brown wren had come up from a narrow crevice splitting the turf at the cliff edge. It flew, calling over the grass and the thrift. Encouraged by the call, another appeared, climbing into the air with less attack than the first. It cheeped and I realised that this was a first flight, a first appearance even, out from the crack in the cliff and the nest where the fledgling had hatched. In a bumblebee whirr, it got itself about five feet off the ground, then turned and flew head-on at me. I expected it to divert and wobble after the adult, but it came nearer and nearer until it was at my shoulder and the whirring and cheeping stopped and it half clung, half perched to the strap of my rucksack. It was four inches from my face. It held on for a few seconds then flew off towards its parent, who answered its calls from a stone wall. For those seconds I had been the fledgling's wall. An indifferent wren at four inches and indifferent killer whales at a mile. The world was good and it didn't need me.

It was midsummer's eve. After this day of bright Shetland light, of puffins, gannets, wrens and whales, I went night-fishing with storm petrels, waiting for that same light to fade enough so that birds might come from the sea and bury themselves in the land.

Proper night lies off to the south. For weeks around the longest day, Shetland dims but never truly darkens. Though it had rained for almost all of my stay and the sun was still towelled by cloud, a silvery light, like developing fluid, lapped down and the islands were floodlit. The time of day or the weather hardly mattered. It was wet but it was light; it was night but it was light.

At eleven o'clock in that night-that-is-not, I waited with some other birdwatchers for a boat to Mousa. The small island to the east of the Shetland Mainland was still lit, golden and warm in the low light, with its ancient Pictish stone broch looking like a tower of honey. It was built two thousand years ago to guard the sound and looks like a squat lighthouse or the cooling tower of an ancient power station. For the petrels to come, the broch must be treacle-black.

A blackbird sang from the twisted fingers of a sycamore in a walled garden next to the sea. That night, with a handful of others through Shetland, these blackbird singers would be the last of their kind singing in Britain. Long after the rest of Europe sleeps, sounds of a suburban summer come from a few wizened northern trees. Elsewhere the blackbird's evening song is a fruited lullaby, but here there was no winding-down to the dark, no last good-night kiss. The blackbird sang like this at three in the afternoon, and it will gather its black cape of feathers and open its crocus beak into exquisite song all over again at two in the morning.

Further north it is even brighter. When I was nineteen, I spent midsummer's night with a girlfriend at Bodø on the Norwegian coast, seven degrees above Shetland and within the Arctic Circle. We had been arguing on the train north. There was next to no money left in our kitty and the loaf of bread we had bought in Copenhagen was finished. Why, Zoë asked, had I insisted we go so far? Just before midnight we climbed a hill, not speaking to one another. We sat on a boulder with a peeling elbow of orange lichen and looked out over the flaming sea. The sun swung low in the sky and hung there. Something in us calmed. To watch the last moments of a sunset and feel our world rolling away from the light is the most obvious evidence of the spinning earth. But here, on the hill, there was no setting sun, and so it seemed that time had slowed. The birds knew it too. There were redwings singing. These were my winter thrushes, the birds that I had heard calling *seep* to one another, flying over me in the dark as I made my way home from Zoë's house through the streets of Bristol in February. As I walked north under their southbound flights, their calls threw a drift net of pinprick coordinates over me. Before Bodø I had never heard them say more than *seep*. Now from the dwarf birches just below the crest of the hill two males sang an evening song, unwinding, fluting and sad. As we watched the sun idle for thirty minutes, they fell silent. Then, knowing as we did that it was time to stand up and start the next day, they sang a dawn song, tightening, perky and assertive. The sun followed and pulled up through the peach sky it had made. The redwings' night was done in half an hour of bright light. Zoë and I walked down the hill happy and restored.

Around midnight on Mousa in June, the sun has gone below the horizon and its light is turbaned enough for the storm petrels to come to their nests. We crossed the sound to the island in an open boat. The ferryman in his sailor's cap led us from the jetty along the shore, though the path was clear to see. In the stretching twilight we arrived at the broch and stood peering up at its darkening bulk, not certain what to expect. I stooped under the low lintel of the sea-facing entrance and through the six-foot-thick walls. Inside, the roof had gone and it was like standing in the hearth of an old chimney rising to the night sky. Between the outer and inner dry-stone walls, a stone stairway spiralled to the top. I began to feel my way up and had climbed ten stairs when I heard the first of the petrels singing. I stopped. In an instant night had fallen.

Storm petrel song is the strangest of music. The birds breed in tiny chinks between the stones of the broch, and from its curving wall came a squeaky skirl as if the stones were being rubbed together. A second petrel made a start-up burp a few feet away, and then another, though it was hard to tell where the sounds were coming from or to imagine how a bird was making them. I stood in the dark on the spiral stone stairs, listening to rock music inside a giant's ear.

All night birds' night songs sound ancient, weird and dark: the reels of grasshopper warblers, the grunts of woodcock, owl yelps, corncrake rasps, nightjar churrs, even the tearing-apart music of nightingales. They come up from a very old earth: the word chthonic manages to look how they sound as well as describing what they are. The storm petrels' song is even weirder: a furry pulse from the back of a tiny throat hidden in a crack in a rock. It is an inward and sibylline sound of swazzle notes and speaking stones. It giggles and rewinds. It clucks and purrs. It sounds like a simultaneous possession and exorcism. It is a noise reserved for the night and the deeper dark of the petrels' nesting holes. It would be unimaginable in daylight and inaudible over even the quietest of seas. It defines the deep contrariness of the midsummer storm petrel.

Shrunken birds, storm petrels are little larger than house martins and superficially similar: their flight is buoyant and they have black backs and a white rump. In the vast space of the sea, they are so small they are very hard to find. Only after hours of looking, when crossing the Bay of Biscay once on a huge ferry, was I able to spot some petrels like particles of fluff pulling their tiny bodies through the troughs of the sea far below me. But at sea, the neighbours of fin whales and sunfish, the petrels live far more happily than on land. Like midget puppet-masters, they seem to hold themselves at a constant height above the water, as if pulling its waves into tides. They are so slight that the sea appears unable to hurt them. They fleetingly dip down to patter their black webbed feet on the sea, tiptoeing over the swell, giving it the gentlest of massages, walking on the water. And from this pattering miracle, and St Peter who did it too, they take their name.

Away from the sea they are disastrous. Seabirds blown onshore or inland are called 'wrecks' by birdwatchers. And so they are. In the spring of 1850 a boy caught a moribund black-capped petrel that he saw 'flapping for some time from one furze-bush to another' at South Acre, near Swaffham in Norfolk; 'exhausted as it was, it had strength enough remaining to bite violently the hand of its captor, who thereupon killed it.' The bird was skinned and stuffed and until 1984, when a corpse washed up in Yorkshire, was the sole British record of this oceanic petrel that breeds on Hispaniola but prefers the pelagic life, far out in the Atlantic. In December 1999, forty storm petrels caught up in vile weather (including birds ringed on Fair Isle in

Shetland and Skomer in Pembrokeshire) were forcibly displaced from the Atlantic to the Jura Mountains in Switzerland. Try to imagine their journey. At the end of October 1952 more than two thousand Leach's storm petrels were funnelled into Bridgwater Bay in the Bristol Channel and wrecked there, half of them dead. I saw my first storm petrel in September 1977 in the same place, on the miserable brown shore of Steart, fogged by the stench of the chicken sheds that cluster at the beach. A broken and blasted bird, its compass shot by the great wrath of a western gale, it tottered on the tidal mudflats, looking like a cripple whose sticks had been snatched away. The bird that can walk on the water is lost on land.

The broch at Mousa is only fifty feet from the shore. We stood around it in a ring and waited. Eventually, black noise from the dark tower coaxed black things from the dark sea. A first bird appeared a few feet above my head and was gone in a pixie bat flap. It flickered and jerked around the tower, as if it was being projected onto it in a damaged home movie. Another bird came and then another. They seemed to rush at the broch, reeled towards it on invisible threads.

The petrels seek a specific crack; some cracks sing and others are silent. The arriving birds are quiet but for their flutter. Can the incomers identify a mate's song – the squashed yodel that they need – among all the hiccups and space noise? Do both sexes call like this? Will the singer leave when the wanderer returns?

Petrels move over the land as though it is repellent to them. Their flight suggests that this necessary short journey from the sea to the shore is forever disorienting. Some find the hole they are looking for right away and scramble in; others begin to spool around the tower, some bashing into the wall and crash-landing, or selecting the wrong hole and falling back down the side of the broch. Two birds collided at a single hole, squeaked and scuffled, and one of them tumbled to the ground at my feet. As I reached down, it spread its wings into the springy turf and managed to launch itself back into the swirl. Another brushed so close to my left shoulder that I could feel its wing beat, a tiny push of air in my ear. I began to smell them. Squid and salt.

Of the birds I could see, most were being pulled to the broch and its sooty night light, but others seemed to be circling it more widely. Were these the birds that had swapped egg duties and had come out from the tower? Three days is the average storm petrel incubation shift. Three days in a damp black crevice. Then, after a rhapsody of squeaks, they tumble into the dark night air, towards the sea and quiet. A midnight flit.

I sat down on a boulder at the edge of the beach. A petrel churred from beneath me. Much of the island was noisy with them. There are six thousand pairs here. The beach snickered and the field walls coughed dry scratchy tunes. I joined the line of birdwatchers and we walked back to the boat along a purring shore. About one in the morning the dark began to ease, and tomorrow yawned awake before we had gone to bed. At five past two, back on the Mainland the blackbirds were singing again. Another black bird, a different midsummer's night dream.

Driving in rain the next day, I stopped at the oil terminal at Sullom Voe. Various hard-core birding friends and acquaintances had travelled to Shetland to work on its construction in the late 1970s. The money for labouring was good, there was little to spend it on and there were wonderful birds – especially for southern birdwatchers – to see. Snowy owls bred on Fetlar, the lone black-browed albatross was still trying its luck with the gannets at Hermaness. Both have gone now, having failed to make their way, and these days, although the terminal still serves as a landfall for much of the ebbing North Sea oil, the place seems near ruined. It has the feel of Eastern Europe and the militarised Soviet world, when rust took charge in the 1980s.

After Mousa broch and its singing stones, I was struck by the weariness of the terminal's buildings. The crumbling sign at the abandoned gatehouse reads 'Su l m Voe Ter in l' and I couldn't get 'petrol' and 'petrel' out of my head: black stuff coming out of the sea, one exhausted within a human generation, another living on in a two-thousand-year-old tower block.

Leaving Shetland the next day, sitting on the runway at Sumburgh Airport, my mind roved towards these thoughts and away from them, accompanying my sweating palms (my fear of flying) and my squinting at the gulls over the Pool of Virkie and the terns above the pier at Grutness. We took off south over a churning sea, past Fair Isle and Orkney. I read some of David Thomson's extraordinary book *The People of the Sea*, with its seal myths and stories of meetings of seals and men and how these survived in Britain and Ireland into the twentieth century. Midsummer, or St John's Eve, was one of these times when seals turned into men and women. I thought of the seals and the whales and the seabirds below and felt gloomy about our separation.

Then I fell into conversation with my neighbour, the friendly manager of a new supermarket in Lerwick. He told me of his banana problem. We have become a nation hooked on bananas; but bananas on northern islands are not easy. Their usual lifespan on a supermarket shelf is only two days. They arrive refrigerated from the tropics in a state of arrested development. Opening the box they have travelled in releases a ripening agent, but from that point the clock ticks fast on their saleability. A banana reaching Shetland would have to be sold the day it arrives and this is too risky for the supermarkets, given the bucking seas that surround the islands and hamper shipping. Therefore Shetland will have the only bananas in Tesco's Britain that will ripen without assistance.

Once, on another Scottish island at a low tide, I had watched a seal curl its head and feet-flippers into a grey smile that looked like a ripe banana. Hispaniola – Haiti and the Dominican Republic – grows some of the bananas that we eat in Britain, and somehow in 1850 an unrefrigerated black-capped petrel had got from that island's tropical slopes to a gorse bush in Norfolk. Meanwhile, in transit at sea that day, beneath me and the man from Tesco, were the storm petrels that had been released from their egg-ripening duties on Mousa. Somehow these birds and those that had swapped places with them at midnight, and their as yet unhatched chicks, would all be flying to the South Atlantic in a few weeks on their six-inch wings.

July

The full moon glided on behind a black cloud. And what then? And who cared?

Samuel Taylor Coleridge

Rusham Road, 6–7.15 a.m. one thrush hammering away at one triple cry, message or whatever anyone else likes.

Edward Thomas

Every day of birdwatching is different. I have been to Wicken Fen many times, but this evening in early July it felt more landlocked than ever before. Though only a few dozen miles from the North Sea, a warm wind blew across the flat plain of marsh and copse as if from an open oven and pushed baked dust, pollen, insects and seeds into the corners of my eyes, my ears and my lips.

Towards dusk, I walked from the fen into a wood of young willows. Cuckoo-spit dripped onto me from the peaked froths of beaten egg-white that smeared the joints of the twigs and branches. The spit was heavier than rain, gummier. The droplets made a soft *silp* sound as they landed. I could hear the whole copse thickening with spit.

The floor of the wood was carpeted with the drifting down of willow seeds and their fine-spun woollen nests. Spiders' webs that had trapped the down looked like Halloween versions of themselves. The wool and the spit. It was like putting on a wet pullover on a hot day.

A cuckoo at the edge of the trees and another down a ride started cuckooing. They turned their heads and threw their voices. The fen was deepened still further. The calls seemed to have arrived from far away in time and space. Each cuckoo apparently held a mirror that sent its rival's call back, thwarted. They sounded dusty and muffled, coming as if being blown, as Gerard Manley Hopkins described them, through 'a big humming ewer'.

It made for a claustrophobic broth – the cuckoos, cuckoo-spit and summer snow – and it drove me back out onto the fen, where it was easier to breathe. The heat was fading and the sky was opening upwards. The day lived on in the clearer upper air and light. Swifts and swallows were cleaning it by dabbing at its insects. They sang as they flew. The swallows' garrulous static rippled as if the birds were mediums channelling the sounds of the sky. Higher up, the swifts screamed their mastery of flight into ecstatic shouts.

I walked through the fen, waiting for it to get darker. The day was reluctant to finish. Two common terns made last flights above the reedy mere, white as ice cubes against the green. In a hedge along a dyke, bullfinches piped their embarrassed music, their soft calls of bloodied regret escaping over their blood-red breasts. Sleepy cormorants flew into the heronry in a tall alder beyond the mere. Their ragged wings, black with a used sheen like an old man's suit, made gashes in the spreading shambolic tree.

The light slipped higher and the darkness rose. A minute before, the low sun had picked out individual stems of the reeds; now, they massed into bigger and bigger plots of dark. A little egret floated to its roost, through the swallow's air and towards the setting sun. It looked like a flying lantern that had trapped light in its brilliant phosphor-white feathers and spilt it into the darkening sky as it flew; just as you sometimes see the golden pin of an aeroplane high overhead still bright long after such colours have drained from the earth. As the egret sailed away, a thirty-year-old thrill and relief at having seen my first in Britain came back to me. As a teenage rarity-hunter, I had taken a complicated journey by bike, train, bus, and several miles on foot, before a distant hunched white sheet on the edge of a marsh near Portsmouth came into view. The egret's white was then a colour not known in Britain.

Below the egret at Wicken was its antithesis. A hidden bird began making a noise like a small mechanical pump. The singing grasshopper warbler sounded as if it was drawing more and more dark up to the surface of the fen. Others have heard a sewing machine, a spinning wheel or a fisherman's winding line in its insect stridulation, but for me the grasshopper warbler's song is the silvery breath of the earth itself, its dark warmth expressed as a reeling drone at the end of the day.

The crepuscular and hidden habits of these birds tie them to a few inches of life just above the wet soil of the world. Inconspicuously drab and streaked olive-brown and buff, they are like a colour chart of the time of day they sing in, the thinning tones and lost pigments of dusk and night, and of the habitat they live in, their winters buried in the grasslands of Senegal, their summers hiding in the reeds of Wicken and their night flights of migration between. You must catch a grasshopper warbler whilst you can. I might only have a handful of summers left when I can still hear them. They are lost to my father; their song is now beyond his hearing range. If you haven't heard one before you are fifty you may never. Seeing them is no easier. They are in Britain just for a few weeks each summer. They are invisible during their silent daytimes at the bottom of a reed bed or scrubby ditch. They often start singing only in the last minutes of light; and when they sing they are usually hidden.

At Wicken two birds sang, the near male in purring battle with a neighbouring one, both hidden, to define and contest the invisible boundary of their territories and to attract an invisible mate. As I listened, the lyrics of Steely Dan's 'Reelin' in the Years' came to me ('Your everlasting summer/You can see it fading fast/So you grab a piece of something/That you think is gonna last') and I thought that here, in this bird that seems to be spooling time with its dancing reel played out and wound in again, was proof of Keats's line that 'the poetry of earth is never dead'. The grasshopper warbler's song comes up out of the earth just as you think the day is quietening down. It has no prelude or warm-up: it starts mid-performance, as if switched on by the dark, as if it had been singing like this beneath the earth until it was dark enough to come to the surface. As if, though we hardly hear it, this singing never stops. The near bird fell silent but the answering male continued across the fen. I waited and stared through my binoculars at the murk of reeds and bushes, but I couldn't see either. The singing continued. The night shift had begun.

I retraced my steps to the dripping willows. Night had all but fallen and there was no colour left on the fen. The dark blue of the sky above the copse had deepened to a velvet stage curtain, and across it was flying a woodcock. He came with the kerfuffle of a Dickensian clerk, hunched and wheezing and crabbed. He looked more as though he was carrying a heavy ledger up Threadneedle Street. It was hard to think that he was in the thick of a sex dance. Against the sky I couldn't make out any colours on the bird, but saw a cut-out shadow puppet with rounded wings, a round thickset head and a long bill angled to the ground. The puppet made a strange jumpy progress and rocked from side to side, a bird manoeuvred on sticks or hoist aloft and held up there by some force – an evening gas perhaps, or a will-o'-the-wisp that had risen from beneath him out of the same wet marsh soil that he lives in, and which had pushed him skywards like an accidental balloon. But go up he must and, above the ride cut through the willows, the woodcock rodes.

As with much else about it, the woodcock has this word – *roding* – to itself. Other birds display during the breeding season at dawn or dusk; the woodcock, alone, rodes. The word seems to come from the old practice of trapping woodcocks by setting a net within a wood along 'cockeroades'.

The bird above me made little *hisp* noises, almost under its breath, like the drip of the cuckoo-spit, and then an even quieter, rather filthy, wormy grunt which transformed it into a flying pig and reminded me of its ties to the soil and leaf-mould where it lives for the rest of its life. These two noises, a snore and a sneeze, are the bird's roding song (an ornithological textbook transcribes it as 'quorr quorr-quoroPIETZ . . . quorr quorr-quoroPIETZ'). Its piggish snuffle might also be the sound they make when their long straight snipe-like bills probe feelingly into the black mud, like a blind man's stick, reaching after worms, seeing in the dark. John Skelton in his poem 'Philip Sparrow' lists 'The woodcock with her long nose', and the *Handbook of the Birds of the World* describes the bill as 'rhynchokinetic'. The flexible tip of the wood-cock's upper mandible has been said more closely to resemble 'the writhings of a worm than a beak' and it uses its worm-beak to feast on a diet of worms, eating almost its own body weight in the course of a single day.

I have never seen a woodcock bend its beak, or eat a worm, or even on the ground at all – yet, the earth defines them absolutely. They feed in it, breed on it and are coloured like it. Flying, they seem broken from it. As if the brightness of day is anathema to them, they appear only when the sky grows earth-dark. Yet their odd limping display is a dance to be seen, and for all the woodcock's weirdness and my sense of them having been yanked from their preferred place, their roding flight is bewitching to watch. It manages to be alien to the bird and yet entirely consistent with it. Roding woodcock can also slow time. As I watched three birds going overhead, or one bird on three rodes of its territory, the fall of light was stalled by the slow rocking flight. Night waited for them as if, in some ancient ceremony, they were the ushers of dusk.

Eating a woodcock, as I did once, was like eating the earth. No wine has ever released its *terroir* to me as that bird did. It tasted like a prune. The bird's dark purple flesh crumbled on my plate like a dried worm cast and I knew that worms made its meat. I had held the bird in my hand before it was plucked and cooked among the white surfaces and steel utensils of a smart London kitchen. Its cryptic moth-wing colours were like a worn fireside rug. To hold its book of browns, the wings falling open on either side of its body, was to sense the humus of dead leaves mulched into a bird over thousands of years; the woodcock as a surviving fragment of an old earth, from a time when leaves became birds, branches grew wings and the dark moved. It shares this quality with only two other birds, I think: the wryneck, an aberrant woodpecker, and another night bird, the nightjar.

Unlike these two, and because it is tasty, the woodcock has been much hunted and much written about. As I write I am sipping a burgundy with a woodcock on its label, an earthy pinot noir from the Cave des Vignerons de Buxy in the Côte Chalonnaise. I browse the entry for woodcock, or *bécasse*, in the *Larousse Gastronomique*: 'its plumage is the colour of dead leaves; it has long been regarded as a delicacy'. I try to imagine tasting casserole of woodcock, or casserole of woodcock à la crème, or cold timbale of woodcock, or cold woodcock à la Diane ('pound the intestines with a knob of foie gras, a knob of butter, nutmeg and brandy'), or hot woodcock pâté à la Périgourdine, or roast woodcock on toast, or sautéed woodcock in Armagnac, or truffled roast woodcock, or woodcock casserole à la Périgourdine . . .

We roasted the woodcock I ate like a chicken. Plucking it sent a leaf-drift of earth into a steel sink. We bent its head beneath it and stuck its ivory bill through its thighs so it trussed itself into an avian pietà. I ate half its breast and a leg, and picked a ball of lead from my teeth.

I don't know where my woodcock came from, but the biographies of others, even from long ago, are readily assembled. We can put together the end of a bird's life in human words if not woodcock terms. In September 1465 a banquet for a new Archbishop of York called for 400 woodcocks (along with 2000 geese, 204 cranes, 4000 mallard and teal and 12 porpoises and seals). On 15 November 1523, Stephyn Percy was paid tuppence for bringing 'a Woodcocke, a grey Plour, and a Snype' to Hunstanton Hall in Norfolk. Gilbert White's Journal for 1 October 1777 records: 'Bright stars. This day, Mr. Richardson of Bramshot shot a woodcock: it was large & plump & a female: it lay in a Moorish piece of ground. The bird was sent to London, where as the porter carried it along the streets he was offered a guinea for it.' Alec Douglas-Home, writing in 1979, has an amazing tale to tell, worthy of a saloon bar or an after-dinner speech, or a second bottle from the Cave des Vignerons de Buxy: 'We were shooting above a railway cutting when I shot a high woodcock which fell into the tender of the Flying Scotsman. I just had time to signal to the driver as he flashed past, and he left the bird for me with his compliments with the station master at Berwick-on-Tweed.' Elsewhere freaks as well as flukes and feasts are recorded: 'In the year 1833, a Woodcock with white feathers in the wings was observed in a cover on the manor of Monkleigh, near Torrington, in the county of Devon. The same bird, or one of exactly the same plumage, reappeared in the same place during the four succeeding seasons, in which period it was so repeatedly shot at by different persons without effect, that it at last acquired among the country people the name of "the witch." In the year 1837, however, it was killed on the property of the Reverend J. T. Pine Coffin, of Portledge, who had the specimen preserved.' In eighteenth-century Cumberland, William Wordsworth hunted woodcocks as a child. The first memory he recounts in the celebrated passage in 'The Prelude' that begins: 'Fair seed-time had my soul, and I grew up/Foster'd alike by beauty and by fear . . .' is of trapping woodcocks (and later stealing other trappers' birds) and he describes getting close to them with an uncanny mimesis that replicates, at least in my mind, the woodcocks' stop-start walk. A walk I have never seen.

> . . . 'twas my joy
> To wander half the night among the Cliffs
> And the smooth Hollows, where the woodcocks ran
> Along the open turf. In thought and wish
> That time, my shoulder all with springes hung,
> I was a fell destroyer. On the heights
> Scudding away from snare to snare, I plied
> My anxious visitation, hurrying on,
> Still hurrying, hurrying onward; moon and stars
> Were shining o'er my head; I was alone
> And seem'd to be a trouble to the peace
> That was among them.

Roding is not the beginning and end of woodcock flights. The summer's reluctant flyer is actually a seasoned mover. Soft soil is vital for woodcocks, and the freezing woodland floors of northern Europe drive them into the autumn air towards the milder south and west. Most British woodcocks are sedentary, but it is a migratory bird for much of its range, and many thousand immigrants join ours each winter. Cornwall and the west of Ireland, where frost is rare, receive high numbers of northern birds. One February dusk I saw one drop hurriedly from the blasting Atlantic sky into a tiny garden of three or four stunted trees on Bryher on the Scilly Isles – about as far from the unending forests of the taiga as I could imagine. Gilbert White reports a great October fall of the birds on the same islands: 'some woodcocks settled in the street of St Mary's and ran into the houses and out-houses', and 'a Gent . . . shot and conveyed home, twenty-six couple, besides three couple which he wounded, but did not give himself the trouble to retrieve.' Think of them, limping there through the streets of St Mary's.

Woodcocks fly fast and direct on migration; so fast 'that a pane of plate-glass of an inch thick has been smashed by the contact, and one was actually impaled on the weather-cockof one of the churches in Ipswich'. Goldcrests – the smallest European bird – which share the northern forests with woodcocks, and likewise need to get out in winter, were once thought too tiny to manage flight for any distance and certainly not able to survive a crossing of the North Sea. They were imagined as woodcock-pilots, riding on the back of a brown and ochre flying carpet. Woodcocks themselves have long been thought to carry their own nestlings between their thighs, away from danger or to water. Many birdwatchers nowadays don't believe this, and today's textbooks turn up their rhynchokinetic noses. *The Birds of the Western Palearctic* is sceptical, recording a flushed female woodcock 'calling and apparently struggling to prop young between feet with depressed tail'.

Earlier authorities were more generous. Alec Douglas-Home is a staunch believer in the woodcock as porter: 'I have several times seen them flopping away with a chick gripped between the thighs, and once with chicks on the mother's back.' William Yarrell quotes several accounts: the brothers Stuart – 'she rose with him in her feet, her long legs dangling and swinging with her little burden like a parachute'; the late Mr St John and Mr John Hancock – 'the young bird was clasped between the thighs and pressed close up to the body of the parent'; Mr R. E. Reeves – 'the woodcock supported her young not only with her feet, but also with her bill pressed over the chick against her breast.' I imagine a woodcock Madonna and Child.

As a young birdwatcher my note-keeping swung from the baldest of logs and the most austere of lists, to winding prose paragraphs that aped accounts I had read in bird reports and books, describing weather conditions, the exact route I took along footpaths to local ponds, and precise counts of commonplace resident birds. My first woodcock was recorded Gradgrind-style. My entire notebook entry reads: '7th July 1974 Thursley Common, hot, woodcock 1.' There is not much to go on, yet I find I can rebuild that bird from those eight words. I was thirteen. It was a hot summer's night. My father and I had gone to the same place where a few years before on a bird club outing we had been shown a nightjar. This time we went home before the nightjars got going. As we walked down a dusty track through gorse and towards a birch wood, a woodcock materialised above the trees, silhouetted against the twilight. It hurried along the skyline for a few seconds before turning away and hiding itself beyond the wood. It was exciting but disconcerting. I was sure of our identification, pleased with how like a woodcock a woodcock was, but it offered so little of itself that I felt I had been simultaneously shown the bird and kept from it. Later I came to recognise this sensation as important and continuing. It is the defining condition of most birdwatching.

Two years later I saw another woodcock. At Hunstanton in Norfolk, I watched one fly in off the sea over the Wash, haring down through salted grey October skies. It was half a mile and 450 years away from the one that Stephyn Percy had carried for tuppence. Seeing this woodland snipe, a piece of airborne leaf-mould, flying from the sea towards the security of some wet muddy spot made me want to understand its past. I began to reverse its story from the point where we had met, sending it back across the unforgiving North Sea and over the mountains of western Norway high over all of Scandinavia to the northern forests of Karelia on the Finno-Russian border. There, in my mind, I made it a nest in the soft summer earth of a forest floor, a woodcock-breast-shaped scrape lined with ferns. I gave it eggs and made it sit on them. Then the bird came towards me again, the eggs became chicks and fledged and the adult woodcock left them. It lifted up to the autumn sky, crossed the Iron Curtain at night and flew over the Baltic and on to our twenty seconds together, five hundred feet apart, under the icy drizzle of north Norfolk.

The Wash is the greatest of the North Sea's jaw bites that open the body of England. In late July, I am in a place as place-less as the open ocean, edgeless, hard to enter, harder still to hold, and full of hidden things and distant birds. It has the colour and mobility of slip, the warm brown muddied water used to keep things wet and moving on potters' wheels.

The Wash's huge square yawn looks big enough to drain every-thing that flows into it, but it gargles instead, holding all the silt of the east Midlands, the Fens and much of East Anglia. To speak of the mouths of the rivers (Witham or Haven, Welland,

Nene, Great Ouse) that drain into the Wash seems absurd; *it* is the mouth. Its thirst cannot be slaked. All the rivers run into the sea; yet the sea is not full. Sometimes the Wash will gulp down what pours in; but just as often it will spit out what it has half swallowed. On one tide the Fens nourish the Wash, on the next they might be force-fed by it.

Following Peter, who had invited me to go out fishing with him, I waded through a mudbath as I sloshed up to my thighs in the retreating tide. The mud seemed to have come from my childhood. The brown cloud I kicked eventually settled like a dreary summer's day on a wet British beach of not-quite-sand. The water was so murky I couldn't see my feet. Like a drunken dowser I stumbled and lurched, feeling my way down channels of sucking mud, bumping between ridges of slippery mud. I wanted water, but there was just mud. Who knows where the shore becomes the sea?

A stick showed above the wave tops, marking the land end of the fishing net I was heading towards. It seemed impossibly distant. I couldn't believe we would be able to walk that far into the water to reach it. But we could, and tangled ahead of me I saw a fish flailing as tidewater drew away beneath it. It had worked; there would be a catch.

We'd had to wait for the tide and it was raining. Peter had chosen a neap, but the north wind blowing straight down the open mouth of the Wash had pushed water higher up the salt marsh and kept it there longer than usual. Held in a great circle of wetness, Peter talked about his Wash: his family on its shore and how he is drawn to its water again and again, the wildfowl he shoots, the fish he catches, the samphire he gathers. Samphire – the word comes from the French, l'herbe de Saint Pierre. Peter and petrels and St Peter and water-walking and samphire swam though my mind.

We sheltered in the lee of a man-made bund, a great round barrow that has pushed the marsh further out into the sea. This mound is a burial chamber of human ambition, the moraine of an abandoned experiment to create a freshwater reservoir at the edge of the Wash, just one of a succession of botched attempts to keep things still in this extraordinarily mobile place.

All is temporary on the Wash. This is a wilderness made of mud suspended in water, perhaps the last wilderness in England, and surely the biggest. Its tides live for twelve hours; it is born and dies twice a day. All life and all energy is in the great estuary's tidal movement from mud disappearing to mud reappearing, in the passage from the edge of the marsh to the sea, from fresh water to salt, from sea purslane to samphire, from green marsh to inter-tidal mud, from muddied brown sea to more salty grey sea, from sea to sky to cloud to rain. All these zones are porous; each leaks into the other.

The cycle of inundation and retreat is endless. The throat of the great mouth can be either the blue-grey open marine sky of the northern horizon, or the black soil of the Fens to the south. Conducting all the business between the one and the other is the mud, a huge tongue lolling in the mouth. Imagine a whale's tongue, grey-brown and wet for ever, fifteen miles long and fifteen miles wide – that is the mud of the Wash.

The conditioning colour here is brown. Everything runs and nothing is fast, but brown dominates from the end of the fields to far out to sea. It is a brown like a jam jar of water after a child's busy painting session, a brown that contains all the colours: the slops of the fens draining green and yellow crops; red poppies; ruddy dust carried from Bedfordshire brick pits via a life in the breeding breast plumage of black-tailed godwits; black soil laid into the heart of heads of green celery; the polar white of Bewick's swans, brought to the Ouse from arctic Russia; pink-footed geese's pink feet ripening like tundra berries beneath them; the shelduck's umber; the dunlin's dun; even the hated mink's black-brown stole. All these raw colours are washed down as silt, salted by the sea, to join the mud. Add any more you like; everything becomes brown.

You have only to be on the Wash for a day to realise the futility of human plans for permanence in the place. What you take to be a fixed horizon is picked up by the wind and disappears. Water vapour condenses just above the fields of wheat and rape at the shore and deliquesces their edges into cloud. A whitethroat flies over the salt marsh from its grassed nesting bank on the most recent sea wall, singing its dry ratchet song over the slippery green ooze; a redshank agitated by a marsh harrier towers inland over emerald wheat fields calling its bleak mudflat alarm. Is there anywhere on these islands that has a less defined edge? This is a place that is no place, that is never what it was or will be. Everything gives and takes, slides and slips.

Peter and I walked out across the mud and into the water, but it would be just as accurate to say into the mud and across the water. After fifteen minutes of trudge we reached the stick that marked the first of Peter's nets. I looked around; I was standing in a sea. The thin line of the marsh and the open mud we started from now seemed so distant and so slight on the vast horizon that I laughed. Two stick figures seeking a third had walked determinedly into the water. We must have looked insane from the shore, except there was no one there. There was no one as far as my eyes could see. We were alone, standing in the lumpy brown water as the tide battled around our legs, the wind pushing sea south towards the land, the invisible moon sucking it away north for its duties elsewhere on the planet.

In the nets were a bass and six grey mullet. We released the two small flounders, or butts, and like miniature waves they snaked back into the water, mud-brown above, sky-grey beneath. The mullet had trapped themselves; Peter unhooked the nylon filament from their bleeding gills and eased their popping eyes of fish panic back through the net. Most of the fish were still alive when we reached them, and being released from the nets gave them a little more twitch. Peter took the wooden fish-priest strung on his waist and hit each mullet very hard three or four times on the head. It was bone-crunching, a loud and finite noise amidst the never-ending soughing and blow of wind and water. As he hit them, Peter talked to the fish in a soft voice. 'I know, I know,' he said. After each of the whacks, their bodies clenched and flexed against his arm before returning to their fish shape. When they died, Peter laid them gently in his shoulder bag. By the time we emptied both nets, the tide was at our ankles.

Gutting was next. Peter turned the mullet belly up, took his knife and pushed it through the fish, just below the gills. He cut bones and pulled the blade up towards the skin, so the fish snapped open one third of the way along its body; then he slid his knife down the fish's belly, opening it in a great gash. The gut in all its warmth bubbled in the sluice of the split. A green vegetable slush creamed out, the mullet's final meal. The viscera spilled into the sea. Four herring gulls detected the offal one hundred and fifty feet up in the wind. They called and jilted in the sky, but wouldn't come down while we were there; perhaps they noted it for later. Peter bent to the sea and washed the gutted fish, his knife and his hands. The clouded water clouded some more.

The sky was fine muslin; the gauzy drift of rain from the north lifted and took the horizon up with it. I looked out towards the Lincolnshire shore and saw it twice, layered on itself. A mirage had raised a line of trees, floating them off the ground into the lower sky, as if to emphasise the impossibility of ever arriving there or reaching anywhere that would be a real edge to this place. Further north, the church tower of Boston Stump hung, detached in the sky, a blurred colour field of brown in grey.

I have seen this effect before, though not when standing in the sea. The *puszta*, with its oceanic grasses and shimmering reeds at the centre of the great Hungarian plain, is an inland dry Wash. It is so flat and has such a wide horizon that you can see the curvature of the earth. I saw that, but in the same place I also saw giant stretched cows sailing through the air with horns prodding the heavens, a magnified image of what lay beyond the horizon, thrown into the sky and projected on its vast screen, a Fata Morgana, or in Hungarian a *délibáb*.

I have often wondered whether flying birds might see things like this, being able to look beyond our horizon, and if so how disconcerting a giant floating cow might be to them. That way Don Quixote's visions lie, but standing in the Wash looking towards Lincolnshire I was also reminded of John Clare, saturated with looking at what was close to hand in front of him, but wandering near the Wash, to the borders of his knowledge, getting to the 'edge of the orison', and thinking he might look over the lip of the world. On the Wash, it seems you can.

Peter is alone out here, but not lonely. His wife worries about him when he is on the Wash, but he likes it, keeping his eye on the work in front of him, untangling the fish and dispatching them, he doesn't notice his isolation. As he got on with scaling the mullet, a solitary grey plover flew over us. It called once, a lone wader flying across a wet summer sky. Most of the grey plovers that winter on the Wash would be finishing breeding now on the lowland tundra of high arctic Russia, but this one hadn't gone. It wouldn't go north this year and wouldn't breed.

Flying here alone across the pallid Wash, with its plumage of courtly black and silver, the bird looked as if it was in mourning for itself. It called again, a plaintive bruised blues made from just one bent note, the saddest call of any bird I know. Peter seemed not to have noticed it, getting on with his solitary task of scraping the scales off the fish, but on the plover's second call he looked up and whistled back to the bird.

As we walked out of the sea with our catch, Peter said he wants his ashes scattered here, on the threshold of the marsh, where the sea runs into it. I thought about what he said: a prospect of oblivion beyond oblivion, ashes mixing with mud in the tide, the thoughts of old age with the memories of childhood, in a wild place empty of people; but this would also be truly moving, a way of casting off the separated self and joining loved things, a passage into this world of constant becoming, breaking waves, rising tides, mullet arriving, geese commuting overhead, knot coming and going. Grey ash to brown mud. I turned to look at the Wash behind us. With the tide out, the great mouth was slack and ribbed, but a few hours later it would tighten at the taste of England, as it did yesterday and will again tomorrow.

I wanted to go out again too, further onto the water. But it is not easy to enter this placeless place. A week or so later on another falling sea, I hitched a ride on a fisheries protection boat making one of its regular trips to collect cockles, mussels and water samples for analysis. We came out of the River Nene and ran across the Wash's fifteen miles of open water while the tide lasted, and then nosed in and out of channels and creeks once it dropped.

I felt like a runaway to a sea that isn't a sea. As soon as the water arrives it begins to leave, and by the end of my second tide it was clear, from far out, as it is inshore, that a kind of walking on the water is the condition of human life on the Wash.

To begin with it was blankly disappointing: empty water and open sky. Then the picture was horribly distorted: the screaming yaw of military jets squeezed and split everything at once. United States Air Force A-10 'tank-buster' planes, painted the colour of the dry brown mud of the Tigris and the Euphrates, dropped their dummies with a *phut*, a flash and a little puff of smoke into the wet brown mud of the Wash's southern-shore bombing range. They left behind another of the Wash's mirages, a cloud from nowhere, seen by no one. Wilderness and government guns have a long history: the Wash is like a plain or a moor, officially perceived as an empty and useless non-place, to be flattened, blind and deaf to the bombers' hysterics. The planes finished their chores; the mud took its punishment.

But the Wash is having none of this; it runs its own time. The tide makes the day, it is the only clock, and there is nothing else. The brown wave on the brown sea is the mud of the sea floor raised by the tide. The mud of the revealed banks is the settled sea. The same mud that cradles the ordnance and sucks at your legs is what gives the Wash its teeming life. Within minutes of sailing out onto the wide water, the mud invited us in. We seemed to be sinking; we were being taught how the Wash fills as it empties. Peter told me that fishermen used to say, 'We're going down below,' meaning they were going out *onto* the Wash. From the boat, I watched as land emerged from the sea, mud strips, then bars, then banks appeared, like the backs of surfacing animals, an otter, a seal, a whale. Sky and sea both had brown in their blue, as if in readiness to deal with the apparently rising land. A brown streak was visible below the falling water, and then a thin brown seam opened between the sea and the sky, like a desert mirage in reverse, a sliver of land shining in the middle of the wet. A plain became a mountain range. Five miles out from the bombed shore the mud began to rise over us; we sank lower into the world, the horizon loomed, the sky shrank. The Wash came alive.

First the land and the sea met in the air. Three gannets, an adult and two immatures, birds of the open sea, and big and bright enough to match it, flew in front of me, drawing their long wings through the wind like turbine blades, and moving crazily south towards the green of the Ouse and the great cul-de-sac. Perhaps they had come from the teeming gannetries of fish stew and aggro at Hermaness where I watched them in June. But why were they pulling deeper in towards the land; where were they going? Then three swifts came, like slates skimmed over the falling sea, five miles from the shore, buzzing the gannets, criss-crossing around them, feeding on insects in their wake, and as at home over salt water as they are around the eaves and crannies of the roofs of Boston town. I was happy to see them. Would these birds, sea swifts, as brilliantly unplaced and unplaceable as ever, be the last I would see this year?

Swifts are nearly legless and gannets are reluctant walkers; both are ungainly on land, and come to it only because they cannot lay their eggs in the air or on the sea. Here over the Wash they met. The brilliant gloss white of the gannets and the black ink of the swifts making broad strokes and fine lines across the grey sky and brown sea, signatures from other worlds.

On the ship's navigation chart in the wheelhouse, the thin edge of true land (only of interest to a sailor in order to be avoided) is marked in yellow. The Wash is coloured green for its salt marsh and inner muds, blue for its sandbanks, and white for its deepest draughts of water. The chart marks a heart shape of white called the Well; it is the only place that holds open water at low tide. All the mudbanks and sandbars have names too; names they carry with them as they drown each tide and as they shift over time.

While half the crew went off in a tender to collect samples to be monitored for algal biotoxins known by their acronyms – ASP (amnesic shellfish poison), DSP (diarrheic shellfish poison) and PSP (paralytic shellfish poison) – I looked out from the deck over the emerging mud-scape to try to identify the banks and bars and scaups (the mussel beds) whose names I had copied from the chart into my notebook. The crew know the mud by its names, though they don't know who did the naming or when. I think of pirate maps of buried treasure, and of Polonius trying to keep up with Hamlet describing the clouds. The mud names record intimacies and fears, stories of hard-won triumph, and magic words to invoke and appease: Inner Westmark Knock, Gat Sand, Butterwick Low, the Scalp, Styleman's Middle, the Ants, Long Sand, Herring Hill, Black Buoy Sand, Thief Sand, Seal Sand, Old Bell Middle, Stubborn Sand, Breast Sand, Pandora Sand, Bull Dog Sand, Scullridge, Blue Back, Mare Tail, Old South, Inner Sand, the Cots, Sunk Sand.

The tide fell further and on the next excursion from the boat I joined the crew in the tender and we nuzzled into the side of a mudbank. Farther along in the afternoon haze, like a stranding of dying whales, were eight fishing boats strung out on the mud. They had been settled there by the retreating tide and were now dozens of yards from the water. For cockle 'hand working', the fishermen run their boats up onto a mudbank like this and wait for the tide to drop. Then, in a controlled abandoning of ship, they throw ladders over the side and clamber down onto the mud to rake cockles. Wandering from their boats, their heads lowered, on a bank miles out from solid land, the fishermen look as odd as icebound arctic explorers, set down on uncertainty. But a good crew on a good site can gather two tons of cockles a day (an eider in the same time eats two kilograms of mussels). In this salty blur of rising mud and falling water, where there is neither sea nor land, fishing has become farming.

As I slid into the shallow water at the edge of the mudbank, a tree floated past. It was a willow, twelve feet long or so, being carried from the River Welland out to sea. Its thin branches were still green and in leaf; they waved in the wind like a ruined sail: a water-loving tree brokering the meeting of land and sea, like an offering from one to the other, adrift but alive.

As we walked up the mud, Dave explained how you age a cockle by its rings, 'just like a tree'. He saw a cockle spit muddy water from its buried home in front of us and grubbed it up. It was five years old, with four distinct lines around its clamped white heart, and a last dark line, marking this year as its fifth, at its still-growing lips. Dave knelt in the mud, scratching and scrabbling with his hands, gathering more samples. 'This is my office,' he said, in his softly curved Norfolk accent.

Back on the boat, we headed towards the bulge of the Norfolk shore, running creeks between the spreading mud. Waders landed all about us. Their arrivals were always like returns, though the sea had only just retreated. The world in front looked new-made, the sparkling mud with its ferruginous glitter and the dappled water that ran from it, but the sureness of the birds' aerial organisation and the accuracy of their touch-downs suggested they had done it before. There were two hundred bar-tailed godwits and five hundred knot. These birds might have bred and returned already from the Arctic, or like the solitary grey plover that flew over on my previous visit, they could be birds that didn't make it north this year.

In 1995, a twenty-two-year-old knot that had been ringed in its first winter in South Africa was shot in the Bay of Cadiz near Gibraltar. At its death it was returning to Siberia to breed, probably for the twenty-first time, and if it had been wintering in the Western Cape all those years it would have flown over 435,000 miles, the equivalent of flying to the moon and back.

Tight flocks of knot thickened above the bank, reflecting down the grey-brown essence of the Wash as they turned. Behind them were leggy gangs of godwits and low twisting lines of dunlin, like mud splashes tossed into the air. Wind-surfing oystercatchers were coming in too. On the mud the waders mixed, but they lifted from it and made their flight decisions species by species. Though they were tangled on the shore, all the godwits went at once, leaving spaces where they stood among the dunlins. In the sky, each species had its own flock shape, but all were part of a flexing cloud. They were like the silver mullet steering through the water below, or the grey-green sueda bushes on the distant marsh edge, touching one another to become a low ridge of wild hedge, or the creamy cockles spitting the slip they had filtered for food, stippling the great whale's tongue of mud.

Into this cloud people have come, nervous and brazen, alone and sticking up into the sky. In 1212 in Cambridgeshire, on the marsh edge of the Wash, King John flew his goshawks at cranes and killed seven. Either the same year, or the next, he flew his gyrfalcons in Lincolnshire and took nine more. Then the Wash claimed its bounty. Somewhere in the mud is John's treasure, ditched in October 1216 in flight from the French, and now sunk, buried or washed out to sea.

Other than mud, I couldn't see any treasure. More knot wheeled and misted over me, and I remembered their namesake Cnut, or Canute, a would-be ruler of the waves, the man who went down to the sea's edge to tame it but couldn't even find it, and met instead something marvellously unbiddable and variously itself, wet, slippery, awash.

August

We were all day hunting the wren;
We were all day hunting the wren;
The wren so cute and we so cunning.
He stayed in the bush when we were running.

Waterford Wren Song

...now he must hold his hand
Like a branch out in the sun and rain for weeks
Until the young are hatched and fledged and flown.

Seamus Heaney

The first living wren I held made me feel I had caught a falling star but, since it was science that had brought us together, I kept quiet and didn't own up to this. We were in a wooden hut at Chew Valley Lake, south of Bristol, on a late August morning and I was processing bags of trapped birds. In any case, it was easy to love the evidence in my hands: the emargination of the sixth primary of chiffchaffs, the blue-grey of the moulted greater coverts of first-year great tits, the reddish iris of adult dunnocks, the fat keels of sedge warblers. Yet I couldn't get over the sensations I had, with the wren in my hand, of holding first an energetic walnut, as its dark brown dwarf body throbbed with life, and then an earthed meteorite, as its midget roundness drew into itself with a density far beyond its weight.

It is fifteen miles from my bed in Bristol to the hut. We gathered early in the morning and unfurled the eight mist nets down by the lake. The lake is really a reservoir; my drinking water sits here like oil in a basin. The nets on the reedy shore billowed for a moment. When they settled they were almost invisible.

We waited for thirty minutes then checked the nets, four of us walking from the hut across a grass field like a mendicant order setting out in search of offerings. We each carried a staff like an odd crozier, a brass hook on the end of a broom handle, used to pull the high-slung nets down to our level. In our other hand, for stowing our treasure, we held a bunch of old faded cloth bags, similar to those used by banks to carry small change, but made from scraps of material, tablecloths, thinning curtains; patchworked stuff that made me think of my grandmothers' aprons.

We reached the nets. Birds hung in them like strange fruit. In front of me were a reed warbler and a robin. No matter how many times I have made that first glance along a mist net and discovered birds hanging there, and no matter how commonplace the birds, this is a magical sight. Trapping birds is like being able to see inside their heads or understand their speech. I felt my fingers prickle. Some old hunter in me was thinking of his supper, or some even older shamanic frisson stirred; we have called down these creatures from their skies and delved into the dark of their migrations. For a moment we will hold them to us, before returning them to their journeys and their secrets.

Skilled ringers are wonderful to watch working a net, untangling the bird silently and fast, like Penelope undoing her weaving day after day, holding back time. The robin and the warbler hung still and quiet upside down, their heads and beaks pointing to the ground, like limp brown flags. They seemed calm but not surrendered. Their flights had been interrupted, not ended.

Like an apprentice surgeon, I was keen to approach and touch the bodies in front of me, but I was frightened of hurting them. I was closer to a reed warbler than I had ever been before. Its eyes pulled me in. The reed warblers' are not unusual, a pair of black beads, but being only inches from mine, they seemed like the deepest of pools. I wondered what they had seen, what they were seeing at that moment. Even this close, birds don't catch our eye; there seems to be no recognition. I felt processed but not known. Their eyes remain quick and keen, unfogged by the experience, as if realness was reserved for them alone.

This blank seeing, with its simultaneous inclusion and exclusion, reminded me of the first milky unfocused looks of my sons more than a decade before, and I began to talk to the reed warbler, as I reached into the net, in a voice that had the same tone and intention as I used to speak to my infant boys. The reed warbler squawked and hissed back to me as I shushed it, trying to hold it steady. Its thin red lips (the inner edge of its beak), orange gape and tiny arrow-pointed tongue were close and active, jabbing and brave, its dark eye severe. I unpicked its pale orange feet first. Its claws had grasped at the mesh and were reluctant to let go of the thing that had trapped them. My shoulders stiffened at the tangle, but the warbler's own elasticity beneath my fingers made me bolder at brushing the mesh from its feet. I was able to hold both legs and feet at the tips of my fingers of one hand, and managed to pull a stitch of the net over the bird's left carpal joint. It wriggled its head back through the square of mesh it had dived into and came free. Its mushed feathers, the colour of warm dust, returned and settled to their reed warbler shape.

I opened the first and second fingers of my left hand to a V and slid them around the bird's head, bringing my thumb and other two fingers around its body and over its legs. Its hissing stopped and I could feel the bird calming just as I became aware of its furious heartbeat, hammering through its thin chest, terrifyingly fast. In my hand there seemed nothing more obvious in the world. I wondered whether it could feel my pulse in return.

There were more birds to extract. While I had been swooning over the reed warbler, the ringers alongside me had already dealt with three or four others. With my free hand I opened the cloth bag and reached into its dark, releasing my fingers and laying the warbler down, quickly withdrawing my hand and sliding it from the bag. Later the same day I was too slow. I worked a great tit free of a net, its beak stabbing my hands like a tiny woodpecker. On the way into the bag, it spotted its moment, scrabbled up my cuff and flew bounding away, calling its freedom and annoyance into the trees.

I collected birds in bags from the other ringers, and gently slung theirs and mine on a lanyard around my neck. Twelve cloth medals hung there. Climbing the stile to the field, I held the precious cargo to my chest with the same caution I remembered from taking my boys out on our first journeys. In the hut the bags were gathered on wooden hooks. Sometimes a bird struggled and the bag rippled like a sleeping bat. Mostly they hung still like bunches of old grapes and, as the autumn goes on, this effect is magnified by the wine stains many of the bags acquire from the blackberry juice that has rubbed off onto them from the birds' beaks or smeared onto them from their droppings. For days after a ringing session, my hands have blackberry birthmarks too.

We took down the birds, one bag at a time, and the gentlest of interventions began. I felt sure I would snap the robin's slight twig of a pale green leg as I tightened the ring around it with a pair of pliers. When all went well I almost cheered. It was thrilling to have put something of ours onto the bird, some evidence of our embrace that would accompany it back to its world. As I measured and weighed it, passing it from hand to hand, I wondered if anyone would touch this robin again. Might someone else from somewhere else take it from a mist net a year from today and rotate the tiny ring on its leg to read the number? Would they marvel at the thought, as I would, that another person had already held this bird, which in the meantime had been who knows where and had done who knows what?

I was clumsy and a cack-handed beginner and in the hut a greenfinch escaped from my grip, and then a sedge warbler, both hurtling towards the windows. It was frightening to see how keen they were to escape. No amount of crooning will ever make them want to stay. I watched the other ringers at work. One is a retired tax inspector and I couldn't help thinking how his fingers were probing the bird for its secrets; another is a potter, his large plate-like hands miracles of delicate touch; a third is an electrical engineer, the bird's functioning technology, how it fits together, is alive to him. My trainer has been ringing for nearly fifty years, but the flicker of his first bewitchment still crosses his face. He moves a bird with the fluency of a card dealer or a magician, switching it from one hand to the other without it leaving the contact of either.

I felt like Gulliver in Lilliput. I turned the birds over onto their backs and blew on their bellies, parting their feathers along their tiny breastbone, looking first for signs of new feathers, evidence of their moult, and then for their fat and muscle scores. The fat on a sedge warbler made me think of pâté. Beneath the warbler's dark pink skin at the base of its throat, and behind its legs, were tiny discs of creamy tallow that might tempt a gourmand or a starving man. 'You could light this one,' someone said, looking at another. The fat will allow the sedge warbler to make a rapid long-haul flight from Chew across Iberia, North Africa and the Sahara Desert without further significant feeding.

Almost all of the migrant reed warblers, chiffchaffs, blackcaps and sedge warblers that we ringed were young birds. They had hatched just a few weeks before; they might have forty-seven days where I have years. They might have come from the same reed bed or scrub we caught them in, or perhaps from many miles away. Their journey south might already have begun, or they might not previously even have travelled as far as the three hundred yards from the reeds to the ringing hut. They were all foundlings, who had never been abroad before, and would have to find their own way to Europe and through Africa. Their parents had already gone, or had abandoned them to wait for them to leave before leapfrogging ahead, flying further more quickly.

The ringers greeted an adult willow warbler taken from a bag. The old bird was a survivor who had made it away and back again at least once. I scrutinised it for its badges of wisdom and experience. Beyond its plumage differences from a first-year bird, a white belly not a yellow one, there was not much to see, but it was wonderful to think that the bird in my hand had flown across the Sahara twice at least, part of the loose green cloud of one billion willow warblers that leave Europe and Asia for Africa every autumn.

I held the willow warbler, as my colleagues in the hut held their birds, in a grip that is a cross between holding a pen and holding someone's hand. I felt the bird between my fingers and palm; it made me happy. I had read it, now I would write with it. Whilst I kept it cradled in my hand, the warbler was like a little grenade, unexploded but with the pin out. Released with the ring, our badge, wrapped around its leg, it would go off. These few grams of bird are a bundled message in the present from the future, unread now, as yet unreadable, but carrying a latent shimmer of meaning that could be deciphered should the shiny ring on its right leg be seen again.

In the first decade of the 1800s, around the time of Wordsworth's first version of 'The Prelude', John James Audubon tied 'light silver threads' around the legs of the pewees (now called eastern phoebes) that bred in his garden in Pennsylvania – the first ringing recorded in America. He wanted to know where they went in the winter and whether the same birds returned the next spring. Trapping them and tying them in this way, he made them his, but he also widened his horizon and stretched his mind. The birds carried the past they shared with Audubon with them. The pewees' air-mail messages flew from and then went back to the garden at Mill Grove, travelling faster and arriving sooner than some of Audubon's letters home to his wife would from his own (later) travels in Europe.

Next to me the tax inspector took down a bag and reached inside. He pulled out a dead chiffchaff, its dusty green head lolling loosely over his fingers. A cat had killed the bird and a neighbouring farmer had brought the corpse to the hut. It was a ringed first-year bird (meaning it had hatched just a few weeks before) and was one of 'ours', a bird the station had ringed. No one else would be touching this one. The marriage must be annulled. The ring was taken off its leg; its body, impossibly small in death, was destined for 'under the hedge'.

I was relieved the chiffchaff wasn't my bird or hadn't died in my hands. A silence hung for a moment in the room. This was a death intercepted at a time when thousands of young birds are ordinarily dying every night, dropping dead from a perch or in flight, to be covered in August dew, then eaten or rotted, swallowed one way or another back into the earth. An X was put next to the bird's entry in the ringing diary. All the information that could be gathered about it had been; all that remained was decay and statistics.

In the warm August sunshine another chiffchaff was singing

from the line of ash trees above the hedge. Chiffchaffs return to song at the end of their summer and, as I listened to the sweet *chiff-chaffs*, it was obvious that there is no mourning in nature. In *Persuasion* (written, in 1816, just a few years after the first 'Prelude' and Audubon's pewees), Anne Elliot, feeling cast down and autumnal, comes across a farmer ploughing, 'counteracting the sweet fruits of poetical despondence, and meaning to have spring again.' By their autumn flights south, leaving their dead under hedges, birds could be saying the same thing.

The nets had to be furled. I walked out to them on a final collection round and, as before, there were birds hanging in them. I could unroll the last half-hour backwards, know what these birds were doing when I was attending to others elsewhere, see into these birds' unseen lives: a song thrush in the bottom pocket, its low foraging hops and short flights under bushes stopped; a greenfinch with blackberry juice dribbling from its thick beak, waylaid on its journey from one bramble top to another; a reed warbler, monochrome sand, frozen in its flight between reed heads; a gang of blue tits on their joint descent to a seed basket, thrown splashes of yellow, blue and green along a net.

We extracted them, took them to our hut and ringed them. Then we let them go. Releasing the birds is as moving as taking them from the nets. Our time together ticks down, the business is over, the measurements noted, and the bird reassembles its quintessence in my grip as I reach towards the little wooden tunnel built through the wall of the hut. The way back to their world is down this dark passage. The tunnel ends a few feet from the hawthorn hedge, the chiffchaff's grave. I opened the wooden flap and reached in and unwrapped my fingers from around the reed bunting I had ringed. I could feel it instantly gathering itself in an ecstasy of repulsion to move away from my hand, towards the light. That was it. It came out of its end of the tunnel at speed, already flying, called once as it gained height to clear the hedge, and was gone.

I was nothing to it. The sharpness of the cut, the bird's un-minded amnesia, was devastating and welcome at once. I thought of the wren landing on my shoulder on Noss. How ghastly if news of where the bunting had been was sent around its reed bed, how lucky for both of our species that it isn't. Yet I love the sense of having held a bird now deep at the base of a stand of reeds, doing what it must do, able to perch above the water on a stem that could never take my weight, in a place that I cannot possibly go, a bird that I have held, now alive in its marsh. A sedge warbler is on an adjacent reed stem, picking trapped flies from an abandoned spider's web for a last meal at Chew, one more dab of fat for its girdle, before it is drawn upwards by dusk and the swing of stars overhead, and it lifts into the air above the lake, my ring on its leg catching the tiniest of reflections of moon silver, as the great glitter of the night sky steers the bird south to Africa.

September

Altogether elsewhere, vast
Herds of reindeer move across
Miles and miles of golden moss,
Silently and very fast.

W. H. Auden

For as long as I have known what migration means I have wanted to be alongside moving birds. Their autumn departures and spring arrivals have made a timetable in my life. To be deprived of an autumn, its chilling lift, its emptying blast, and all its atmospheres between, held indoors shuttered from the wind and the light, or exiled to the seasonless tropics, would be a kind of death. My children have been born, my parents have grown old, relationships have been made and foundered and made again, my work has flowered and soured and rallied – all these human adventures are what my life has been built from. Yet my years throughout have been rhythmically driven by the step up into spring and the swing away into autumn and the movements of birds through them. Comings and goings. Windfalls.

Seeking migrant birds, seeking migration, I spent two Septembers on Fair Isle, one at the threshold of adulthood, one in my forties. Isolated in the middle of violent seas, halfway between Shetland and Orkney, it is a port in the storm of autumn for migrating birds.

We locate the onset of autumn somewhere between the parties of swallows gathering themselves with conversational twitter on telephone wires in late August, and the back-to-school tang of the air in early September. But to witness migration, as you do on Fair Isle, is something else. Through yellowing crops and fading grasses I walk south towards the lighthouse on the small island's southern shore and the heaving salt water beyond. As I stand at the schoolhouse, a movement in the corner of my eye becomes a single swallow flying level with my shoulder, dipping and rising over the fences and stone dykes, pulling its blue-black wings repeatedly through the cooling air. It sweeps up for a moment as it reaches South Harbour, momentarily slows as if punctuating its flight with a comma to mark land's end, before casting off alone into the oceanic blow.

Fair Isle has been known for its migrants as long as anywhere. It was one of the first places in the world where passage birds were logged and studied, and where the secrets of migration began to be investigated and unlocked. As a boy I had obsessively studied old reports produced by the island's bird observatory, and memorised red-letter days when tiny bundles of feathers took shape as the first recorded example in western Europe of a warbler from North America, or a pipit from eastern Siberia. I dreamt of walking its crofts and cliff edges, its dykes and geos, the sheltered green clefts along the island's coastline. I saved money and went for a month in 1980, before I started university, determined to wipe clear my head of home and school and fill it with birds and movement, before I sat still and read books for three years.

In 2007 I went again to Fair Isle. I was curious about my youthful self and the sights it had banked then. After that first month on the island, I pretty much gave up birdwatching for ten years or so. I was interested in reading and human politics and lived in Budapest and London with my eyes turned from birds. But they never left me; there is no unknowing the kind of knowledge birds bring. In my forties, my own autumn coming on, I was keen again. I wondered how the delicious paradox of rejuvenation through departure, the sight of birds being chased by death out of the north, drifts of lost young birds and family parties of others moving south together, would seem to someone with children, a mess of relationships, wounds and fresh starts.

Nowadays many birdwatchers fly to the island, hoover up its rarities and dash away. But there is still a ferry, a boat always called the *Good Shepherd*, which runs south from the Shetland Mainland across twenty-five miles of sea to North Haven, the natural harbour near the observatory. I took the three-hour ferry on both my trips, eking my savings, but wanting also some sense of distance and journey, some equivalence to put alongside the flights of the birds I hoped to see. On both crossings I was horribly sick, and so, twice over, began my education in the awfulness of passage.

On my first visit, some other birdwatchers shipped with me. As the – old – *Good Shepherd* turned a corner in the sea, from the calm of the Shetland harbour south towards Fair Isle, an invisible hand from above slid the hatch and from then on we were locked in the cabin. All young men, we'd nodded to each other as we had assembled on the quay, but had barely spoken. Standing there, hiding behind our binoculars, staring at the sea, each of us had in turn undergone the male trial of cautious performance ('Storm petrel at two o'clock'), asserting our place as birdwatchers without addressing anyone directly. Within minutes of trying to float on the furious sea we were filling sick bags in front of one another. I regretted my last cheese roll very much. The hand, like a god through cloud (where was *that* good shepherd?), appeared in the hatch space and we understood, broken and gut-wrenched as we were, that we should pass up our wretched offerings to be tossed overboard, as a defeated gull would disgorge its dinner for a skua.

I tried to peer through one of the tiny portholes, clutching at its brass fitting, remembering some advice about keeping the horizon in view to allow it to work as a spirit level for the stomach. But the sea was everywhere. The boat seemed to be in a permanent trough, with no horizon and certainly no longed-for land anywhere to be seen. The windows were small, I realised, because the sea wanted to come into the cabin and kill us. Nothing other than a floating coffin, sealed and dark, had a chance of getting to the other side.

Twenty-seven years on, I was again scourged by the crossing. There is a new and bigger *Good Shepherd*. In the passenger cabin the portholes are slightly larger than previously. They made me feel optimistic about the voyage. Then I noticed the seat belts.

As I had waited for the boat at Grutness at the edge of the sea I had spotted a huge rusting iron urn, three feet across, held in a stone harness over the remains of a brazier. It looked like an inverted giant's helmet; Achilles might have worn it. Neil Thompson – the skipper of the *Good Shepherd* today – told me that his great uncle, fishing after herring, had sailed open boats hundreds of miles from Shetland to within sight of the Faeroes. Ordinary life back then asked for extraordinary efforts. The urn was used on their return to render down herring livers. 'They saw a lot of waves,' Neil said. I told him about my first trip south to Fair Isle. 'It's a bigger boat but it's the same sea,' he replied. My stomach knocked at the base of my throat.

We started out and almost immediately the sea came to the

boil. Cold but molten lead was being cooked, the colour of the pot at Grutness. I was to be rendered in it. I had shunned the seat belts, choosing to stand again at the portholes, my watering eyes pleading with the gods and my innards. It was ghastly. Forewarned, twenty-seven years previously, I hadn't eaten breakfast, but still the skua-sea found some vinegary bile to take from my stomach. The boat could not keep sea time. Nor could I. Thousands of years of ships and sailing, human endurance and ingenuity, had nothing to answer the continuous rolling of the sea except repeatedly to smack into it. Hence the seat belts. We saw a lot of waves.

Back on the shore, I had seen a migrant snow bunting huddled near the pier. It prompted a memory. Four years before on the lava beaches of Surtsey off the coast of Iceland, I had seen breeding males dropping themselves in charming and delicate song flights, like tumbling black and white lacy handkerchiefs, onto sea-smoothed boulders of grey-black pumice. I had allowed myself to imagine that the bird in front of me was a grandchild of those Icelandic buntings.

Before the ferry, at the Pool of Virkie, just around from Grutness, I had seen a rarity: my first killdeer in Europe, a striking North American wader like an oversized ringed plover, with triple black bands on its neck, throat and upper breast, a deep orange iris and a diamond-shaped tail with feathers at its centre coloured in exquisite warm sand tones. These are the same colours as the dry prairie earth and short late-summer grasses of central Ontario in Canada, where I'd seen a killdeer just a few weeks before. This bird – was it too a relative, perhaps? – had been blown over the whole of the North Atlantic to find the sand of a Shetland sea loch.

Now I was on the same Atlantic that the snow bunting and the killdeer had crossed, whose miraculous journeys had moved me when I had thought about them just an hour before. But the knowledge that I was sharing a sea with the birds was useless to me. I couldn't see any birds. I couldn't imagine any bird like a snow bunting here. It seemed impossible. Sea-watching from the sea is very different from standing on a cliff top, letting the sea first wipe then fill your open mind. Here the message is that holding on to whatever raft you have – your wings or your good shepherd – is the only thing that matters.

The churn and retch of the engines brought us to the middle of the crossing, to a stretch of water called the Hole, where, free of the currents around the islands north and south, the Atlantic Ocean meets the North Sea full on. I tried to recall the calmness of the Well in the Wash. I tried to picture the snow bunting's migration, imagining one outside the porthole, but I could only think the last thing in the world I wanted to think about: that my stomach was a hole, emptied of its ballast, and floating horribly close to my mouth.

We arrived after another hour of mind and body warp. Birders who go to sea looking for pelagic petrels and other seabirds *chum* for them, dribbling buckets of rotten fish from the back of their boats to attract the birds. I was chumming too but nothing came, until at last a dark slice of solid green rose up out of the waves. Fair Isle never looked fairer. I felt I had swum the twenty-five miles and it had taken me twenty-seven years. Staggering from the boat, my queasy lurch giving way to steadying bliss, I understood as never before the meaning of *landfall* and *haven*.

I looked up and saw a party of meadow pipits arriving from the north, from where I had come across the sea. They called with what I heard as relief as they wound themselves down to the grass headland at Buness. Every autumn day the island proves that tiny land birds cross the open sea without a seat belt, a cabin or a piloting skipper. I hadn't been able to see them from the boat, but there had been birds there, above me and alongside me: migrant thrushes, buntings, warblers, wagtails, part of a vast and scattered flock, heading south, all the way down the entire western seaboard of Europe, every day from August to October.

A few weeks before, many of them had been eggs. Just days ago, in the brief northern summer in Iceland or Scandinavia or further east, these young birds had left their nests and fledged. Surrounded by the encouraging buzzing of their brothers and sisters and parents, they had learned to fly from that nest to a tree, perhaps a dwarf birch, a willow or a fir, a few feet away. Their next journey would be on their own and might take them as far as Africa. None of them would have flown over the sea at all prior to launching themselves up into the air, in the dark, one night in early September. They go, and once they go they cannot turn back. 'Tracing a memory they did not have/until they set out to remember it' is how W. S. Merwin puts it in his poem 'Shore Birds'.

What must it be like to be so sensitive to the magnetism of the earth that you are able to taste the iron in the air; to be drawn up into that air as if evaporated; to feel the inching creep of longer nights pushing you away from what you know towards what you don't? What must it be like to hatch from an egg and look up from a nest and know the stars already? As if your paper-thin skull were a planetarium, along with the smooth curve of your late-abandoned eggshell and the cup of your nest too, as if the skies and the stars had pressed their map into everything there is of you.

Migration cannot but seem a mystery. There have been decades of studies from Fair Isle and elsewhere: ringing and radar, tracking and tagging; robins kept in cages flooded with artificial sunshine; pigeons fitted with magnetic skull caps and opaque contact lenses;

Manx shearwaters transported from their nesting burrows in west Wales to be tossed back into the air outside St Mark's in Venice to see if they can make it home. But migration eludes us more than ever. We begin to be able to explain it, but because in our time we feel it less and less, we cannot grasp it. We couldn't do it and we cannot fathom how birds can. Its reality is as hard to hold as any idea of it. Try to comprehend what the earth is busy with in autumn and spring, in its exchange of light and feathers between the north and the south: on this day, say the third of September, there will be 45 million swallows in the air on their way out of Europe. We are in the middle of it, they fly right through us, but we hardly notice.

If we feel migration at all, it flickers in our imaginations like a story from the beginning of the world. If its rhythms and energies still flow, they do so like the sunken memories of folk tales or nursery rhymes. I think of W. H. Auden's lines about reindeer running silently and very fast across golden moss on the other side of the world. Migration's ghost lies deep in our minds and bodies, a shadowy thread running from the earth to the sky and back to the earth. For most of us nowadays, any connection with it is at best muted. On Fair Isle it was brightly shown to me. We are an island people who have moved over the waters, who have stepped off the land and taken to the sea. Migrations are hard and risky, but migrants are at home in the world and move between homes in ways that no amount of holiday cottages or air travel can replicate. We once moved with the sun like swallows. And to witness them doing that is to realise what we have lost.

Sea-holed and bleary I was safe on land once more, and my nausea rolled back into the mucus-coloured surf thrashing the jetty at North Haven. My stomach settled with every step, and it seemed abundantly clear, as I carried my bags up to the bird observatory, that walking and not sailing or flying is what we should do. How wonderful our way of movement felt after the crossing – my easy mastery of it, and the truth it offered about the world. The horizon that had been either invisible or mobile for the last three hours solidified in front of me: the brown hills of the north and the softer green south.

For the next weeks this was to be my place, my migrations were to be local and on foot. Walking is what I did. I wore wellingtons and trudged the island every day. Once, at the end of my second stay, while hurrying to see a newly found vagrant, I was offered a lift in the bird observatory's car. I clambered in and as we zoomed south at a terrifying 20 mph, I felt like a Manx shearwater in a wicker basket being flown to Venice.

My life on the island, like that of the birds I had come to watch, was determined by the weather. All arrivals and departures depended upon it. Rock was beneath me and water surrounded me, but the air decided everything. For two Septembers of my life I was a connoisseur of the wind: its swing around the compass watered my eyes and after a single day of walking the island's paths, I learned by charting my tears' coursing progress down my cheeks to plot the wind's direction and strength, its salted northerly gales, the sweeter westerlies, and if I was walking south and my left eye wept harder than my right, I knew the wind came from the east, the best quarter for a fall of birds.

My first trip had been blessed with easterlies. On one day my nineteen-year-old body stepped back towards some ancient knowledge. My cold left cheek made me hopeful and my ears showed off their barometric skills, registering some thickening isobars from a deepening low. I felt the air twist and darken and detected movement above and behind me, and I turned to find myself in the middle of a cloud of birds condensing out of the sky and descending all around towards the rough fields and croft gardens. They were thrushes – redwings, robins, ring ouzels – heading south from their northern breeding grounds. The ouzels all the way to warmer places around the Mediterranean, the redwings and robins to a milder British winter.

Watching these birds pour earthwards out of the sky, breaking from it, was exhilarating: migration was visible, had a shape and was happening in step with me. I too was on my way, moving from home, and I was in the midst of the passage of these birds that were doing the same thing. I knew I couldn't reach across the gap that separated us, but this didn't diminish the thrilling sense of community. Flying kept them from me, and our separation – so obvious as the flock tumbled down, sown from the sky like rain – was both saddening and enriching; the impossibility of joining the birds made being tangled up with them even more precious.

The loose flock swirled around me. The wall ahead was dotted with birds that had pulled up after hours in the air, like galloping horses coming to a halt. Here was the planet at work. The birds were exhausted, they wanted to rest, preen and feed, but their eyes were bright and intensely alive; they had brought something from the sky down with them, an imprint, a picture or a reflection of the whole globe beneath them. The male ring ouzel in front of me was beautiful, like a dusty blackbird with a gorget of white across its breast. Its bright round eye and sharp black beak pointed back into the air from where it had just dropped, making it look like a figurehead on the prow of an old sailing boat. Movement was its life, and even as it rested on the stone wall, I felt how the earth is turning us all.

I had seen my first ring ouzel ten years previously at the other end of the bird's year, on one of my first proper birdwatching trips. I was eight. My father, who shared my new interest in birds (within months I was in the grip of an obsession that left him miles behind), had arranged a permit to allow us to visit Beddington Lane sewage farm a few miles from our home in Surrey. One of our first visits had been on an early April morning. It was cold and the sky was miserable, but the grass on the banks around the sludge pools seemed incredibly green. The spring was coming.

New to all this, we didn't quite know what to do. We walked the banks and peered at the settling ponds of sewage. There were a few mallard. A kestrel pulled away towards a factory tower. Pied wagtails bounced along in front of us. We walked on and met another birdwatcher. Not as steeped in spurious protocol as I was to become (witness my caution in 1980 on the *Good Shepherd*), we asked him what he had seen. He said a pair of ring ouzels were on one of the far banks. At this stage of my birdwatching life, the only thing I knew about ring ouzels was that I hadn't seen one before. But being beginners, we accepted their arrival as we would the appearance of any bird in our path, with grateful bemusement, and didn't hurry to look for them. We carried on scanning the sludge.

Then, jumping through the long green grass on a bank, was the male ouzel, with the female not far behind. I peered through my binoculars and I remember the male raising its head, and its bright white breast band simultaneously drawing me towards it and pinning me to the spot. It was as if a wire ran between us. I identified the ouzel and fell in love at once. It was a rare bird, but it wasn't its rareness that hooked me, it was the sharp tang it gave off of having come from somewhere else. I looked at it and felt I could see its past, its life in the places it had been, so far from the sewage farm and the bank of green grass.

That evening when we got home I read all I could about ring ouzels and felt the thread still taut between us as I discovered how in all likelihood, that same night as I was reading about them, the birds would lift from the grassy bank up into dark air and plough north towards their summer home in the uplands of Britain, or perhaps to higher latitudes across the North Sea in Scandinavia. They were already on their way to becoming one of my best birds.

On Fair Isle ten years later, at the other end of my childhood, here was another ring ouzel, stopping briefly alongside me, once again casting its scintillating thread. More birds slipped down from the sky ahead of us both, and time turned over again. The wonder of the moment became part of a story of movement; the birds had come from somewhere and they were going on somewhere else. The ring ouzel on the wall turned away from me, flicked its long wings and flew on.

I walked further south down the island, trembling with happiness. I saw many other birds in my month on Fair Isle, far rarer ones: I found a woodchat shrike that should have been on the other side of Europe; I became adept at listening for the soft calls of common rosefinches, the blandest of birds with the beadiest of eyes; I knew where a buff-breasted sandpiper blown from North America roosted. One night something drew me out of the observatory and I saw for a few moments a green flickering along the edge of the northern sky, the shaking curtain of the aurora borealis: the north electrified and harrowing birds south. Another day I watched the islanders gather at South Harbour to collect the flotsam of a tide. A ship had lost a container overboard which had split to release its contents. Training shoes and lumber were expected. These were charged days and nights, but after the ring ouzels and their ruddy train of robins and redwings, I didn't really need anything else. I'd had an audience with nature's everyday sublime, and was ready to leave home and make my own tracks through the world.

For more than a week in September 2007 the wind stayed in the west, the autumn refused to be autumn and very few migrants arrived. I continued to walk the island, a pilgrim waiting for revelations, being tutored in patience. My devotions were simple. My feet remembered stiles and paths from all those years before as I moved from the rough heather moor of the north to the green crofted south. I reminded myself of the lovely string of names of the cliff edges and offshore stacks, the Reevas, the Geos, the Kames. I stopped at every altar and shrine, the tiny stand of pale oats at Shirva, the nettle bed at Pund, the vegetable patch at Quoy, a miniature plantation of stunted sycamores and dissolute pines, the squelching bog beyond the Post Office. These sacred groves and holy wells were where clouds of migrant birds had previously fed and recuperated, where amazing rarities had taken shelter and been found. But this autumn such sanctuaries fed the resident twites and house sparrows and shone in the warm sun, the grasses and leaves bending lightly beneath the creamy mild air from deep in the Atlantic.

At last the wind changed. First it blew so hard from the south-west that it seemed to exhaust itself. There was a storm. A terrifying sea built up with slabs of muscled water. A huge swathe of sky thickened to a metal plate that slid over the island. The sea was running its own foundry and seemed to rear upwards. It looked solid and yet able to pour itself somehow into the sky. As the rain broke from the clouds, the horizon came towards me with terrific speed. The sea and the sky were no longer separate. The ocean I had seen from the porthole of the *Good Shepherd* was nothing compared to this – here it was utterly opaque, a thick and malign overcoat made of lead, the size of a barn door and held two inches from my face, dense and deadly and very old. A doomsday sea, too frightening to watch through binoculars.

I ran away and hid in the island's phone box. As I sheltered I thought of what I could least imagine doing at that moment: being launched from a hundred feet up with my arms pinned to my side to dive headlong into this sea – a gannet's life; or a swallow's – trying to fly through the storm, struggling headlong into a wall of wind, unable to avoid the lashing rain or the ghastly rolling tar of the sea.

I walked back towards the observatory. The rain came over me like a cruel jazz solo. It stung. In the fields the sheep all turned north-east in unison and then stood stock-still. I was soaked. On Buness, the wind pushed a waterfall uphill to become a waterspout. Spating streams rushed over the sodden grass to the cliff edge, but the wind was stronger than gravity and forced the water back up into the air to fountain in a great arc, one hundred feet of sparkle through the grey, a blowing whale's back made from a cliff top. It was beautiful, but I cursed and dripped through the blasting, hectoring weather. Through the spray came twenty-four black and white snow buntings, rising from the grass ahead of me, birds that had made it over the sea, but here forced to drop to the ground, to bivouac against tiny rocks like arctic soldiers in unseasonal weather.

The next day everything had changed. The storm, or *gynda-gooster* (one of many Shetland words for the wind and sea I had learned when hiding from the weather in the bird observatory), was spent and birds came in behind. Often the best birds – if that is what the rarest birds are – come out of weather like this, ruined and wrecked, blown off course, wrong and moribund. And this is what happened. The wind dropped to nothing. A thin high sky, the colour and texture of a much-worn, much-washed blue shirt, lifted my head, and seemed to pull the whole island south and east. It was patterned with cloud that was being blown from different quarters at different heights. Some upper-atmosphere realignment was under way. The autumn, made in the east, came to the western edge of Europe.

It started with geese. The sea had settled, long calming waves (called *da mother* waves in Shetland) rolled in. The day grew sweeter still. After a storm that made me believe in hell, heaven was advertised; the sea grew so calm it seemed loving. I watched fulmars fall asleep on it, bobbing in its lightest of swells, their heads swivelled behind them and tucked beneath a wing.

Having walked south as usual, in the cemetery by the South Light, I looked for warblers and read the gravestones and remembered the storm: James Wilson 'who died from exposure in a boat' 3 September 1897, aged 20; Stewart Stout 'accidentally drowned' 11 February 1946, aged 35; Karl Arne Emanuel Sundblom 'who perished on a raft through the sinking of S. S. Signe of Mariehamn off Fair Isle' on 2 April 1940, aged 20. Against the back wall of the graveyard is a small metal cross, a memorial to the Spaniards of the Armada ship, *El Gran Grifón*, which tried and failed to get back to Spain around the north coast of Scotland and was wrecked at Stroms Hellier on the east coast of the island on 28 September 1588.

I lay on my back in a grassy *naust* near the cemetery to stare at the beautiful sky. *Nausts* are small dry docks cut from the turf where the islanders used to haul their *yoals*, or fishing boats. Lying in one reminded me of the bumps and dips of the fields on Bardsey off the Welsh coast, where you can lie looking up at the sky for birds and feel yourself held by the dead bodies beneath you of the many pilgrims who journeyed to the island and died there. I remembered Coleridge too, walking in the Lake District in June 1801 and finding 'a hollow place in the rock like a Coffin – exactly my own Length – there I lay and slept. It was quite soft.'

I was nestling in the *naust*, a perfect combination of a nest

67

and a roost, warmed by the sun, out of the breeze, and feeling drowsy, when overhead I heard the beginnings of the distinctive yapping of barnacle geese. Out of the sky they came, a family party of ten birds, talking their soft and conversational dog-speech, shepherding themselves south. They dipped towards me but didn't stop; I could see their black necks and white faces leaning down to look at the island, but they could also see Orkney from up there, off to the south, and the air was mild and good ahead of them and on they went.

Wherever they had come from, it was as if they opened the door of the sky. Almost the next bird I saw was a redstart on a stone wall next to the red barn at Kennaby, the same gorgeous rust colour pulsing between the bird and the barn, making my day as redstarts always do, and confirming its place as my favourite of all birds.

The redstart has all I need in a bird. Every one I see has a bloom on it from the times when we are not together: it migrates; it breeds amongst the freshest, greenest leaves in the sweetest oak valleys of western Britain; it winters in Africa, in that ideal landscape of gently undulating grassland with scattered trees; it is shaped like a small and perfect thrush; it perches with an intense upright alertness; its song is thin but fine and beautifully apt, like the first glances of sun after rain; both male and female are exquisite to look at; males have a slate-grey back and wings, a brick red breast, a soft black throat and a brilliant narrow white fringe running around their faces above their eyes, females are a lovely soft brown; and best of all both have a warm orange-red tail that shimmers continuously. Nobody really knows why. The moving tail and its redness is commonly the thing that first draws your attention. The blurry red seems to hang in the air in front of you, as if alive independently of the tail and the bird. It's what Gerard Manley Hopkins would call the redstart's instress, or a birder its jizz, and it is beautiful. The redstart is quivering its tail on the worn carpet of lichen that covers the top of the dry-stone wall at Kennaby. A month from now it will do it from an acacia branch in the savannah belt south of the Sahara in western Africa. Next spring it will do it at the edge of its breeding hole in a tree fresh in leaf anywhere from Spain to the far north of Russia.

After that firetail, my last two days on Fair Isle were as perfect as they could be. I had loved the resident wrens and the star-lings, the seabirds, the gannets and fulmars, but now the island came to life in a different way, as earth, not sea; not sky, but earth, *our* place that land birds need, that we share with them, where they stop and rest and live among us for a while. The observatory emptied. All the birdwatchers combed southwards. The *chack* of the first fieldfare of the winter came close behind the last swallow of the summer, and we were in the thick of it.

There was sunshine and a soft easterly wind. It wasn't a Siberian wind icing the west, but it was more than enough to start the birds off. Where had they been waiting, what anteroom in the skies had they been held in, that they might respond to the slightest change of wind direction within hours? Or had they been able to cross the North Sea from the Scandinavian shore in that time? Perhaps, but these arrivals seemed miraculous. I *pish*ed – sucking air through my teeth, chacking and tutting – and a bluethroat appeared from behind a pigsty, a beautiful sort-of-redstart for me, almost equally good, its next year's blue inti-mated in its delicate pinpricked necklace. All around me redwings lowered themselves from the sky ('wind thrush' is an old name for the birds) and I remembered my first visit to the island and the descending thrushes of September 1980.

On that day – 23 September – when ring ouzels dropped around me, 120 were recorded; on the same day blackbirds dotted the island's field like rooks and there were 70 redstarts, 50 black-caps, 300 siskins, 400 redwings and 550 robins. The numbers were smaller over the two magic days of 2007, when I saw only one ring ouzel and that single redstart, but the island was still stippled with birds: there were thrushes all up the cliffs, robins along the stone walls. A goldcrest like a northern European hummingbird fluttered at a leaf edge, having made it this far on tiny wings and without a woodcock to ride on. Then, typically for Fair Isle, though there were relatively few birds, some of the island's vagrant specialities appeared and complicated the magic.

Along a fence at the cliff edge at Klinger's Geo, dancing before my eyes was a yellow-browed warbler. Its diminutive green and yellow sherbet fizz of energy seemed to have escaped from the lush shelter of the cleft of the geo just below. Geo is the Norn (the old Shetland medieval Norse language, with Scandinavian accentuation and pronunciation) word for a narrow inlet. The cliffs of the island are indented with them. There are no substantial trees on Fair Isle and the geos with their green and moist skirts of moss and lichen and ferns and their insect-rich warmth are the best place for bird repairs. Yellow-browed warblers breed no nearer than the Siberian taiga. The bird in front of me, almost certainly only a few weeks out of its nest, should have flown in the opposite direction to winter in open deciduous forests anywhere from Nepal to the Malay Peninsula.

In the first decade of the twentieth century, the early student of migration William Eagle Clarke was amongst the first to suspect and then prove that Fair Isle was a magnet for migrants. He published his findings in two volumes called *Studies in Bird Migration* in 1912. He visited the island several times and went searching the cliffs and geos with his shotgun and some crofter assistants from the Stout family. Think of the scene in September 1908, the men perched and clinging to the geo like a yellow-browed warbler, a bird Eagle Clarke described as 'a favourite with me'. Then a bang that is lost in the wind and sea roar, and a tiny body somehow collected or a corpse out of reach falling to the waves below.

The yellow-browed warbler I saw wasn't going to be shot, but it had made a mistake, and it is probable that no amount of nurture on Fair Isle could truly rescue it. Vagrancy is a death sentence. Almost all the rarities that arrive on the island (and almost all vagrants anywhere) will have the same fate. They are wonderful treasures from far away that we cannot keep and cannot save. Rarity-hunting is coffin-chasing. There is very little evidence that vagrant birds reorient themselves and correct their journeys. Having gone south-west where it should have gone south-east, it seems most likely that the yellow-browed warbler would continue in this aberrant direction and fly on west out over a ocean that has no refuges, no green skirts for thousands of miles. That would be the end of it. It was soon to be home-less. I was watching a lost child at death's door.

The day ended with a lanceolated warbler in an isolated patch of oats right at the sea edge of the southern tip of the island at Skaddan. Close relatives of grasshopper warblers, lanceolated warblers are as skulking and as hard to see. They are the birds for which Fair Isle remains best known in the birding world. Like the yellow-browed warbler they are Russian, most breeding east of the Urals across Siberia and wintering to the south. Almost all of the few dozen British records have been from Fair Isle, since Eagle Clarke shot the first on the island on 9 September 1908 'as it rose from some rough grass'.

The worn out, scraggy fields of Fair Isle in September are still the most reliable place in Europe to see a lanceolated warbler. A text message that had travelled who knows how far, bouncing between the sky and the earth, told me one had arrived from equally unfathomable distances, and had been found just a mile south of where I watched a bluethroat. Already I knew that it would be a first-year bird (all those trapped on Fair Isle since 1908 have been), and already I knew that, like all those others, a watery grave was its certain destination. But still – or perhaps *because* I knew all that – I turned and ran towards it in my wellington boots.

Though it had flown from Siberia, the warbler now preferred to walk, or rather not move at all and walk only if it must. Familiar with this behaviour, the warden waited until the whole island of birdwatchers had gathered, and then with a colleague stepped over the fence at the far end of the oat crop, and the two of them began slowly to drive the bird out. They got closer and closer to the line of waiting watchers, until a thin strip of crop was all that remained. Surely the bird couldn't be there, but it was. The warden spotted a tiny movement and the warbler crept away from his boot out into the open and then back into the yellow-brown mess. I saw it well for about five seconds. My first and very possibly my last. It moved with the jerky progress of a mouse, a lovely bird full of bright character, like a runt dunnock, severely streaked but with a cocked tail and a beady eye, and just four inches long. I thought of Eagle Clarke's lead shot and the lead sea that waited offshore. I wanted the child warbler to live for ever.

I could still see it inching through the oat stems when I heard the whales. Our backs were to the sea but all of us gathered there turned as one. A family of five killer whales, a bull, cow and their three calves, were surfacing and blowing only a hundred feet offshore. It is possible these were the same whales that I had seen on Noss. The line of birdwatchers gasped as if we were all breathing in what the whales had breathed out. The bull's black dorsal fin seemed to fill the sky like a huge pirate flag; the brilliant white of their flanks effervesced in the green sea. As one rolled under, another was surfacing, so a lovely serpentine ripple plied the calm, turning the family into a single beast, inseparable now as they will remain for life.

Another year, another day in September, I was crossing the Bay of Biscay on a ferry. I had seen storm petrels. We were straining our eyes looking for spouting whales miles out across the silvery water towards the horizon. The wind was chasing us hard south and it was attending to the sea's surface with diligence. It picked at acres of water, and as it rose in strength it seemed to go back over the sea to work on smaller and smaller patches until every square inch had its drama. I thought of Kafka's vignette on the sea god: 'Poseidon sat at his desk, going over the accounts.' There was so much sea and each roll or wave was made up of these inches of water, each with its own ridges and furrows, mountains and valleys, wrinkles and frowns. The wind farms the sea in this way and makes a vast extension of the skin of the earth. And through this, barely over this, come flying migrant land birds.

There were two miles of water below me. It is a distance that is less known and less knowable than its equivalent in any other direction. By comparison, the thin air of birds' lives seems solid and well mapped. Up from the sea's depths came fin whales; we slid past one another, their jaws and undersides lighting the sea with an otherworldly blue. Though the ferry was bigger, the vastness of each whale was stupendous. Its back broke the surface and it blew, and the sun caught its breath. The whale rolled forward and went under. Far away, it surfaced and blew again and then again. Through these fleeting rainbow clouds tiny things appeared in my binoculars and grew to gannets as the ship reached them or they passed it. Then there was a tiny thing that didn't grow and that suddenly was upon us, whizzing overhead, somehow drawn towards the ferry and to me. I lowered my binoculars and turned my head, and two inches away from my face, perched on my left shoulder, was a willow warbler.

It seems unlikely that twice in my life whilst watching whales a tiny bird should land on my shoulder. Yet it happened. To see a land bird at sea is one way to feel how the earth is made, and how it can fit a whale and a warbler together. The warbler weighs less than ten grams and has come from miles to the north: perhaps it was the bird that sang along the railway cutting at the back of my house this spring and lifted my journeys to work; perhaps it had passed through our trapping area at Chew Valley Lake, missing the nets and my grip by inches; perhaps it was a Norwegian bird, the descendant of the three or four in a gully that I had helped flush into a funnel trap on Fair Isle nearly thirty years before; perhaps it was just a few weeks old and had never seen the sea, nor a man apparently standing on it. Its washed green back was the same colour as my coat; for a moment we were a bleached and shrunken version of Long John Silver and his parrot, sheltering in the lee of the ferry's funnel. A second later either the bird realised where it had landed or the wind whipped it from my shoulder, and it let itself be lifted into the air, out to the side of the boat, south over the whales and over the sea.

October

Hope, Joy, Youth, Peace, Rest, Life, Dust, Ashes, Waste,
Want, Ruin, Despair, Madness, Death, Cunning, Folly,
Words, Wigs, Rags, Sheepskin, Plunder, Precedent,
Jargon, Gammon, and Spinach.
> Miss Flite's caged birds in *Bleak House*

No, no, no, no! Come, let's away to prison.
We two alone will sing like birds i' th' cage.
> Shakespeare, *King Lear*

At Troy in western Turkey, you can see and feel the Asiatic
steppe reaching the sea. The rolling open land ripples
one last time just behind the shore where the Greeks
landed their fleet, and made their camp. On this ridge behind
the beach is a huge mound; Achilles might be buried there. From
the top you can look far out into the silvered Aegean, but the
view inland is far more arresting. This is the view the Greeks
would have had looking towards Troy. In the dusty lemon light,
the ruins of the city lie far off to the north-east, just visible to
the naked eye, raised on a promontory on the other side of the
plain. Between Achilles' tomb and the city he brought down, the
country undulates into some of the most beautiful, benign miles
– with or without the *Iliad* – I have ever seen. There are wide
arable fields, rough grasslands, smaller meadows and orchards

with scattered oaks sown naturally between them and, at the Scamander, the flash of river silver. Shade and light and shelter and sustenance are woven into the plain.

Trucks on dirt roads throw up dust and these moving clouds catch the sun and flicker with specks of mica. Homer described the advancing Greek army becoming visible to the Trojans in the same way. In October the fields are earth-brown, scratched with stubble, and the grasslands are pale citrine yellow. Everything has dried. Most things have died. Tall silver-grey thistles are snapped and broken across the plain in sharp-angled agonies, a dead army on barbed wire. The skin of the earth has been stretched and pulled tight. Olive trees shimmer and the oaks – the local Trojan oaks – are a dusty hard green and rattle with their bearded acorns in the endless wind that blows from the land, as if from the past, a wind that has crossed grass all its life and that has never tasted the sea.

The miles of open country below Achilles' tomb seemed made for the *Iliad* and the poem could be read in the plain. I sat for a while with my microphone switched on – I was making a radio programme – sucking the wind into my tape recorder. As I listened to it coming and coming and coming, I watched Troy through my binoculars and picked up a swallow flying through the nearest oaks. A single bird on the point of leaving the land, like the swallow on Fair Isle. As if all the air of Turkey and of central Asia were at its tail, it flew fast and committed, knowing where it needed to go. The tomb seemed a way marker. It flew right over me, two feet above my head, forcing me to swivel sharply to watch it streaming on over the beach and then out to sea, flying at the height of Achilles' tomb south towards Africa. This swallow then, not the one on Fair Isle, would surely be my last of the year.

I walked off the mound and the next bird I saw was a redstart.

A drab first-winter bird, it called once from a fig tree – still fresh green and humming with fruit-gorged insects – and flew out ahead of me flashing, as ever, its irresistible trembling tail. Its red was as warm as the sherds of terracotta pots that were crushed into the track beneath my feet. It dived into the crown of an oak, and that was the last I saw of it. Goats had gathered and were nibbling at my microphone cables and I had to move on. The next bird I saw I thought at first was the same redstart, but it was a robin. Hidden in some tamarisks on the beach, it *ticked*. Like the swallow, the redstart was on passage south to Africa. The ticking robin had come from the north, perhaps from northern Turkey, or from Russia or Ukraine across the Black Sea. It would probably stay on the beach in these bushes for the winter.

The rusty red of the robin's bib and the rusty red of the redstart's tail reminded me that Aristotle thought that the summer redstarts of Greece turned into its winter robins. He called redstarts 'red tails' and the bird's scientific name *Phoenicurus phoenicurus* means 'red tail red tail', as if the name must itself quiver. Aristotle identified the similarities of the two species and noted that redstarts departed at about the same time that robins arrived. On the beach, the robin ticked on, bringing the winter around, sending the redstart off, proving Aristotle wrong, proving him right.

On 10 May 1940 at Hemnes in northern Norway the Germans captured a British soldier called John Buxton. Before the war he had taught English literature of the sixteenth and seventeenth centuries at Oxford University. He was also a poet and a serious bird-man. He spent five years, the rest of the war, in south Germany in prisoner-of-war camps. At Laufen (Oflag VII-C) and later at Eichstätt (Oflag VII-B – close to the limestone quarry where the first archaeopteryx remains had been found) he watched birds, which came through the camp wire to breed.

> In the summer of 1940, lying in the sun near a Bavarian river, I saw a family of redstarts, unconcerned in the affairs of our skeletal multitude, going about their ways in cherry and chestnut trees. I made no notes then (for I had no paper), but when the next spring came, and with it, on a day of snow, the first returning redstarts, I determined that these birds should be my study for most of the hours I might spend out of doors.

In 1950 Buxton published (as part of the celebrated New Naturalist series of books) a monograph based on his wartime studies of the bird. It is called, simply, *The Redstart*. I think it is one of the finest bird books. I also think it is no accident that what is one of the most poetic works of ornithology should be about the redstart. After the war, Buxton returned to Oxford. It is reported that he 'owned the best handwriting of the New Naturalist authors'. He died in 1989.

The redstarts in Bavaria shared their summer home with two thousand prisoners of war. Buxton recruited other prisoners to help with his observations. Remarkably, there were several bird-watchers incarcerated with him: one, George Waterston, founded the bird observatory at Fair Isle after he was released, and another, Peter Conder, later became the director of the RSPB.

The prisoners weren't allowed outside before six thirty in the morning, so Buxton missed the two hours of spring-dawn bird activity. Yet the redstarts he studied must be candidates for the most watched individual birds ever. In 1943 one pair were observed for 850 hours over three months. For days at a time the birds were in view and watched by the men as continuously as their German guards allowed. There is remarkable detail in Buxton's book, and his account remains the key reference on the bird to this day.

His ornithology was good, but what makes Buxton's book so unusual and distinguished is his beautifully expressed humility in the face of what he sees. Before the book has got under way he is saying he hasn't really written a work of natural history at all: 'These redstarts . . . I loved for their own sake and not for the sake of adding to men's knowledge'. His modesty, his gently expressed jealousy of the redstarts' freedom, his assertion again and again that the birds might not be doing what he thinks they are – all make for remarkably tender science.

I must be understood to refer only to my redstarts . . . My redstarts? But one of the chief joys of watching them in prison was that they inhabited another world than I; and why should I call them mine? They lived wholly and enviably to themselves, unconcerned in our fatuous politics, without the limitations imposed all about us by our knowledge. They lived only in the moment, without foresight and with memory only of things of immediate practical concern to them – which was their nesting hole, and which their path to it, where lay the boundaries beyond which they would not go; memory also, perhaps, of the way back when their one necessary urgent purpose was done, to the hot sun of Africa.

Buxton's quiet confidence allows him to be serious and playful at the same time. The prison fence and the redstarts coming and going through it proscribed the parameters of his research. Their much longer journeys beyond Buxton's view, on their migrations to and from Germany, become a kind of shadow book to the actual study. He literally cannot go with them, but nor can he scientifically, and this opens his mind. He doesn't stop being a scientist, but as with his studies hedged with doubts on the breeding birds, he writes about redstarts in Africa with a curiosity accompanied by what seems like a generous shrug. It is as if he is smiling at the unknown: 'I wish that some naturalist with a pair of eyes might visit some of these places, or that I had done so myself; but since that has not happened, there seems little point in trying to guess what the redstarts do during these three winter months when they vanish.'

The book is full of moments like this of approach without capture. Its overriding image is the freedom of the redstarts. No amount of scientific scrutiny or torn-down prison wire can bring us truly closer to the birds.

There is scarcely any point at which his mind and mine can touch: how, then, could I write this book? . . . This book is therefore not objectively about the redstart . . . the bird remains ultimately as unknown and unknowable as ever, and the most that I could hope to achieve was to show to a few of my fellows how much delight is to be had from watching a little bird with its tail constantly aquiver. For

> He who binds to himself a joy
> Does the winged life destroy;
> But he who kisses the joy as it flies
> Lives in eternity's sun rise.

Buxton quotes Blake here and elsewhere cites Wordsworth and Racine and Lucretius, Aristophanes and Marvell. Helen Macdonald has studied the notebooks and papers of Buxton that are now held in Oxford at the Edward Grey Institute. She has kindly shared her transcriptions and notes with me. The papers include a letter from Julian Huxley, one of the four editors of the New Naturalist library, who wrote to Buxton in 1948 as he was preparing his book: 'I don't quite follow your point about not wishing to pretend to knowledge you haven't got and not wanting to acquire the scientific knowledge to write a scientific treatise on redstarts.' A similar query was raised more strongly in a letter later the same year to Buxton by James Fisher, another of the series editors: 'You have definitely over-done the "mere naturalist and not a scientist" attitude, almost to the extent of inverted whatnot. Can you please do something mildly about it?'

Huxley and Fisher were great naturalists and understandably allergic to preciosity. And Buxton's book now seems both ahead of and behind the idea of the series he was writing for. Ahead – because the book makes an account of our separation from nature (metaphorically dramatising it even, since the watchers were prisoners), and it records a yearning to close the gap between us while knowing that no such closure is possible. Behind – because it appears not to want to know everything, wants indeed the unknowableness of the redstarts to be part of what a redstart is. This is Buxton as romantic poet. He wanted to be an amateur because he knew the etymology of the word, that an amateur is a lover, and that his love for his redstarts lay at the heart of his experience of them. He quietly insists that a telling of the particularities of his relationships with the birds has to be central to his book. He couldn't write in any other way. This is like Gilbert White or Coleridge, but it is also like Ted Hughes or J. A. Baker, author of *The Peregrine*, the hallucinatory account of a winter watching or imagining – no one could or can tell – hunting peregrines along the coast of East Anglia.

Buxton writing about the redstarts' tail-flirting captures the richly contrary drives of his watching and thinking. Here is romantic science, poetry-saturated observation and a sophisticated self-reflexive anthropology that knows that there is no such thing as objective looking. Yet it simultaneously conceals these ground-shaking truths with a modesty and reserve that could help you survive prison, and obtain the permission of your captors to build the best possible getaway machine: a bird to watch and love that came through the wire every day.

Young redstarts, Buxton discovered, start quivering their tails on their tenth or thirteenth day. The only birds that do it are the redstart species and the closely related rock thrushes. Buxton says they would call themselves redstarts if they needed a name, 'since it is by this that they recognise one another'.

> The action is performed so often that I do not think it can be said to occur in one particular set of circumstances and not in others, and this fact suggests that it is not a form of display, in that it does not represent any emotion or excitement in the bird itself. Rather it is a means of exhibiting the characteristic red tail to other members of the species ... the movement brings the tail down and then quickly back to the line of the main axis of the body: it may be imitated by holding the tip of a knife-blade on the edge of a table, depressing and then suddenly releasing the handle.

Buxton looks hard at the birds in front of him, but it seems the red tail and its quiver will not give up a meaning beyond what we can see and guess at. Our looking and noting cannot contain it. It is beautiful, it is vivid, it moves, it says 'I am here'.

The displaying male, with his bright tail fanned and pressed down on the branch, his rosy body flattened, his black face and white cap thrust towards the hen; with his wings held straight up to show their undersides as he 'waves in his plumes the various light;' his wild, darting flight after the act, accompanied by a sweet warbling song as he flies – all combine to make one of the most strikingly lovely scenes I have ever watched in the lives of birds.

By the end of the book Buxton comes close to apologising for what he has done:

> Perhaps it would have been better to have remained content with what I saw, to have rejoiced alone in this Ariel delicacy and grace which my book, paying too ponderous attention to such human trivialities as statistics and maps and dates and comparisons, has inevitably missed. For what mattered to me is that the redstarts lived, and lived untroubled except by their own necessities, where I could see them.

This is very different bird writing from what passes these days, but it was provocative in those days too. James Fisher, Buxton's editor, was a great lighthouse and foghorn in post-war bird life. He wrote a monograph on the fulmar and the still unsurpassed *Shell Bird Book*, a vade mecum of the cultural and natural history of British birds. When I got my copy around 1972 it scared me. I remember thinking that there was just too much in the book for me, and that I would never be able to know birds as it did. Geoffrey Grigson prompted a similar reaction. He also wrote extraordinary petrol-backed encyclopedias such as *The Shell Country Book*. Now I think of Grigson and Fisher as the two last men who knew everything. The trouble is, I think, so did they. There is a loftiness and patrician hauteur in Fisher's prose. He marshals his chapters for our benefit like a headmaster and writes with the slightly bored swagger of imperious certainty.

The Shell Bird Book has many words on music and poetry, but its underlying drive is to say that birds are over there and we are over here and science has sorted this out. Some of the best things in the book are also the most troubling for me. Fisher approves of John Clare – who was much less well known and read then than he is nowadays: 'of all our major poets he was by far the finest naturalist . . . He wrote of about 147 wild British birds, 145 from his personal observation, 65 of them first county records . . . All Clare's bird work was entirely overlooked by Lord Lilford in his supposedly full account of the birds of Northamptonshire (and the Soke of Peterborough) a quarter of a century after Clare's death . . .'

This is exhilarating stuff if you are a bird lover and keen on poems too. I had never heard of John Clare before I read about him in *The Shell Bird Book*. The thought that a poet was actually good at birds was exciting. In 1972 I was a tentative newcomer to poetry reading, and not that experienced a birdwatcher either. I was uncertain how the two might meet and I knew both to be risky pursuits for a young man to own up to. I mostly kept my mouth shut. I will always remember the horror of starting to read the Molesworth books and finding the weedy nerd Basil Fotherington-Thomas bouncing into unwanted view with his distinctive call at the beginning of *Back in the Jug Agane*: 'Hullo birds, hullo poetry books . . .'

James Fisher remarking on Clare's 65 first Northamptonshire records now seems interesting for two reasons: to think of a poet adding to science (especially something as exacting as a local avifauna) and to think of someone, a scientist (presumably

Fisher), working out what the poet has done. Sixty-five, not sixty-four, species. But this is where my worry begins. The birds and the poems are being sieved for their facts. James Fisher, I am sure, would have no qualms about that. But John Buxton, with his redstarts, wasn't ready for this empirical reduction.

> Nor would I change this mystery of the redstart's life by trying to make it seem familiar. That may be the method of science: I do not know. But the method of poetry (and that is my concern) is to make things familiar be as if they were not familiar, to make this too much loved world more lovely.

Buxton wanted poetry to be able to touch what we carry away of his birds. He wanted poetic insight to be as meaningful to our total knowledge of the redstart as scientific information. He achieved this, in part, by keeping in front of us the individuality of the birds that were in front of him. His concern with specifics and particularities connects him to Clare, perhaps the greatest poet of the particular in English, and he quotes Clare's poem on a redstart's nest. At the end of his book, Buxton writes,

> Yet even now, how little I know of these strange creatures that, merrily busking about the trees which shaded us, or perching on the wire that kept us close, delighted us, as they must have delighted the inmates of Belsen, by the very incomprehensibility of their lives. They lightened (if only for a little while)
>
> the weary weight
Of all this unintelligible world

simply by their unconcern in our affairs, and by the beauty and pathos and vivacity of their lives.

I am deeply drawn to this writing – its precision in retreat and its curtailed ambition, its quiddity that makes it neither lush nor parched, the way it holds itself back whilst opening itself to the world. Buxton puts his discovery of the border between him and his redstarts into the centre of his life. It isn't the fence (neither the German wire nor the gap between men and birds) that makes him a good neighbour, but the way he looks across it. His book would love to reach and make contact, but it knows that it cannot fully hold on to anything.

I think of Buxton as a man of 'negative capability' in Keats's term, 'capable of being in uncertainties, Mysteries, doubts, without any irritable reaching after fact & reason'. This needn't imply the hackneyed polarities of science and poetry – it could be, as with Buxton (a scientist and a poet), a way of bringing both together and letting each inform the other. Science makes discoveries when it admits to not knowing, poetry endures if it looks hard at real things. Nature writing, if such a thing exists, lives in this territory where science and poetry might meet. It must be made of both; it needs truth and beauty.

Our habit of seeking truths with birds is deeply human. Collection and classification lie at the origins of all thinking about birds, from cave paintings to the *Handbook of the Birds of the World*. Aristotle was doing it with the redstart and the robin, and so were the haruspices and augurs and other readers of nature of the *Iliad*, foretelling what was to come by birds' guts or birds' flight. But much nature writing – especially poetry – has been hostile to the tyranny of the notebook and the ringing pliers, and has sought other less measurable truths. In a letter, Edward

Thomas wrote, with unusual vehemence, how 'the way in which scientific people and their followers are satisfied with *data* in their appalling English disgusts me, & is moreover wrong.' John Clare wrote of the cuckoo:

> Artis has one in his collection of stuffd birds but I have not the sufficient scientific curiosity about me to go and take the exact description of its head rump and wings the length of its tail and the breadth from the tips of the extended wings these old bookish descriptions you may find in any natural history if they are of any gratification for my part I love to look on nature with a poetic feeling which magnifys the pleasure I love to see the nightingale in its hazel retreat and the cuckoo hiding in its solitudes of oaken foliage and not to examine their carcasses in glass cases yet naturalists and botanists seem to have no taste for this practical feeling they merely make collections of dryd specimens classing them after Linnaeus into tribes and familys and there they delight to show them as a sort of ambitious fame with them 'a bird in the hand is worth two in the bush' well everyone to his hobby . . . I have no specimens to send you so be as it may you must be content with my descriptions & observations.

Behind these splenetic outbursts is the idea of man as a fallen creature who has acquired knowledge but lost feeling. This is Adam's curse and we are all descendants of the first name-giver of the animals who traded proximity and connection for separation and classification. Clare and Thomas are central to my mixed life of birds and words, but both seem wrong to me. Yes, we need to guard against the sterilities of knowing too much or allowing knowing to supplant all else, but we must still know.

Not knowing our birds keeps us from them – at Reading railway station, yards from industrial units occupied by companies with names like 'Flowtech' and 'Phoenix', I watched as three red kites, like flying crucifixions battened to the blue, flew just fifty feet above the platform while dozens of people walked unseeing beneath them to their cars. Removed in this way – not looking up – we can only aestheticise nature like Tennyson's eagle ('He clasps the crag with crooked hands'). Indeed, both Thomas and Clare habitually wrote poems that are far subtler than these prose responses, and their writing is characterised by the continual mingling of *data* with *poetic feeling*.

As a young birdwatcher I wanted none of this. I was more interested in nature's writing than in nature writing. Books of words about birds that tried to say more than how to tell them apart seemed secondary and for after the event. It was the event I wanted, and for much of my first decade of birds I lived with raw facts of hard matter: flight lines, skywriting skeins of geese counted, logs of numbers, the hieroglyphs on eggshells labelled, annotations of feathers, and lists – day lists, my back garden list, my Godstone Pond list, my summer migrants arrivals list, year lists, my life list, even a list of birds heard and seen on the television; I was simply taking down – one bird after another – the way they wrote themselves onto the world. Nothing in print could answer or match the four tufted ducks on Godstone Pond or the marsh tits on our back garden bird table that I counted week in and week out. My simple notes on these birds formed accidental phenological accounts – immersions in places that started as a list but became a way of feeling nature and landscape and time, the lived life of the earth.

The only nature writing I admitted to liking at this age was exotic. When I was eight or so, Gerald Durrell and the Hal and Roger series of Willard Price (*Lion Adventure, Safari Adventure,*

African Adventure) transported me to the savannah and a dream of a future life. From twelve onwards I began to notice that a few poets took birds into their minds and remade them there without the acuity of observation being lost (when it was, I knew the poem failed or the experience was faked). I allowed Ted Hughes and a handful of other poets (I especially liked the *Voices* anthologies that Penguin produced) to cook my nature for me.

I continued to read, but nature writing – the apparently wholesome picnic of seeing and language – tasted mostly off to me; there were only a few books and a few voices that weren't embarrassing, only a few who saw it as I did or more interestingly than I had, and who had managed to get it down. Even these successes had the air of marginal literary activity somewhat guiltily carried out by rather apologetic writers. This quality – it will always be both their strength and their vulnerability – they share with John Buxton. I read Kenneth Allsop, his book of collected newspaper columns, *In the Country* (1972), and his two novels, *Adventure Lit their Star* (1949, in Penguin 1972) and *Rare Bird* (1958, dedicated to Henry Williamson), J. A. Baker's *The Peregrine* (1967) and *The Hill of Summer* (1969), Desmond Nethersole-Thompson's *Highland Birds* (1971) and Richard Mabey's assorted (and happily continuing) writings. One or more of these books saw me to sleep most nights. I memorised whole swathes of some of them; I had several pages of *The Peregrine* off by heart and paragraphs of *Highland Birds*. My stories at school were heavily indebted rip-offs.

Though my principal reading matter was still the annual reports of the Surrey Bird Club or, a little later, the monthly bulletins of the Bristol Ornithological Club, I was aware that I was reading more widely than most of my bird friends. Watchers rather than readers surrounded me; if we talked at all whilst we were out, it seemed best to stick to the known world of names and numbers. I read my favourite bird poems alongside the monthly bulletins, but apart from the sense I had of these two currents meeting in me, it was hard to see a way to bring the streams together. Basil Fotherington-Thomas sat reproachfully on my shoulder. To talk about John Clare's poem on a yellowhammer's nest to my friends in the Field Club at school seemed twee, and, a couple of years later, to talk about the accuracy of Clare's observations in a tutorial at university seemed tweedy.

My nickname at school was Tweedledee. At university it was Scared Chicken. My fellow students hardly knew of my bird obsession. Though I joined the Cambridge Bird Club and couldn't stop noticing birds, I cased my binoculars and kept quiet. My friends watched my close-cropped head, my jerky walk and my general skulk, and saw a defeated bird. When I discovered what they called me, I was doubly upset. *Gallus gallus domesticus*: a bird that is not really any longer a bird.

Twenty-five years later, in October at Birdlip in Gloucestershire, I went walking with my sons. I like the name of the place. The wood, which wraps the hillside of the western scarp of the Cotswolds, looks down over the Severn Valley. It had been raining and the trees were dripping. Several had their own scarves of cloud they had made, snagging on their autumn branches and drifting slowly out over the valley. There was not much bird lip: a robin *tick*ed and some redwings flew off in front of us *seep*ing as they went. At the crest of the hill the wood gives way to fields, and a yellowhammer called and flew along the hedge. I had been thinking about nature writing and birds' lips, and I remembered John Clare's description of the yellowhammer's nest in a poem: 'Dead grass, horse hair and downy-headed bents / Tied to dead thistles,' and how excited I had been to find this so close to the description in *The Handbook of British Birds*: 'built of stalks, bents, and a little moss, lined horsehair and fine bents'; and how I also loved Clare's note on the yellowhammer's eggs: 'a fleshy ash color streaked all over with black crooked lines as if done with a pen and for this it is often called the "writing lark".' I told the boys that a yellowhammer had been the first special bird I had noted on my very first proper (rather than back-garden) birdwatching outing aged seven, and how my dad and I had struggled to clinch the identification. At Birdlip we didn't see much else. I *pish*ed at some long-tailed tits as they came around us, and the boys laughed because I was caught in flagrante, sucking and chacking, as another walker crossed our path. We chatted as we wandered back through the waterlogged light, beneath the dripping trees. I tried to explain the sequence of my thoughts and my enthusiasm for spotting ways in which nature has written itself in the world, but the boys were not that interested. Summer holidays and seabirds on cliffs came up and I sensed that Dominic, aged fourteen, was searching for the word 'puffin'. He tried 'toucan', then 'pelican', then 'mongoose', and finally had to be helped out.

Nowadays, I am most interested in and moved by Dominic's kind of nature talk – writing or speaking of birds that doesn't identify itself as 'nature writing'. In May 1940, the same month John Buxton was captured, the Germans also caught up with Olivier Messiaen. His 'Quartet for the End of Time', featuring his musical accounts of a blackbird (played on a clarinet) and a nightingale (a violin), was premiered in Stalag VIII-A in Görlitz in January 1941. Listening to it is like being able to hear with another set of ears, perhaps even with a blackbird's or a nightingale's. Walter Scott extends what nature writing might be, when 'out hunting and with some good lines suddenly in his head, [he] brought down a crow, whittled a pen from a feather, and wrote the poem on his jacket in crow's blood'. A single letter from D. H. Lawrence, to Lady Cynthia Asquith in November 1915, gives the finest account of autumn in England that I know. Bruno Schulz's stories, from under the eaves of Drohobycz in old Galicia, of his relatives transformed into condors and other birds mean a lot to a scared chicken. Yves Klein's photographed leap (*Le Saut dans le Vide*) from a wall in the Rue Gentil-Bernard, Fontenay-aux-Roses, in October 1960 says things to me about flying (we can't) and falling (we will). The lysergic shamanism in Ted Hughes's crow poems turns looking at birds into a kind of bad trip, or a gruesome hangover, that I hadn't realised I'd had. Brancusi's 'Bird in Space' sculptures look to me as a bird feels in my hand. Joseph Cornell's box constructions, like Central Park in an aerial view of Manhattan, with their cut-out parrots and collaged landscapes, remind me of nature tables at school and my mantelpiece today with its line of bird skulls, a world salvaged and in retreat, like a nest but also like a coffin. Peter Szöke on his bizarre record, *The Unknown Music of Birds*, slows down woodlark song and makes a soloist from the Budapest Opera sing it so beautifully that I weep to hear it. Ian Dury rhymes and associates 'gannet', 'the Isle of Thanet', 'prannet' and 'Janet' to great comic effect, and every gannet since I heard 'Billericay Dickie' has been marked for me. Rimbaud kept a list of pigeon names and terms in English that he collected when he was living in Reading prior to his great escape out of the European world. It is hard not to hear him, amongst these carrier pigeons, shuffling his own wings in preparation:

Pigeons: homing – working – fantails
             pearl-eyed tumbler –
             shortfaced – performing tumblers
             trumpeters – squeakers
             blue, red turbits – Jacobins

baldpates – pearl eyes, – tumbles well
high flying performing tumblers
splashed – rough legged
grouse limbed
black buglers
saddle back
over thirty tail feathers

For a few decades through the twentieth century, we weren't sure how admissible this great flock of birds – noted and then re-imagined – could be to our lives. Nature writing was dismissed as being hopelessly elegiac or sentimental, overdone and out of date. William Boot's 'Feather-footed through the plashy fen passes the questing vole' (in Evelyn Waugh's *Scoop*) did for grown-ups what Basil Fotherington-Thomas did for me as a child. But, though their binoculars might have been packed away, all sorts of observers went on noticing birds.

Just north of Pisa in a prison camp on the other side of the Alps from John Buxton and Oliver Messiaen, Ezra Pound was held after Italian partisans caught up with him in May 1945. He had been making pro-Mussolini radio broadcasts. For a time Pound was kept outdoors in a wire cage with minimal protection from the elements. Afraid of losing his mind, he watched birds. Some of his Pisan cantos, the poems he wrote after his confinement, contain his field notes of birds – swallows mostly, I think – seen on distant wires of the camp. Canto 79 has a running list, one of its punctuations, of birds seen:

with 8 birds on a wire
or rather on 3 wires (*ll.* 37–8)

4 birds on 3 wires, one bird on one (*l. 66*)

5 of 'em now on 2;
on 3; 7 on 4 (*ll. 74–5*)

2 on 2 (*l. 104*)

3 on 3 (*l. 107*)

with 6 on 3, swallow-tails (*l. 115*)

The birds move freely and Pound in his wire cage writes them down. In Canto 82 he sees the settled birds as silent musical notes on the stave of wires:

> 8th day of September
> f f
>   d
>   g
>   write the birds in their treble scale
> Terreus! Terreus!

Old birds and old poems come to Pound in prison. The nightingale cries 'Terreus!' – Tereus raped Philomela who, transformed into a nightingale, called his name – and another canto (75) is almost entirely a transcription of the score of the French composer Clément Janequin's 'Le Chant des Oiseaux' from around 1500. The song is an extraordinary and delirious imitative round and chorus, that creates the sensation of falling through a spring wood at dawn, with one bird chasing another in song, and has you catching again and again at species (nightingales, starlings, cuckoos, blackbirds). It is cool and green and happy and it comes from far away. '*Détoupez vos oreilles*', bend your ears, the lyric instructs. In Pound – in the midst of poems begun in captivity – this speaks of the double impossibility of capture. The musical score (my description comes from listening to a recording not interpreting Pound's scribbles) joins his various languages and alphabets and references as another more or less concrete poem that is difficult to grasp. And the human mimicry of nature can only be that – an imitation. We can be captured but the birds cannot; they fly onto the wire but are not caged by it. At Metato – the site of Pound's prison camp – nothing remains of the wire or cages today but, when I visited, there were swallows flying freely over the maize fields and singing from the wires along the riverbank.

In the early 1960s on the Neringa, or Curonian Spit, in Lithuania (then part of the Soviet Union) an ornithologist, D. S. Lyuleeva, carried out experiments on swallows. Her findings were published in a scientific paper in 1973. To determine the energy costs of birds' flight, she caught swallows, house martins and swifts near their nests on the spit and released them 40 or 70 kilometres south. Hirundines and swifts feed as they fly, but to ensure they couldn't, their bills were tied shut with a thread passed through their nostrils. Before they were thrown into the air, they were kept for three hours and deprived of food to empty their guts, and some 'measure' was taken to prevent them defecating on the wing (similar experiments with tippler pigeons involved their cloacae being 'sealed' somehow). Those birds that made it back to their nests were retrapped and had their mass losses calculated and their bills untied. Not all the birds returned. One house martin was found thirty-three hours after release; it had lost a quarter of its body weight. Lyuleeva described what she did and what she saw: 'It reacted to shaking and pushing with a feeble fluttering of its wings. Despite the fact that it did not appear excessively emaciated, it perished after some time. This episode suggested that considerable losses of weight, characteristic of swallows deprived of food for a long period of time, induce torpidity and subsequent death.' Perhaps I am missing something, but this doesn't seem a major scientific breakthrough – if a bird cannot eat it dies.

In the 1960s, at the time of these experiments, the Baltic shore of Lithuania, Latvia and Estonia was a military zone, a heavily policed frontier of the USSR, with patrol planes, watchtowers, border guards, and just a few permitted scientists from Leningrad stitching shut the beaks of swallows. The three countries (then republics) were cut from their shore, their people kept from their sea. The edge of the Soviet Union here was soft: thinning pines and dunes flattening to pale golden beaches, the shallow Baltic coming and going with the slightest of tides. Declared out of bounds to ordinary people, the bow-line of sand became a slowly shifting northern desert.

In a decade of concrete and iron, walls and wires, weaponry and rust, on a cold Soviet shore an ornithologist is sewing a thread through the nostrils of a swallow, a bird that had come freely into that pallid spring from its winter in the skies of South Africa, another country then savage towards its own people. It is hard not to see some human envy, unspoken but deep, at work in these experiments. The birds come and go, we are stuck here, let us catch them and tie them to us.

The wall has fallen now; Lyuleeva's paper is still cited in ornithology books; the swallows are still nesting along the Baltic shore. I saw them there one midsummer night – the sun once more stalled along the thin horizon – hawking for insects between the ruins of a watchtower, picking at the flies a crane disturbed as it walked through a meadow of yellow and purple flowers that held the sun like a million light bulbs. Flying just above the flowers and the crane, the swallow sang as it hunted.

Through the Second World War, German ornithologists were studying redstarts at the same time as John Buxton watched his. Breeding birds were ringed in the Magdeburg and Dresden districts in 1944 and recovered in Spain and Portugal the same autumn, yielding information about the birds' routes out of Europe. Earlier research on what triggered migration urges in redstarts had been done at the bird observatory on Heligoland, the curious island (British from 1807 until 1890, when it was exchanged with Germany for Zanzibar) off the German coast in the North Sea.

John Buxton's brother-in-law was Ronald Lockley – another great bird-man, an island-lover, pioneer student of migration, devotee of seabirds (his film on the gannet made with Julian Huxley won an Oscar in 1938) and a champion of bird observatories (he set up the first on Skokholm in west Wales in 1933). It was he who posted Manx shearwaters from Pembrokeshire to Venice. In October 1936 Lockley went to Heligoland to watch some autumn passage. He arrived at the same time as a large fall of southbound birds: 'Song thrushes and robins predominated. We passed one woman scrubbing the roadway – all citizens must keep the road outside their houses spotless, for dirt is forbidden and litter must be jettisoned through a chute into the sea. There were two robins perching, exhausted, upon the woman's head.' That day 752 birds were caught in the observatory's four traps. Wrecked migrant birds falling accidentally down rainwater pipes made the drinking water on the island taste gamey. The next day 350 woodcocks were shot (one man alone got sixty) and sold for two shillings each to be exported to Hamburg.

Lockley reports a trip to the cinema on Heligoland where he watched a Nazi newsreel with 'goose-stepping, and fierce speeches'. He also visited the bird observatory and was shown an experiment where the responses of trapped redstarts and robins to day-light and day-length were being studied, and the caged birds' attempts to migrate were being recorded.

Dr Shildmacher showed me his redstarts and robins living in special cages with delicately poised perches, which by means of electrical contacts register the restlessness of the birds at night when the migration fever causes them to vibrate their wings and jump about the perches. Every quiver breaks the inked record which revolves slowly over a time graph, showing the exact second the fever began and ended each night. By this means it is proved that the direct cause of migration is fever or intense physiological rhythm of energy which seizes the bird. No matter if confined in the darkest cage, when the hour comes – usually beginning towards midnight and ending just before dawn – it must expend that energy in violent wing trembling and beating.

The German word for this migratory nocturnal restlessness or fever – wing-whirring, perch-hopping, body-turning – is *Zugunruhe*. The term is still used by ornithologists. Wing-whirring is what the redstarts do when they have adapted to their cage. It stands in for the flying they have been prevented from doing, and has been described as 'migration in sitting position'. Another experiment involved would-be migrants themselves writing their intentions – inkpads were placed on the floor of their cages and the birds' feet scratched marks on the papered walls that revealed their levels of activity and directional preferences.

*   *   *

John Clare had been incarcerated in madhouses for thirteen years when, in 1850, he wrote a few letters in code from Northampton General Lunatic Asylum. His code is relatively easily cracked, though a few ambiguities remain. Clare wrote to several women. Two letters to Hellen Maria Gardiner have been published. In one he writes of wanting to kiss and cuddle her and to take her flower-picking and bird-nesting. But he cannot, he says, because he is trapped in a prison. The code makes his words look chopped up and boxy. On the page his writing could be mistaken for hasty field notes or the semblance of a song transcribed, the best that can be done in the wrong medium. His letter is an escape telegram scratched from a cage – an indication of Clare's directional preferences. The poet who didn't punctuate his lines, whose child-hood and youth had been unenclosed, who made nature's mess his ms – his manuscript – is here hedged, edited and confined. Torn from his right mind, he has been tipped from his nest.

> M Dr Hlln Grdnr
> Hp t wll n hppnss nd hlth – nd tht r prtt fc kps the rs blm s t ws whn mt – b th frdls – xxxxx xxx xxx xxx kss's hw s Crln r Sstr – M drst Hlln Mr hw lng t pt m rm rnd r btfl nck nd r chk nd lps – 'Thn drst Hlln ll lv n mr' – M dr hlln hw shld lk t wlk wth n th bnks f th rvr & gthr wld flwrs nd hnt brds Nsts – bt hv bn tn rs n prsn – nd cnnt s n thng f plsr r pstm – Lv nd nj yr slf m dr Hlln Mr nd b rslf fr hr w e hmd [? tll] m scrl m wn nm – stll m mslf snsbl s ver ws
> m drst Hlln Mr | m rs sncrl
> Jhn Clr

This, Clare's editor, Mark Storey, transcribes as:

My Dear Hellen Gardiner

I hope you are well in happiness and health – and that your pretty face keeps the rosy bloom as it was when I met you by the firdales – xxxxx xxx xxx xxx kisses how is Caroline your Sister My dearest Hellen Maria how I long to put my arm around your beautiful neck and your cheek and lips – 'Then dearest Hellen I'll love you een more' – My dear Hellen how I should like to walk with you on the banks of the river & gather wild flowers and hunt birds Nests – but I have been ten years in prison – and cannot see anything of pleasure or pastime – Live and enjoy yourself my dear Hellen Maria and be yourself for here we are homed [? till] I am scarcely my own name – still I am myself sensible as ever I was

my dearest Hellen Maria | I am yours sincerely

John Clare

Twenty years earlier, in May 1830, Clare had recorded how his son found a nightingale's nest. He describes it in detail and with an accuracy that is as good as anything ever published on the nightingale. The precision of his looking and the quality of his thinking about what he sees makes his imprisoned desire to 'hnt brds Nsts' even more upsetting to contemplate.

May 29 My Frederick found today saturday a Nightingales nest in the bottom of the orchard hedge with 4 eggs in it and tho there is but one oak tree as I am told in the Lordship she has got some oak leaves about her nest – in the woods she generally nay always uses dead oak leaves very plentifully at the bottom or outside of her nest and seldom or rarely puts any within side but here she had got dead grass on the outside and a few old oak leaves eaten

bare to the fibres by insects withinside her nest and I never
in my life as yet saw a nightingales nest without oak leaves
and I have found a many and as many as seven one May
in Bushy Close and Royce Wood at Helpstone

In 1850, when he felt himself to be 'scrl m wn nm', Clare was
still certain a nest was the best possible haven in the world – the
only desired enclosure – but he also knew he was far out at sea.

November

Look through my eyes up
At blue with not anything
We could have ever arranged
Slowly taking place

W. S. Graham

Only one ship is seeking us, a black-
Sailed unfamiliar, towing at her back
A huge and birdless silence. In her wake
No waters breed or break.

Philip Larkin

On the cliff top, six elderly men are sitting in a line of low-slung deckchairs. Two tend a camping cooker on which a kettle is cocked; others ply their thermos flasks. When not attending to their hot drinks, all of them look ahead, as if in the front row of an outdoor theatre. Spread and settled in their seats, they are waiting for something to fall from the sky into the gorge in front of them.

The Avon Gorge cuts at the western edge of Bristol like an injury, a three-mile-long, quarter-mile-wide, two-hundred-foot-deep gash through dirty limestone that bleeds brown mud and tidal water. Its plunge is most startling just where the watchers are sitting at the edge of the Downs, an open city park of mown grass and scrub, fringed with stolid Victorian villas. There is a last football pitch and then the sudden calamity of a sheer cliff face. I must have walked to the edge there a thousand times, but every time the falling cliff tells me that my journey, however flat and inconsequential to this point, has nonetheless been made across the surface of the earth. For here the surface has been cut open.

The Gorge marks the edge of the city. Where I stand and the watchers sit there are feral pigeons behaving like rock doves, tumbling over the cliff. On the far side of the Gorge, along the gentler heights of Leigh Woods, there are wood pigeons breaking cautiously from the canopy of trees and hugging the brown edge. Neither species, urban or suburban, seems keen to cross the open air between.

There are two reasons for this. The Gorge is a wind machine. The bash and thrust of air funnelled and collected by its cliffs and slopes makes its own wind, separate from the surrounding city's, and all sorts of local peculiarities blow: gusts, eddies, thermals, vacuums, up-draughts, whirlpools and aerial maelstroms. The Gorge does what it wants with air, and its birds know this. The pigeons cope as best they can; the Gorge's jackdaws and ravens are at home in its turbulence; but one bird knows how the machine works and how to crank it up. It also wants to eat pigeons.

The watchers are waiting for peregrines. A pair has fed and bred in the Gorge since the late 1980s. When I moved to Bristol in the mid 1970s there were none here. I hardly ever saw peregrines then. One, a dark arrowhead, flew fast along a slate mountain ridge high above me in north Wales, as if it had chiselled itself from the cold rock beneath; another, I saw for just a few seconds one winter, a heavy falcon flicking past the stinking henhouses at Steart in Bridgwater Bay.

For a time it seemed that the peregrine and the henhouse were not so far apart. Close to extinction in Britain, the most powerful falcon was also the most vulnerable. Mastery of the air hadn't been enough to save it from the insidious creep of pesticides up the food chain, concentrating in the falcons' bodies and poisoning them, or weakening them so that the females' eggshells became so thin that they were broken by the adult birds as they incubated.

I grew up thinking of peregrines as sickly. They were rare and remote things glimpsed in distant or severe places, but I knew them to have been ruined by the malign human idiocies that were contaminating the whole world. The peregrine was Porton Down and chemical weapons, Agent Orange and napalm, a nuclear missile head and a neutron bomb, death delivered by stealth out of thin air. The magnificent hunter, the apotheosis of the wild, the falcon on the king's gloved fist, was becoming as helpless as a spastic battery hen, a bird that broke its own eggs.

This was true, but the peregrine in my young mind was also built by J. A. Baker's *The Peregrine*. I read it when I was eleven, it stole into my head and stayed there, and I then reread it compulsively. At that time it was mostly ignored by birdwatchers; more recently, it has been noticed by poets. The book has been in and out of print several times since it first appeared in 1967. Next to nothing is known about its author. Though steeped in what seems to be real observation, there are times when you feel you might be reading fiction. Over ten seasons of watching, Baker says, he found 619 peregrine kills. He isn't specific about where and when. Might he have made it up?

Baker's prose seems bruised by his encounters with the hunting falcons (and perhaps also by illness – the book feels written in the knowledge of sickness). It takes on purpled tones and at times is too rich, blood-drenched and strewn with corpses, like

Ted Hughes's bird poems. But it is also wonderful: a grounded man's love affair with the airborne, a story told by a downed Icarus long after his fall, earthed, haggard and self-loathing, traipsing through marshes, crouching in ditches and lurking on field edges, and looking up before a greater creature.

At eleven o'clock the tiercel peregrine flew steeply up above the river, arching and shrugging his wings into the gale, dark on the grey clouds racing over. Wild peregrines love the wind, as otters love water. It is their element. Only within it do they truly live. All wild peregrines I have seen have flown longer and higher and further in a gale than at any other time. They avoid it only when bathing or sleeping. The tiercel glided at two hundred feet, spread his wings and tail upon the billowing air, and turned down wind in a long and sweeping curve. Quickly his circles stretched away to the east, blown out elliptically by the force of the wind. Hundreds of birds rose beneath him. The most exciting thing about a hawk is the way it can create life from the still earth by conjuring flocks of birds into the air . . . In long arcs and tangents the hawk drifted slowly higher. From five hundred feet above the brook, without warning, he suddenly fell. He simply stopped, flung his wings up, dived vertically down. He seemed to split in two, his body shooting off like an arrow from the tight-sprung bow of his wings. There was an unholy impetus in his falling, as though he had been hurled from the sky. It was hard to believe, afterwards, that it had happened at all. The best stoops are always like that.

Baker seems to want to lose himself completely, perhaps even to become an object of prey for the birds. At one point he drops to his knees and creeps through frosty leaf mould towards a peregrine that has just killed a woodcock. He gets within four yards, 'but it is too far, a distance as unspannable as a thousand-foot crevasse. I drag like a wounded bird, floundering sprawled. He watches me . . .' An even stranger meeting of bird and man occurs when Baker is sheltering in a barn and a wood pigeon, struck by a stooping peregrine, hits the roof and slides down in front of him almost dead. He kills the pigeon and tosses it to the ground, where the peregrine collects its prey.

You can see why some bird-men were sceptical about the book's authenticity. The weirdness of *The Peregrine* cannot be overstated, but Baker writes with an extraordinary authority. There are no notes, nor references. Along with things he has seen or appears to have seen, arcane lore from books is included (there is an aside on the crow catchers of Königsberg) and facts that he might have invented (surplus meat from abandoned pere-grine kills helps to support, he says, 'tramps and gypsies'). He says long-tailed tits use the feathers from peregrine kills in the construction of their nests: 'I have found an unusual concentra-tion of such nests in areas where many kills have been made.' This is a unique observation, as far as I know, not supported by any reference anywhere in the ornithological literature.

The book's heart is hunting, and specifically the peregrine's skydiving stoop. Baker works over many kills to find some written equivalence to what he has seen. His obsessive nature as both watcher and writer makes the peregrines' daily hunting habits seem obsessive themselves. Obsession, though, is meaningless to the birds. They hunt all the time but have no conception of hunting as an all-consuming activity. But Baker needs the extremity of his driven life as falcon-follower to be matched by the bird. Early on, he says the peregrine is 'inhibited by a code of behaviour . . . if the code is persistently broken, the hawk is probably sick or insane.' Insane? How would he know? This seems more like a veiled announcement about Baker's own code-breaking, his stepping away from the human world. If his peregrines seem mad, it is because he made them so.

This is nature writing's Goya. At times there is an iron-cold sadistic brutality to Baker's writing: 'The odd are always singled out. The albinos, the sick, the deformed, the solitary, the imbecile, the senile, the very young; these are the most vulnerable.'

> I found myself crouching over the kill, like a mantling hawk. My eyes turned quickly about, alert for the walking heads of men. Unconsciously I was imitating the movements of a hawk, as in some primitive ritual: the hunter becoming the thing he hunts. I looked into the wood. In a lair of shadow the peregrine was crouching, watching me, gripping the neck of a dead branch. We live, in these days in the open, the same ecstatic fearful life. We shun men. We hate their suddenly uplifted arms, the insanity of their flailing gestures, their erratic scissoring gait, their aimless stumbling ways, the tombstone whiteness of their faces.

At other times and for much of the book the imagery is of great precision and it anchors the weirdness: a heron trying to land is like 'a man descending through the trap-door of a loft and feeling for a ladder with his feet'. Baker's best writing is about the flight and fall of the birds he sees above him. He is wonderfully good at going up with them, though he is always at pains to stress his – our – earthbound life: 'Imprisoned by horizons, I envied the hawk his boundless prospect of the sky. Hawks live on the curve of the air. Their globed eyes have never seen the grey flatness of our human vision.'

The Peregrine was written when the catastrophe confronting the bird was taking hold, when it was thought that it could not survive and could no longer retreat to the wild places because the pesticides found it wherever it went. In the book's grimmest moment a peregrine falls back to earth, dashed down from the skies like its own prey, stunned by what has hit it, poisoned by chemicals, and clutching skywards with its yellow claws.

For me this was the greatest and most needed bird book of my youth. For years I ate it up again and again, returning to loved and memorised passages, and breathing its poisoned skies with a shared horror at the coming vacuum, the air without the birds that give it shape.

In 1973 I moved with my mother and father and sister from Surrey to Bristol. I was twelve. Things weren't good at home. My father had tried to relocate his business from Croydon to Bristol, but it went wrong and he ended up losing his job. He had had an affair, it turned out. He was sacked. He was also drinking too much.

One evening back in Croydon, my sister and I had met him after school and the three of us had gone for a meal near his office. By the time we left the restaurant he was too boozed to drive, but we had to get home, fifteen miles away out into the southern edge of suburban Surrey. He drove. My sister climbed onto the back seat of the car and fell asleep. I sat next to him in the front, wide awake and terrified.

The roads were dark along the wooded hills of the North Downs. On a previous night ride home my sister had called these *hairy woods* because of the way, in the car lights, the branches of the trees rather scarily seemed to be plaited together above the road. This night a tawny owl suddenly breathed out of the wood, dusting the edges of the beams, flying down the meshed tunnel in front of us in its brown field of gathered quiet, showing us the way for a few yards before disappearing through the black curtain of the woods at the side of the road.

The owl knew where to go and my father sobered for a moment. But within a mile he had arrived at the fond rambling stage of his drunkenness interspersed with gulfs of silence. I was trying to keep him talking. On a back road, out of the woods but still a few miles north of our house, he nodded forward, his head dipping to his chest. There was a parked car in front of us at the side of the road. I watched it float towards us for a second, like the owl in the lights, then reached over and pushed the wheel to the right with a twelve-year-old effort at steering. The jerk of the car woke my father enough for him to finish the manoeuvre.

We made it back. My mother had been waiting for us. I started crying as I saw her sitting on the foot of the stairs in the hallway, watching our bleary and hooded return into the lit world of home. My sister and I went to bed; I fell asleep to the already familiar night music of my parents shouting.

In this state we arrived in Bristol and were immediately stranded. My parents were in crisis. My father couldn't find a new job and had to go on the dole. We had to move to a cheaper home. I watched my family: horrified by what my father had done, terrified that my parents would separate, desperate to escape the corrosive air around them both.

I watched birds. They always seemed to know where to go and never bumped into one another; only people clashed and collided. At the time I didn't – couldn't have – put it like this. Then, on my paper round one afternoon, I saw a man jump into the Avon Gorge and I learned as deeply as seemed possible, then and now, that we cannot fly and we must make our escapes in other ways.

I had had a morning round but I liked the afternoon one more. It helped fill a drifting hour between the emptiness of school and my cautious return home to our unhappy house. It also took me towards some birds. I cycled with a bag of evening papers over the Gorge across the Clifton Suspension Bridge towards the houses of Leigh Woods where I had to make my deliveries. There were almost always jackdaws out in the middle air of the Gorge as I crossed the bridge. It was hard not to think that they loved the testing winds. The birds, grouped in a conversational cluster with their powder-grey heads and black bodies, like drifting ink and soot, would drop hundreds of feet simply by folding themselves up. Then, flicking open their wings in unison and as if powered from beneath, they would rise up to the handrail of the bridge from below, coming to my eye level and *chack*ing. Their garrulousness always made me feel lonely: how wonderful to live like a jackdaw, always among your own kind and surrounded by reflections of yourself; to be a single organism and a community at the same time – wasn't that a definition of a family?

I looked beyond the jackdaws at the cliffs like marbled meat on one side of the Gorge, the bosomy trees bucking in the wind on the other, and far down to the hemmed-in river below, toiling muddily through the slash it has cut, wanting to be an estuary and to escape to the sea, and meeting a daily silt-thick tide of salt water, wanting to be a river, pushing deep into the heart of the city. Some days a briny tang came up the Gorge and I felt I could taste the Atlantic; on others it was a stink of all the rank socks and rotten vegetation of the West Country. I saw oystercatchers on the mud, black, white and orange like marine buoys, beneath the green oak and ash trees of the riverbank. They piped their seaside yells into the landlocked woodland chorus of songbirds.

On the far side of the bridge in Leigh Woods, the middle of the afternoon was quiet; the place seemed buried into itself, like a sleeping cat. As I cycled up the switchback of the wooded road,

I felt I was opening it up to its evening, bringing something of the jackdaws with me, pushing air into a somnolent world.

The birds helped. There were always birds. On summer afternoons song-thrush and blackbird song was just starting up again at four o'clock, spilling beautiful woodwind descants from the trees. On winter dusks, robin ticks and wren flourishes made percussion for the settling wood. The autumn was full of feeding movements of tits and finches; the spring, of warblers' sung arrivals amidst unfurling leaves.

The woods in the 1970s were still good for two special but secretive birds: wood warblers and hawfinches. They divided the year for me. Wood warblers were spring and summer visitors, and hawfinches were mostly autumn and winter birds. If I saw either bird, the day was made. Once I had found them and knew them to be there, my entrance into their places – the final stretch of my delivery round, three hundred yards of road at the wood edge – was never less than charged.

Both birds were hard to see. In a second-hand bookshop I had found a pamphlet published in 1907, *Some Common Birds of the Neighbourhood of Clifton* by Herbert C. Playne, that described the wood warbler as 'extremely abundant' in Leigh Woods, but they certainly weren't by the 1970s. There were no more than eight birds, they were there for just a few weeks from the late spring, and they lived high and hidden in the top branches of the newly green trees. I found them only when the males sang and made their parachute song flights through the leaves that shuffled and flickered in the breeze with the same colour and movement as they did. After that they disappeared silently into the canopy, like just another leaf, before their invisible departure later in the summer back to Africa.

Hawfinches were even more elusive. I saw them fifteen times in five hundred delivery rounds. They were very shy birds, the colour of autumn leaves and ripe hazelnuts. I knew them by their exits: their short wings and short tail flying away quickly through the trees, rebuking me for having broken into their Arcadia, for catching them at their bath in a woodland puddle like Diana; or once trying the tarmac of the road, stepping like fire-walkers over hot coals.

Hawfinches have a voice as near to silent as any bird. Their call is a tightly squeezed *pissp*. It is very easy to miss. The birds seem to be in a permanent reverse out of the world. But for their beak, you would think there was something apologetic about them, with their gentle tones of camouflaging green and brown, their whispered call and their swift retreat from view. Their beak, though, is enormous, the largest and most powerful beak of all the European finches. It is a colossal tool, an anvil and hammer at once and very serious. You might call it out of proportion, except that nothing is in nature. The books told me that a hawfinch could exert enough pressure with its beak to squeeze a cherry stone until it popped and surrendered its soft heart. Their call makes this very sound.

At best I got fleeting glimpses, but both birds had great power for me. On an ordinary weekday afternoon, with my bag full of local news, just a few seconds with them opened another world. On the back road I felt that only I knew the wood warblers and hawfinches were there, and that their quietest of dramas, whispering itself out of existence, was shown only to me. Sure enough, they have vanished now. I haven't heard wood warblers in Leigh Woods for twenty springs, and the hawfinches have gone as well.

There was a bird missing then, too. The Gorge needed another performer. As I crossed the bridge every day I always thought there should be peregrines. All the extra air the Gorge put into the world seemed made for them. A stooping peregrine would fully chase it into life. I looked and hoped and craved a stoop, and made one in my mind and replayed it again and again: that hinge in time when the peregrine reaches its tipping point and the accumulated knowledge and energy of the bird's hunting life – its eye on its prey and its height above it – rolls it from effortless horizontal flight into a near vertical dive. It stops in the air, appears to raise itself slightly, folds its wings over its back and, from the most casual of starts, slips forward. It drops down in the shape of a smooth pebble, fast, faster, falling in an ecstatic arc towards something far below that the falcon has seen and singled out, but which will probably never know or see what is about to hit it. The stoop is a piece of site-specific theatre, a superb stunt that is ordinary but beyond our imagination, a free fall made by a controlling intelligence beyond our comprehension.

One November afternoon, slicked with rain, I was looking out for peregrines as I cycled to Leigh Woods, my newspaper bag over my shoulder. The day was quiet. The air in the Gorge loured. Bikes had to go on the pavement of the bridge. Walking about twenty yards ahead of me was a youngish man with thick and tumbling black hair. He wore a dark brown corduroy jacket. I began to catch up with him and as I braked, preparing to go around him, he turned his head to the right and glanced over his shoulder. Perhaps he saw me, maybe he didn't. As he turned his head, he brought a cigarette in his right hand to his mouth and dragged on it; its tiny fire throbbed brightly back to me. Then, still walking, with the cigarette in his mouth, he put both hands on the wooden railing of the bridge to his left, and vaulted over the side.

I knew at once what was happening and what had happened. In front of me, a man was jumping off the suspension bridge to kill himself. I stopped my bike, dropped it beneath me, knowing that I needed to hurry. I didn't look over the railings, I couldn't.

It was as if a steel wall had grown up from them high into the sky, stopping me from looking down after him.

I turned and ran back to the tollbooth about one hundred and twenty yards behind me. I leant through the glass slits into the booth, where pedestrians passed their 2p fare, and said to the man inside, 'Someone has jumped off the bridge.' I was hurrying, because in my head I thought it might be possible to stop him, to catch him even.

There were two men inside the booth. They both pointed to its side door and I came round into their little room, with its tea mugs and transistor radio and low piles of copper coins waiting to be given as change. One of them was already on the telephone. I remember him saying, 'We've got one over.' His voice was grey like old paint. I was breathing hard. The men were calm. One asked me if I'd left my bike on the bridge and I said that I had and he said he would come with me and get it. We went out across the bridge. The steel walls were still up for me, but as we got to where my bike lay, he put both his hands onto the varnished railing, just as the man before had, and peered out, over and down to the river and the road, two hundred and fifty feet below. I couldn't look down, but looking back towards the end of the Gorge, where the river arrives from Bristol and the high ground gives way to ordinary England, I could see that far below there was a line of cars on the road that ran beneath the bridge.

We went back to the tollbooth, me pushing my bike, the bag of papers still around my neck. I couldn't form words in my mouth without swallowing hard. The men didn't speak to me; they finished their tea. An ambulance arrived outside the booth. I thought it might be for me, but one of the men went out to explain that it had come to the wrong place. The newsagent appeared – the men must have telephoned him – and he took my bag and drove off over the bridge to deliver the papers. It grew dark. In the booth, I waited. A policeman came in, big and clumsy with his helmet. He asked me what I had seen and my name and address, and wrote a few words in his notebook. He said he would come and see me again and that I should go home.

Apart from glimpsing the line of cars backed up on the Portway, I had no sense of the end of the man's jump. All I had was the beginning. As I cycled home, a silent film of his leap began to play in my head. It ran again. Then again. I told my parents what I had seen. They were kind, but I could see them struggling to know what to say or do. That night was terrible. I needed to clean my mind and stop the film and I couldn't. That leap and the fall. The leap and the fall. The leap and the fall. I slept in my parents' room on a camp bed.

The next day I had to do my paper round as usual. Someone was walking ahead of me on the bridge again. I got off my bike and waited for them to get to the other side so that I could cross. There were jackdaws, but I couldn't look down over the railing at them as I had done before. Since then, I never have been able to.

As I delivered my papers, I became preoccupied with thinking that if I had been there a minute earlier or later, I wouldn't have seen anything. This was a thought-game I was used to playing because of birds. The hawfinches on the road were only there for a few seconds. If I hadn't been there then, I would never have seen them.

The second night was worse. I couldn't close my eyes without the half-turned head, the glowing cigarette and the athletic vault flashing there again and again, stuck in the gate of my mind. I felt I'd been got at, contaminated somehow. The world was calling on me. Life and death, already. Everything felt speeded up.

A few days later, a policeman and a policewoman came round

to our house and asked me to describe what I had seen. It didn't take long. They wrote it down. The policewoman told me that there would probably have to be an inquest into the cause of the man's death and that I would have to give evidence. No one said the word 'suicide'; no one said anything about what would make a man jump off a high bridge. It was as if I had witnessed an accident, not a decision.

As I waited for the inquest, I began to extend the man's fall in my mind. I think this was because I wanted to get beyond the endless replay of its starting. But it had to do with birds too. His launch, and then what? There was a moment of energetic push, out into the air, powered by the kick of his legs off the bridge and his hands on the railing, and then maybe he registered the thinness, the nothing, as the air failed to hold him. But my man – he became 'my' within a day or so, as I grew aware that I was carrying something of him with me whether I liked it or not – my man didn't want to stay up.

My thoughts closed in on the moment when the energy of his push from the railings equalled the force of gravity and the air's collusion with it and his body felt weightless in space. There would have been a moment like that – that was what it felt like when I used to jump from the swing in our old back garden. I loved that feeling. For a fraction of a second you have the tiniest intimation of flight.

A peregrine could have shown me this if I had seen one begin its stoop. A man did instead. The peregrine uses its own falling weight to bring death to its pigeon prey. My man used the same to kill himself. It didn't matter that he couldn't fly. It mattered that he didn't have wings. There was nothing to hold him up. The peregrine folds its wings away so that the same thing happens, falling and killing. The man fell and died.

Weeks later, a policeman called at the house to deliver a

notice about the inquest into the man's death. I had to attend the coroner's court in Bristol. It was on a school day, in the morning. I wore my uniform and my father took me. We arrived without being certain of where to go. We went into the building, its municipal wooden doors with crinkly glass and polished brass plates giving onto a stone hall with a desk. We were directed to a room, which was carpeted and half panelled with wood. The stone busyness of the hall was muffled and everyone in the room was whispering. There were only a few people there. One was a youngish woman, her hair tied up, wearing a black dress. Her eyes were rimmed with red as if a razor blade had shaved a single layer of skin in a fine circle, taking her eyelashes away to show what was beneath. We waited in the quiet.

We were ushered into the court. There was wood everywhere. The floor was wood, there was panelling up the walls, the court furniture and its strange low fences and gates, which had to enact some separation of parts of the court – all of it was wood. I can't remember the order of events, but quickly, it seems, I was called up to the witness stand. I had to swear on the Bible that I would tell the truth. An official held a card in front of me with the oath that I had to say. My throat was dry and I tried to lick my lips discreetly to help me get the words out. The coroner in a dark suit sat like a judge behind a wooden desk on a dais. The only windows were behind me, set high in the wall. A neutral light came through them, as if the city had been able to order a civic sky.

The hush was like a library or a museum. I was on show, standing up and expected to speak loudly. I knew that amongst the people sitting below me in the public area of the room would be – surely – someone who knew the man. The youngish woman with the eyes was there.

The coroner asked me to say what I had seen on the bridge. I was allowed to read from the statement the police had taken. It was only a few sentences long but it was hard going. I never seemed to have enough breath. Each sentence fell away and was lost in the hush and the wood of the court.

I got to the end of my statement. The coroner said, I remember, 'That wasn't very impressive, was it?' and he looked across at me. He said the court needed to be able to hear me clearly and he made me read it out again. What I wanted to say was that I was frightened of what I had seen on the bridge and that I hated the man for doing it in front of me. But I felt under some official pressure to send this dead thing out of our world. The job had fallen to me. I tried again with the words. The wood of the room soaked them up once more. I was a disappointment, I knew, and I hadn't been able to do what I should have done. I could tell that the coroner was still not impressed but had decided he had got from me as much as he could. I was allowed to sit down.

The court went on. There was another witness. A middle-aged lady had been driving along the road under the bridge. Something had hit the rock face to her right and bounced onto the road in front of her. It was him.

Someone, perhaps the coroner himself, told the court about who the man was. I don't remember his name. He had parents who lived somewhere in the Caribbean; they hadn't come to the court. He had been depressed for some time. His business hadn't gone well. He had run a shop on his own, just up from the suspension bridge in Clifton. As this was described, I remembered walking past the shopfront one day and catching his eye as he looked up from behind his counter. He had had a moustache.

Ten years after my falling man, when I was gathering information on the threatened birds of Africa – a catalogue of rarities and extinctions substantially made from information taken from the labels attached to dead birds' feet – I was struck by a sense of something familiar in the atmosphere of the Natural History Museum's bird collection. As I went into the building at Tring for the first time, my breath faltered. The drawers of the dead birds that I opened, the wooden and metal cabinets and the hospital-clean corridors between them, the place's institutional quietness and the feeling it gave of being in some giant tomb – I had been somewhere like this before. The thought rose up in me, drying my throat, that the dead birds of the museum were taking me back to the coroner's courtroom in Bristol.

After fifty years of absence, peregrines came back to the Gorge, and now they are easy to see. The watchers sitting in their deckchairs on the cliff top will point them out to you. I have often seen them in the Gorge, but I still have never seen one stoop there.

December

An Airy Crowd came rushing where he stood:
Which fill'd the Margin of the fatal Flood.
Husbands and Wives, Boys and unmarry'd Maids;
And mighty Heroes more Majestick Shades.
And Youths, intomb'd before their Fathers Eyes,
With hollow Groans, and Shrieks, and feeble Cries:
Thick as the Leaves in Autumn strow the Woods:
Or Fowls, by Winter forc'd, forsake the Floods,
And wing their hasty flight to happier Lands:
Such, and so thick, the shiv'ring Army stands:
And press for passage with extended hands.

Virgil, translated by John Dryden

. . . as we take, in fact, a general view of the wonderful
stream of our consciousness, what strikes us first is the
different pace of its parts. Like a bird's life, it seems to be
made of an alternation of flights and perchings.

William James

D usk on the winter solstice: the shortest day and
longest night of the year. I was cold and alone on
a track on the Somerset Levels, looking towards
the dying light in the west. Moving across the sky in front of
me, like the breath of the earth, were thousands of birds –

starlings arriving to roost, to put away their day, and so too, on this day, the year. From the next dawn the glorious creep towards spring would be under way: more light; a future; repairs; song, nests and eggs.

The year had drained to this pinching day and its paltry hours of watery sun. In the middle of the afternoon, a cold, iron-hard dark arrived from the east and pushed all the light away to a buckling golden foil fussing on the western horizon. There the day launched a last flare like a crack of magma seamed through lava. The year was burning down.

It was freezing on the old track across the peat moor at Westhay. Last night's unmelted ice thickened and reached towards tonight's dewfall. It frosted the tiny flashes of the puddles, the lank grass around them, and my boots. Molehills along the track had frozen mountain-hard with little ice caps on their summits. The sky was clear and harsh. High ice crystals prinked its blue like a snowfield. Night was coming and I shivered, but from all points of the evening skies the starlings came over me like warmth.

Westhay is part of the watery grid of the Somerset Levels. They are level or flat only relative to the hills that rim them on three sides. Their flatness is like the flatness of the sea out to their western edge. The land buckles as if it remembers it came from this sea. Around ten thousand years ago, at the end of the last Ice Age, when the sea rose, Westhay became a salt marsh. Six and half thousand years ago, as the sea receded, the marsh silted up and became, in slow succession, a freshwater reed swamp, then wet fen woodland, and then a raised bog.

Millennia of rot laid down peat that cloaked these new flatlands with a deep black soil. More than five thousand years ago, people built the first trackways – like the one I stood on – across the spongy soak so they could pass to and from adjacent higher ground, the hills of the Mendips and the humps and mounds of Glastonbury. At Shapwick, near Westhay, in the spring of 3806 BC, the Sweet Track – a wooden road – was laid, using cut (and probably coppiced) oak, ash, lime, hazel, alder and holly. It is amongst the earliest pieces of woodmanship in the world. Later, people began to dig the peat. Walking on the track, I could feel the earth's plastic bounce, its five-thousand-year-old give.

Nowadays, something of an old, low-intensity life lingers on the Levels in the slow suck and churn of mud and grass, in the drip and spread of water and sunlight. I could see where an abandoned orchard's unpicked cider apples fermented beneath the skeletons of their trees, red globes of bright treasure in a damp grave. In the fields, bullocks chewed an endless cud. Their hot breath hung at their nostrils, as they breathed out their own local weather systems, making clouds from a cast of their lungs.

People, starlings, cattle and peat-cutting lived side by side until the recent past. In the last few years commercial digging finished, and the gouges cut into the land were abandoned and allowed to fill with water and new vegetation. At Westhay the old peat workings left flooded mires and swampy pools with reeds growing across them, making a perfect night-time sanctuary for roosting birds.

Every evening, through the winters of the past few years, thousands, even millions, of starlings have come to sleep here. Eight million were counted, somehow, in one roost here a year or so ago. This may be the largest ever gathering of birds in Britain. Imagine Hyde Park Corner in failing light and the entire population of London arriving there from all points across the city.

At Westhay some starlings were local birds, others flew in from miles away. Arrow-headed echelons of them had shot south above me as I drove to the Levels hours before. Starlings are sharp and pointed, and the first flocks they form on their way to their roosts are sharp and pointed too. They were already heading purposefully towards Westhay, raking the sky. In midwinter the starling's day is even shorter than the few hours of light. Not long after midday they are thinking of bed and their assembly flights begin.

Other starlings spend their winter days in the fields adjacent to the reed-beds where they will roost. Flocks of a hundred or more were already out on the Levels. Local birds and arriving birds mixed, squabbling, feeding and talking. In the fields they looked older and more purposeful than they did as village starlings an hour before. They seemed to be joining some necessary action. A call-up was under way.

That evening, summer was further off than it would ever be. Stowed sunshine from months ago was rationed, like the last grains of sugar in a siege. Its light and heat survived in only the flimsiest of things: the feathered seed heads of the reeds that engraved fine scratches onto the plate of the sky, and the tiny contact calls swapped between parties of long-tailed tits as they moved through the willow tops, living in the warmth of their own talk. Everything else was, or soon would be, a shade of black.

The light had nearly gone. All that was moving looked shadowed: the great spotted woodpecker whose bouncing flight ahead of me echoed the folds and dips of the fen path appeared to have lost its white and red; the buzzard that planed alongside the ditch looked so dark I thought at first it was a melanistic bird; the gulls beating north were as drained of colour as the cormorants flying the other way.

Black had overtaken the starlings too. If I could separate just one bird from the lines flying above me, or the legions in the fields, I could find their daytime sheen of pearl-spotted oily iridescence, but the massing birds took on a generic darkness. It was not the furred black of wet peat; that came later. For now, the starlings' black was the feathered brown-black of drying peat, the soil at the surface, not the buried earth.

From all sides there were lines of starlings, in layers of about fifteen birds thick stretching for three miles back into the sky and coming towards the reed beds that surrounded me. They came out of the furthest reaches of the air, materialising into it from far beyond where my eyes or binoculars could reach in the murk. All flew with a lightly rippling glide, as if the net they were making of themselves was being evenly drawn into a single point in the reed bed.

Their arrival and accumulation had been eerily silent. From the early afternoon, first in the villages and then in the staging fields, there had been great noise. A collective telling and retelling of starling life rose through those hours of pre-roost talk to a complicated but loquacious rendering of all things – idiomatic adventure, mimetic brilliance and delighted conversational murmur. Once this annotation of the day was done, the birds grew quiet and lifted up and off to begin their thickening flights towards the roost.

There were thousands of mute birds around me, their wheeze and jabber left behind. Many thousands more were too far away to hear, but their calm progress towards the roost suggested they flew in silence. Closer, the only noise was of the flock's feathers. As they wheeled and gyred en masse, the sound of their wings turning swept like brushes dashed across a snare drum or a Spanish fan being flicked open. The air was thick with starlings, inches apart and racked back into the darkening sky for a mile. Every bird was within a wing stretch of another. None touched.

A rougher magic overtook them as they arrived above the reeds. Great ductile cartwheels of birds were unleashed across the sky. Conjured balls of starlings rolled out and up, shoaling from their descending lines, thickening and pulling in on themselves – a black bloom burst from the seedbed of birds. One wheel hit another and the carousels of birds chimed and merged, like iron filings made to bend to a magnet. The flock – but *flock* doesn't say anything like enough – pulsed in and out.

I could feel my eyes being forced to deepen their field of view to take in birds behind birds behind birds; I could feel my brain slowing as it tried to compute the organising genius of what was in front of me. Floating above a peat bog in the dark, I was to sit a maths exam in a room drawn by Escher. I couldn't do it. I failed O-level maths twice and optical illusions make me feel sick. To describe the flock is like trying to hold on to a dream in daylight – it slips from me, it cannot be summoned except in fragments, and they cannot be transcribed. Try singing it.

I thought of Thomas Tallis's forty-part devotional motet *Spem in alium* from 1570. For as long as I have known it I have loved this piece, especially the recording made in 1962 in King's College Chapel in Cambridge. Could its eleven and a half minutes of singing light the black midwinter night and the black midwinter starlings?

Spem in alium doesn't describe what the flock does. It is the flock. The music – unaccompanied singing, or rather singing that only accompanies itself – comes in, opening its throat before us, beginning with some tentative note on some frontier of sound, arriving into a space from a place without space, from far away. It might be one bird flying, or the sound of a wave beginning far out in the Atlantic. The sound catches and swirls towards us, becomes a striving, and folds into itself and floats and opens further with a beautiful frail young solo which twists my ears and then gives onto a landscape like the great heave of an abstract painting, making me think of Peter Lanyon's sky masterpieces, as well as starlings hatching from the evening. It is huge and everywhere, but tilted and very close. And all along there is the strangest of pulses, a breathing, a flexing continuo, that rises into the heights of the chapel at King's College, climbing around the stone like a filling bath. The voices arrive from all corners, unfolding and bending, in relay and alone. Forty throats open. They sing together and against one another, and then against one another and together again. It is a wind blowing out of paradise. It is a vast river of warm stone and dark skies, of sea silver, of black and sheen and matt and dust and lisping and echoes and news and pain, and it deepens beyond voices until the great stone room is singing its own song, and its sound goes brightly down beneath the building into the earth and then rebounds, coursing up the vaulting out into the winter night. There are snake whispers and dead leaves rustle; there is music for outriders and prophets, songs for latecomers and dreamers. It is a coffin and a bed. Then: a resolution, the first of many sung 'Domines', that wrestles with the flex of moving song, which wants to gather the word in right away and take it home, but cannot; the word repeats and rises and wanders beautifully out into terraced voices, with vistas that stretch as far as the mind can go, pushing back the night, opening the earth, and then the lit dark comes, its stars thrown over you the moment the sun goes, the soil sings. And big and kind and at the right time it ends, calming to begin with, an embrace and a decision, and then the wild shriek of a single young voice climbing and breaking back out into the sky for one last flight, loud, and screaming, and elated.

Standing under the storm of starlings, I wondered about the moment when a single bird commits itself to the collective swirl. You can see it. Individuals hurried towards the flock; one came quick and low just over my head from behind and it surfed into the fabulous mêlée. I tried to keep it in view and for a few seconds

I had it. Then its singleness was taken into the whole; it angled its wings as all the others did around it, and the scattering shot of birds shifted and I lost it. We cannot watch this without thinking that the flock becomes a single organism, but why should it? There doesn't need to be one god up there, there could be eight million.

I could feel the starlings wanting to go down into the reeds towards the safety of the soil. Each flick pushed them lower – as if they were obtaining successively closer approximations towards the solution of a problem – but still they rose and folded upon themselves. The pressure snap of the flock just above the reeds set off water rails below, its whiplash forcing open a door so that eight spook sirens (of a torturer or the tortured, I am never sure) could escape to squeal across the marsh.

It was almost dark and getting colder still. Freezing mist rose from the gelid pools. Wigeon whistled like boatmen hurrying to pack away their oars. Pied wagtails *chissick*ed about me on the track, loath to settle before the starlings.

And now they began to disappear. The lowest birds brushed down over the reeds again. Half continued, but under the flowing cape of the larger flock a phalanx invisibly dropped down. Starling fission. Arrows were becoming anchors. Why those ones, I wondered, why there? Had they been pushed to the ground by the bulk of massed birds above them, had they finished something those birds were still occupied with? Had this been a purposeful dance, were they leaders or losers, were those reeds marked as theirs, was this their dormitory? It is known that starlings' roosts are organised with adult males predominating at the centre and young females pushed to the periphery, but how was each bird filed into place?

There was a rumpus. The birds that slipped from flight down

between the reed stems at the edge of an iced mire disturbed a bittern. It got up like a sleepwalker (*myre dromble* was an old name for a bittern, meaning a sluggish bird of the marshes) and flapped heavily away through the flying starlings, an old unrolling brown carpet, until it was able to slump down in another patch of reeds.

The combing and pleating of the master starling flock continued. But the exit was quick and simple. The gathering preamble, the flying and flocking, had been the main event. Deciding to go to bed takes much more time than getting into it. More and more starlings dropped into the reeds; all were immediately hidden from view.

As they arrived at their roost they began talking again. The encore took one minute only. They shared their last words and a simultaneous full stop. The water rails quit squealing the moment the starlings fell silent. Shush. The loudspeakers were switched off at the same time as the light. The show was over; everything had been put away into the black box of the earth. Goodnight.

I stayed on the track in the midwinter dark, looking across the reeds in front of me that now held thousands of invisible sleeping starlings. I remembered the storm petrels on Mousa waking at midnight in midsummer, the black tower and the black birds that came from the sea. Now at its other corner, the year was ready to shut. Behind the reeds at Westhay, the last vestige of light seemed to keep an auroral trace of the starlings. For a few moments there was a kind of black starling light, like winter pollen, twinkling amongst the starlight, an after-image (as starlight is itself) of what was once there.

I walked back and was surprised to see shadowy figures joining the main path from other tracks across the moor. Unnoticed by me as I stared at the starlings, others had come to see the spectacle. A scattered crowd watching an assembling crowd come down to earth amongst them. Starlings, ordinary starlings, *Sturnus vulgaris*.

I drove home in the dark and they seemed to be everywhere still; I passed the Harptrees, the two villages East and West, and I thought of the starlings I'd seen there on my way out gathering in bare winter trees and making their noise, and of Coleridge, who also watched starlings, writing 'The Eolian Harp' in Clevedon just a few miles west of the Harptrees. And I remembered that in 1904 Cecil Sharp had collected bird 'starving' or scaring cries there too: 'Hi! Shoo all o' the birds/Shoo aller birds/Shoo aller birds'.

Back in Bristol, I wanted to do my own starling diary before bed, as they do. I pulled books from the shelves and scrabbled in notebooks and plundered my memories, and while the Westhay birds slept I gathered and wrote down as many of my starlings as I could:

- the starlings running over the snow-covered lawn of our back garden, doing their human walk but printing their bird feet in the snow, one of the first birds I identified, aged five or so;
- starlings weaving through flocks of parrots in Los Angeles, the Europeans jiving with the Brazilians;
- the starlings of Fair Isle that go south in their first winter, return home, then never leave;
- Nero's starling, as told by Pliny, practising its Greek and Latin and managing 'ever longer phrases' every day;
- starlings in the rain on the back of sheep in Scotland, like people riding elephants;
- Bobby Tulloch's scientific note on starlings from Shetland using sheep as towels, and another of a starling drowning on Yell in a bowl of custard;

- rose-coloured and regular starlings in a thistle field at the foot of a Turkish mountain, children in starling-pink and starling-green watching me watching them there;
- a starling singing its song of songs, including an oyster-catcher's yelp and a curlew's summer bubbling, on the roof of the house where Van Gogh lived in south London, telling me where it had been that summer;
- starlings at the railway station in Bristol baffling a preda-tory sparrowhawk, by opening and then closing their roost flock around it;
- introduced starlings, the first birds I saw in South Africa, when being met at the airport by Claire, who grew up in Cape Town calling them Eurostars;
- Bertolt Brecht and Rosa Luxemburg identifying starlings with the urban proletariat;
- starlings in Dante compared to the damned, 'As starlings, when the evenings draw in,/assemble in tremendous seething flocks,/so are those dark souls gathered by the wind . . .';
- Edward Thomas in France in March 1917 describing German shelling 'over our heads into Beaurains all night – like starlings returning 20 or 30 a minute';
- starlings flying across Columbus Circle in New York City in 2008 towards Central Park, where they were first released in 1890–91;
- Rachel Carson, standing up for the maligned introduced starlings of North America – which only did what other Europeans had done: arrived, moved west, succeeded – and writing an article in 1939 called 'How About Citizenship Papers for the Starling';
- an English roost of starlings detected on a radar screen in the Second World War disturbed by German V-1

bombs flying over it and 'causing a scare that the enemy had invented a new form of radio jamming';

- starlings blamed for £100 of damage to a reed bed in Lincolnshire in the eighteenth century, after one night of a roost and its 'abundant excrement';
- spotless starlings laughing at me, so it seemed, from the roof of a holiday apartment, near Alicante in Spain, as I tried to learn to dive, aged forty, in a swimming pool below them;
- Laurence Sterne's caged starling in *A Sentimental Journey* that speaks its confinement: 'I can't get out – I can't get out'; Sterne's own name, close to *starn*, a dialect word for starlings;
- the starlings that bred this last summer opposite my flat, in a roof crack above the Creation Nail Studios ('Full Eyebrow Waxing £5.00') and wheezed from the gable through the rain and traffic slush to my desk;
- 'Starlings!' shouted derisively to the men on the quay, by passengers on ships from the northern isles of Orkney as they steamed into Kirkwall;
- Coleridge keeping starlings in mind, a letter from him explaining why he wasn't writing, remembering Sterne (as well as Macbeth), and comparing himself to a starling, 'self-incaged, & always in the Moult, & my whole Note is, Tomorrow, & tomorrow, & tomorrow';
- Coleridge two years before that, watching winter starlings from a coach travelling south to London and writing starlings as well as Tallis sings them, 'I saw Starlings in vast Flights, borne along like smoke, mist – like a body unindued with voluntary Power / – now it shaped itself into a circular area, inclined – now they formed a Square – now a Globe – now from complete orb into an Eclipse

– then oblongated into a Balloon with the Car suspended, now a concave Semicircle; still expanding or contracting, thinning or condensing, now glimmering and shivering, now thickening, deepening, blackening!' and two days later, in the turmoil of London, Coleridge contrasting 'the harmonious System of Motions, in the country & every where in Nature . . . [with] . . . The immoveableness of all Things thro' which so many men were moving';

– starlings dropping down to my sister's lawn seconds after she has scraped the crumbs from a bread board onto it;

– starlings hovering at a seed dispenser in my parents' garden, irked but cunning, trying to work out how the tits manage to feed there;

– a young starling with its legs splayed like a baby in nappies going head first down the stretched throat of a lesser black-backed gull near my home in Bristol;

– a shambling family of starlings on Coll in May, debauched and chaotic and moaning about winter, next to a corncrake still stoking up the year with its *crex crex* song ('endorsing summer' as Louis MacNeice says, with the 'sourdine in their throat' as Andrew Marvell says);

– the 'brabbling' starling, as John Skelton describes their noise;

– the charivari of morning starlings on countless roofs of my life, jangling and gasping and putting the kettle on, always installed in the day long before me;

– fir trees full of starlings, common grackles and American crows in Fergus, Ontario, defragging the day before going to sleep;

– starlings perched but swimming with their wings and heads up with their spiky beards of feathers in spring on a farm near Bordeaux, singing their sex songs, mimicking a tawny owl's *kewick* (did they dream it?), a golden oriole's torrid whistles, a green woodpecker's yaffle;

- W. B. Yeats's 'stare', and John Clare's 'starnels' that 'darken down the sky', and him in his lunatic asylum thinking he is in prison: 'I am still wanting like Sternes Prisoners Starling to "get out" but cant find the Way';
- and my childhood sleeping under starlings, listening to them dragging junk for their nests into the cracks of the roof above my bed, their scuttle noise up there at dusk and dawn;
- my starlings and yours, always going home, all of them, at home everywhere, all of them, running with the grain of the world.

I started writing this book in an attic room in my parents' house in south Bristol. I had fled there sad and distraught in the middle of a winter. My domestic and emotional life was a mess. Trying not to feel sorry for myself, I sat at a table under a window and began to write about what I remembered of birds and my bird-watching forty years before, when I had lived with my parents as a boy. As then, gulls trekked into the city along the lines of water that flowed through it, like flakes of gold leaf against the evening sky. In the morning they went the other way, their marine bleats tugging Bristol out to sea. From the high window I looked north beyond the gulls and back towards the city and the steep bowed hillside of Clifton with its Georgian terraces like sculpted continuations of the Gorge's limestone cliffs.

I had lived in another attic in a house up there as a child. Starlings scratched in the roof an inch away through the plaster behind my bed; below me, I had watched spotted flycatchers in

July breeding in the garden wall, coming to and from a nest in a crack between the stones where the mortar had loosened and crumbled to dust. The snap of their beaks was the only sharp noise in the hum of hot summers. There too, one May, I had identified a garden warbler singing hidden within a huge candled horse chestnut that spread its great branches across the road as if it was holding its own skirt. For three springs this bird or its children sang from the tree. I never saw them once, but their singing filled my room, a rich and convoluted slurp of a song, which still sounds to me like a commentary on the colour of their life, 'a green thought in a green shade'.

Forty years on, I repaired myself as best I could and after a few months in the new attic found somewhere of my own to live. A year later my parents also moved. I came back to help them clear the loft space of years of family clutter that had been shipped from house to house in Bristol. Among my old school books and some Victorian stuffed birds – which I rescued and have around me now – there was also a box of fifty small plastic bags of soil. Some were peaty black, like dried mole skins; others had a more southern Somerset ruddiness, a colour that to me always seems old, like cheese rind, or the face of a red deer. Each bag had had a label stuck to it, with scrawny writing listing a grid reference and sometimes a field name, but many labels had lost their glue and had slipped off and gathered in the bottom of the box.

Thirty years before, I had collected and bagged the soil as part of a barely begun and never finished school geography project on the land use of the Somerset Levels. Only when I saw the bags did I remember having done this. I had forgotten I had dug all that soil at the age of seventeen with my mother's garden trowel from fifty fields between Westhay and Wells, intending to map its qualities and correlate this with land use. Did cattle need richer soil than apples? How moist a loam could vegetables tolerate? It was a ludicrously ambitious project and I ended up doing two days of sample collection and nothing more. I don't know why I had held on to the soil. After it slipped my mind it had found its way up under the roof. The whole house had been living under the soil of the Somerset Levels for years. And I had come back there seeking refuge, a roost, and had slept and written in an attic room beneath the earth: black thoughts under black soil.

In the Campo Santo in Pisa, the city's beautiful colonnaded burial ground, I once followed a house sparrow that had been picking at the earth in the central garden of the building as it flew in through the open tracery of a stone window, along an arcade of graves and tombstones, and out through another window. The Campo Santo was founded at the end of the twelfth century when Archbishop Lanfranchi returned from the Crusades with a cargo of soil from Golgotha in order that eminent Pisans might be buried in holy earth. The sparrow moving through the building made me think of Bede and his image of life's journey as a sparrow flying through a lit hall. The echo the stone gave to the sparrow's chirps as it flew made me think of Nick Drake's home recording of his song 'Fly' (released on *Time of No Reply*) made in 1969 at Tanworth-in-Arden in Warwickshire. Before he begins to sing his song – which is about discovering that the earth is where we belong – you can hear house sparrows chattering outside the room where he made his tape. Against the sound in the gutters he sings 'It's really too hard for to fly.' And I thought of the sparrow above the dead of Pisa, and Nick Drake dead now, and all the sparrows that sang from his gutter dead too, and again Keats's line from his letter of 22 November 1817 to Benjamin Bailey came to me, a talisman ever since I first read it years ago, 'if a Sparrow come before my Window, I take part in its existence and pick about the Gravel'. Keats's sparrow is dead. Yet every time I read his words, as every time I hear Nick Drake and his sparrows, or hear the singing made in King's College Chapel in 1962, I am restored to life, as I was in the dark of midwinter, at the year's midnight, on Westhay Moor amid starlings.

January

You acid-blue metallic bird,
You thick bird with a strong crest,
Who are you?
Whose boss are you, with all your bully way?
You copper-sulphate blue bird!

D. H. Lawrence

What birds were they? He thought that they must be swallows who had come back from the south. Then he was to go away for they were birds ever going and coming, building ever an unlasting home under the eaves of men's houses and ever leaving the homes they had built to wander.

James Joyce

The new year began with dead things, with blown eggs and dried skins, on a tobacco farm in southern Zambia where an old British army major, poleaxed with illness, deplored the end of all good genealogies amid his cabinets – the best collection in the world – of eggs and skins of cuckoos and other avian cheats.

It started with me feeling disinherited and estranged. I was, at best, third in line to a throne. Lazaro was first. That morning, before his work as a farmhand in the Major's tobacco crop, he had found the tawny-flanked prinia's nest. He led us through the tall wet grass of an abandoned field towards a marker flag of red tape, splaying his wide bare feet as he went, knocking the silver rods of rainwater from the grass stems to the earth. Behind Lazaro was Claire, in her hat and long sleeves, guarded against the heating sun, and shouldering a bag of equipment. She is an ornithologist, the farm is her field-site, the prinias and cisticolas and the cuckoo finches that parasitise them are her study birds. I had come to see her and them and brought up the rear, sweating and lost in Africa.

Then a party of four swallows flashed past, drawn by the insects we stirred. They dipped near the grass heads between Lazaro and Claire and flew on, their dark blue backs catching my eye. Something shifted and I could see again. They were barn swallows, my swallows.

The night before I left Britain to visit Zambia I was in bed in Bristol surrounded by my half-packed bags; I hadn't shut the curtains as a big near-full moon was riding the night sky. Like a bed-ridden astronomer, I lay in the dark looking up at it. It was a cold ash-grey winter moon with none of its yeasty summer curd. As it barged through the thinning clouds, I picked up my binoculars. It looked like a hole cut in the sky's black curtain. It was that in my childhood fantasy, an escape hatch, a way through and out. It itself was nothing, just a hole, the mouth of the cave we all lived in, from which a stone had been rolled. Through the hole you could see a circle of the world that lay at the end of the deep space far beyond our space. I wanted to go there.

As I watched through binoculars, three birds crossed the moon's light, silhouetted, turning towards it as if to go through its hole. I lost them. They were probably redwings; the sky of Bristol is pricked with their thin wiry calls most winter nights. The invisible sun's light reflected off the moon, making backlit shadow puppets of the three birds, picking them out from an otherwise hidden flock, all carrying on their migratory business in the dark. The moon was once thought to be the destination of migratory birds like these thrushes. Watching, for a moment, the redwings crossing this lunar stage, it was possible to understand where such ideas came from.

The journeys the swallows had made from northern Europe to fly above us in Zambia seemed as incredible as the prospect of a redwing flying through the moon's hole towards the silvered light of a world beyond. When our summer birds leave us in the autumn it is very hard to follow them in any way, to imagine their journeys south, their wintering quarters, their new neighbours, the way they become African. We let them go, taking up with newcomers from the north, such as redwings, who have arrived to fill the spaces left by the departed. What is in front of us becomes the truest and most arresting thing. A swallow in midwinter would be a mistake, a lost or sick bird.

But in Zambia there are plenty of swallows in January, all of them at home. The four above Lazaro and Claire were part of the fine black mesh of swallows, martins and swifts – half European wintering birds, the others local migrants or resident species, all of them loosely stitched through millions of acres of African sky. Seeing a swallow above the long grass of a Zambian farm brought on a kind of happy vertigo in me. I might have seen the same bird above the reed bed at Chew Valley Lake last summer, might even have ringed it there, held and measured and released it back to its sky there.

Before I saw the swallows I was struggling to see anything. Flying south from London, I knew that all of Europe's summer birds were spread out below me through Africa. This should have been reassuring, but I felt disconcerted. As we crossed the Mediterranean, five miles up, I peered out of my porthole and looked down at the beginnings of the Sahara, the citrus-peel soil of Tunisia and Libya giving way to an antelope skin, pulled taut over the bony skeleton of Niger and Chad.

There were fields that from the air looked like blank pages dropped from a book, and I could make out the dotted grids of orchards, each an uncountable abacus. I wanted a bird in the bush, a legible mark on the earth like 'the three orange trees at the edge of a field near Guadix' that Saint-Exupéry writes about, guiding flyers through Spain. But all I had was an idea of unknown numbers in an unreadable place. Down there were all my redstarts, but the landing lights of their quivering red tails were snuffed out by the brightness of the day and the vastness of the place.

After the dry fields and trees came the sand, shadeless burning miles of it, with long-running ridges of rock making scarified marks on its otherwise featureless face. It takes a willow warbler between twenty-nine and forty-four hours of continuous flight to cross the desert. Some do it without stopping; others drop to the sand in the heat of the day and rest, flying on in the cooler dark. I thought of the sedge warblers I had trapped at Chew and ringed, blowing apart their breast feathers to assess their fat reserves. The tiny sachets of it laid along the birds' keels were the same colour as the desert below me. This fat, less than a teaspoon's worth, had to see them across the sand.

I slept, and then woke even more bewildered over the Congo Basin. The vast dry swatch of threadbare desert had given way to a thick sweating blanket of damp, dark, hairy green forest.

To fall into the desert's sand and grit, as thousands upon thousands of swallows and redstarts and sedge warblers must do every autumn and every spring, would be to die by desiccation, the warbler's tongue parched to silence, the swallow's fat cooked to nothing. I thought of the red dust, the colour of a redstart's tail, which sometimes blows north from the Sahara and falls with rain back in Britain. Perhaps it brings with it some revenants, returning particles of migrant birds that die in the desert.

To fall into the forests of the Congo, as many thousands of birds must also do, would be to crash through the lush canopy, then rot and slide in shadow into the dank earth, carried off by mould and maggots. The forest hides more than the desert and is hungrier. Bodies are dusted and rolled in the sand and preserved. Saharan oases are graveyards, heaped with the tiny bones of fallen birds. But the forest eats bodies entire; and it also hides the living.

Somewhere, in the thousands of feet of wet air between the treetops and me, are Europe's house martins. All cross the Sahara for their winter, but of 290,000 ringed in Britain and Ireland to date only one has been recovered south of the desert. The bird that builds its house on ours, whose selection of our eaves we regard as a benison, whose 'pendent bed and procreant cradle' on Macbeth's castle makes King Duncan happy to go inside – all the house martins of Europe are lost to our eyes every winter somewhere over Africa.

We landed but Africa still felt shut, an illegible terra incognita. I was once sent on a hostage survival course designed to help me cope should I ever be captured while on BBC business. Before they put a gun to my temple and made me beg for my life, the ex-soldiers who taught us pulled a cotton sack over my head, spun me around a Surrey heath on a hot summer's day and pushed my clouded face into the soil. Africa did the same.

A kind of continental claustrophobia came over me, familiar from Canada and Minnesota and the Moscow oblast: trees formed the only horizon and gave no sense of ever ending. A hot rain fell. I started to sweat and the sweet smell of animal and vegetable decay didn't leave my nostrils for a week. My body mouldered in minutes and lost its compass.

On the hundred-mile journey to Heathrow Airport from my home I had noticed just one species of bird, four matt-black carrion crows pulling away from the mess of a motorway verge like rag-and-bone men. After such a scant and monochrome spread, Africa's birds were refulgent and chaotic. Rainy-season Zambia is wet and warm and green, and its birds, mostly invisible to my untutored northern eyes, seemed wet, warm and green as well. They showered welding sparks and fizzed with electricity. They sounded like frogs, insects or children. I knew *my* birds – those wintering in Africa that I understand – were there, but they were lost in the riot.

I learned a call, but the next time the sound came I dumbly asked for its name again. I thought a pink bird on an emerald treetop a bee-eater; Claire corrected me, naming a weaver one quarter of the size. After half an hour of listening, I managed to pinpoint an African broadbill that had been singing only a few feet from me in a riverine thicket that seemed to go on for ever. Deep from the shade, it burped its buzzing frog-speak and simultaneously turned backward somersaults from its perch, flashing a white marshmallow puff of feathers, like an acrobat magician. An African bird.

Rescue came from the swallows showing themselves to be African and knowable at the same time. Towards evening, I walked through more warm wet grass to a fishpond with a dam at one end and a smallish reed bed at the other. Orange light was being ladled like pumpkin soup over the surrounding yellow fields. In front of me a sedge warbler called. It was the same dry harsh note that sedge warblers make while attending their nests in the reed beds at Chew Valley Lake, six and a half thousand miles away. This one, at least, had made it across the Sahara and the Congo. It called again, then fell silent. Palm swifts scudded high into the sky. Below them, slowly lowering themselves to the reeds, were two barn swallows.

Two birds barely count as a roost, but these swallows were telling enough. They made wherever they existed in the world into their home. Their last flights of the day turned imperceptibly from hunting sorties, hawking after insects, to a final minute of a more sweeping flight of great beauty back and forth over the reeds. Describing in the air the shape of a rope or a rein by which all things might have been tied under the sky, the flight seems to throw over the traces of the day. Now everything must be released to the dark. Swallows do this wherever they roost, but here they were dipping down to sleep through a thick quick dusk of tropical insects, a warm dew, a virtuoso frog chorus, tiny cigarette-glow fireflies lighting up, great thunder-headed clouds darkening on the horizon and pulses of lightning from far beyond it. And they were sharing their sleep with drongos and hamerkops, babblers and jacanas, all flying to their places through the same air.

I couldn't follow the swallows down into the reeds, but they were at home in this marshy valley of a Zambian farm. What I couldn't imagine before – the disappearance into Africa of the birds I thought of as mine – was happening in front of me. Something of the swallows' last flight reminded me of the seamstress I had watched earlier that afternoon, on the verandah of the Manila Clothing Factory in Choma. She pedalled her ancient sewing machine, black with gold inlay, and turned clothes beneath her fingers, all the while peacefully looking through the crowds that thronged the streets and alleys of the outdoor market around her.

As one of the swallows had flown over my head on its way to its roost, it sang a full round of swallow song: the lovely purling that signifies the beginning of spring for me. I had never heard it in January before. I wondered if the singer above me had hatched last year and had never sung before now. Was I hearing the first creaking-open of its red throat, like a barn door it might fly through? Would it fly to a shed on the outskirts of Liverpool or to the Chew Valley and into a farmyard singing the same song? It didn't matter. To have seen the swallows at home and singing here was enough. I could add a swallow winter to my swallow years.

The nests of resident birds helped me too. A nest is the sole fixture – and that only temporary – in a bird's life. It marks the longest joining of a bird to a single place. Just as albumen (egg white, part of the nest's *raison d'être*) worked as a binding fixative in early photography – the stillest part of a bird being used to arrest movement – so the nest holds the bird to the world. It is an anchorage in the comings and the goings, a sanctuary tied to the earth, a refuge to start from and return to. But the nests at Choma are more complicated still. Claire studies tawny-flanked prinias and red-faced cisticolas (both small streaky warblers) that have been parasitised by cuckoo finches laying eggs in their nests. These, intended as homes, have become battlefields.

In the old fields at the Major's farm at Musumanene – the big tree next to the river, in Tonga – a prinia or cisticola nest parasitised by a cuckoo finch will earn Lazaro and two other farm workers, Kiverness and Collins, twenty thousand Zambian kwacha (about £3). A prinia nest without a cuckoo finch egg is worth one thousand (15p), a red-faced cisticola, three thousand. A day's wage for a farm labourer is around five thousand kwacha.

The nests are beautiful, domed like grass skulls and tied by just a few strands of grass twisting out of the back to the stalk of a woody flax-like plant. Red-faced cisticolas incorporate living leaves into their nests for protection and further camouflage.

Using their beak as a needle, the birds weave fresh leaves onto the dry-grass underlay of the nest. It looks as if tiny green rugs have been thrown over the dome.

The men are incredible nesters: by listening for the parent birds' alarm calls or watching them back to their particular corner of vegetation, each of the three manages to find ten nests or so every day of the three-month breeding season. They look for them at the beginning or end of their hours working in the fields or orchards of the farm. Knowing the fields and knowing the birds, they seem able to walk to the nests as the prinias or cisticolas leave them – quietly, unfailingly and direct. Lazaro moves like his namesake, up from the earth as if back from the dead, unencumbered, hurrying towards life, nest after nest.

To find a nest anywhere is a revelation. It feels like an intense trespassing – the parents fly off, the eggs start to cool or the chicks are unfed, and the season stops. Walking behind Lazaro, I thought of John Clare once more, another consummate field-worker, a farm labourer, gooseherd, egg-finder and nest-lover. Nests made poems for Clare. A nest was a cottage, a bower, a place of happiness, of sex, of nature's nurture. He wrote dozens of poems about them, obsessively recapturing and restating the moment of discovery and of sharing the shelter they offered, the comfort of their tether to a place. Every nest poem is a field note; you arrive in his poem, and he is already there, simply seeing things, without binoculars, close up. He wrote how as a child he would make his own nests with 'moss from apple trees' and 'bits of straws', thinking 'that birds would like them ready made.' He wrote how even non-breeding birds like to 'nestle' in the autumn. Through his long and catastrophic final breakdown, he continued to write about nests and called what was to be his last poem, written in the winter of 1863–64, 'Birds Nests'. Like the chaffinch's nest in it, it isn't finished:

Tis Spring warm glows the South
Chaffinches carry the moss in his mouth
To the filbert hedges all day long
And charms the poet with his beautiful song
The wind blows blea over the sedgey fen
But warm the sunshines in the little wood
Where the old Cow at her leisure chews her cud

We dropped Lazaro back at the farm workers' compound. Children, with scraps of maize meal porridge around their mouths, ran towards Claire's truck. Their faces reminded me of the rattling cisticola's nest Lazaro had shown us. These birds gather spiders' webs to line their domed nests and plait them around the rim of the dark grassy hole like a milky mouth. We said hello to the children. Then we stepped from a world of hatching and birth into a dark where cuckoos were king, a dark that was at the other end of the story.

The farmhouse where Claire works on her eggs had its curtains drawn. On a metal bed raised to the height of a desk in a darkened living room rested the farmer. I imagined him having been laid there on his iron litter by African bearers after a tortuous crossing of the continent. But the English Major has been in Zambia for many years. Gaunt and yellow with illness, he livened up at our arrival. His young wife, Royce, smiled and offered gin. The Major apologised for the curtains: 'We were being carried away by mosquitoes!'

Claire went to work on his farm partly because its ramshackle outer fields are full of prinias and cisticolas and cuckoo finches, and partly because the Major has amassed an astonishing collection of bird skins and eggs. The collection has enormous scientific value. In three rooms – his living room, a spare bedroom and his bird-room proper – there are 10,000 clutches of, mostly,

African birds. The Major has between thirty and forty thousand eggs, every one taken, blown, catalogued and stowed. It is perhaps the largest private egg collection remaining in the world.

The eggs are cleanly blown and the skins are beautifully prepared; the labels on the birds are neat and so is the minuscule writing on the eggs, the registers immaculately kept. The collection is an orderly mass grave, but it is also a hecatomb. The epic, African, scale of it – the strange quiet fields of eggs laid out, in their original clutches, in ersatz nests of cotton wool, in the starless dark of drawer after drawer – left me wondering about all those birds that never became, the unhatched thousands, blown to oblivion out of the single tiny hole made in their eggshells.

For the Major the collection is life-giving. Talking of his clutches, the sick man rallied, like John Clare half-rescued in his asylum by his memory of nests. The Major got up from his bed and walked, pulling open a drawer to show me his Levaillant's and Jacobin cuckoo's eggs. The cuckoo's secret was plain to see: the deceptions that allow its eggs to be fostered. Some eggs showed astounding mimicry, being perfect sky-blue matches for the sky-blue eggs of the arrow-marked and white-rumped babblers the cuckoos were parasitising; others were flagrant impostors, the wrong size and the wrong colour, but they had been laid where the cuckoo could have deposited an ostrich's egg in a hummingbird's nest, because the host bird (bulbuls in this case) couldn't or chose not to distinguish the parasite's unwanted gift. It is a war.

In other drawers I looked at the Major's set of cuckoo finch eggs and his prinias and cisticolas. Elaborately and beautifully patterned, no two were the same. The prinias' eggs have three layers of markings. The background colour can be blue, white, reddish-brown or olive-green; brownish blotches are smeared over this undercoat; and finally, squiggling lines, often extending from tiny pools of ink, run pell-mell across the whole egg. They look like miniature globes seen from the other end of space.

All eggs start white. The shell gland in the bird's uterus begins the painting, the colours coming from old blood cells that have been broken down into porphyrin pigments in the bird's liver. As the shell is formed, the egg background colour is deposited. Then blotches and squiggles – each egg having a unique pattern – are painted into the outer coating of protein molecules, or cuticle, of the egg. The cuckoo finch can mimic the prinia's backgrounds and blotches but it cannot – as yet – do the squiggles. Sometimes the prinia notices a cuckoo finch's egg in its nest and jettisons it. The cuckoo finch meanwhile – across millions of years – works on its reading and replicating of the globes beneath it in the prinia's nest. The war goes on. Looking at the eggs, I thought of the language of co-evolution – of how *host* and *guest* share the same etymological root, as *hospitality* and *hostility* do too.

Outside, thunder was coming and lightning flashed through the brief Zambian twilight. Inside, the electrical supply was wonkier; the power flickered hopelessly on and off and then gave up. The fridge warmed. The television draped in a Union Jack tea towel looked as if it was due a state funeral. The Major shouted 'Candles, Julia!' to his temporary cook, and took comfort by speaking of Churchill and the Blitz. Julia arrived, wheeling a wobbly cake-trolley across the carpet.

There are no drapes in the bird-room to hide the dead. They are everywhere. Wooden drawers containing two thousand bird skins cover the walls. A huge, seven-foot tall, free-standing cupboard of eggs takes up most of the middle of the room. The skin-preparation table is the only other piece of furniture. Here the birds are gutted and their eyes are removed; they are then stuffed – often with weavers' old nests – back to some approximate shape. Perhaps a dead weaver in the Major's collection has been plugged with the grass it was hatched in. Perhaps its eggs are in a nearby drawer.

Scientific study skins are not mounted in a lifelike pose, as are stuffed birds in the public galleries of a museum. They don't really look like birds at all. In the skin drawers the birds lie on their backs, their wings folded tight to their bodies as if they have wrapped themselves up. Each has been skewered in death on a wooden kebab stick. Each has a label tied to its feet. None have eyes, glass or otherwise. Where he has a male and female, the Major has arranged his bird skins like the marble effigies of recumbent knights home from the wars, lying alongside their loyal ladies in an English church. Nothing is going anywhere from this room.

Claire and I retreated to where she works. Here the Major's parallel interest in human genealogy is stored alongside his overflow skin collection and yet more eggs. Next to a pink double bed were three chests of drawers of eggs; the nearest to the pink pillows were labelled 'Doves', 'Cormorants and Darters', 'Auks, Petrels' and 'Penguins, Pelicans, Storks, Gannet'. On the shelves were journals, food supplies and tools, as well as books and birds: *Still to Decide* by Enoch Powell; *Genealogy Magazine*, volume 6, 1932–34; an unbound run of *The Spectator*; skins of a pied crow and a black-necked heron, with cotton wool for eyes, both looking like huge, feathery, cumbersome lollipops; some oxtail stock cubes and boxes of UHT 'Supa Milk'; a hammer; *The Pedigree Directory 1917*; *The Coat of Arms*, volume 8, 1964–65; *Monumental Inscriptions of the British West Indies* by Captain J. H. Lawrence-Archer; *Burke's Dormant and Extinct Peerages*; seven volumes of 'Bristol Marriage Licence Bonds' 1820–1837; four pairs of binoculars; *Men and Armour for Gloucestershire in 1608* by John Smith; a glass jar of Italian herbs; a plastic bottle of raw linseed oil; an iron; *The Auk* 1970–76; *Diccionario Nobiliario* by Julio de Atienza; and a 'hunting autobiography' by Cecil Aldin, the author of *Dogs of Character*, called *Time I Was Dead*.

Resting on the shelf in front of *Time I Was Dead* was a single large grey and black feather like an extravagant quill, the primary of a secretary bird. Its shaft had been pushed through a piece of cardboard cut from a box of mint imperials. Written on the cardboard in a fine calligraphy, as if the feather had been its own amanuensis and inscribed its own label, were details of the find: 'picked at edge of miombo & guava orchard north of homestead, 10 February 2005, a very local species seldom seen at this property'.

There were two copies of Enoch Powell's book in fact, but between them was a Penguin edition of Defoe's *Journal of the Plague Year* of 1722. I took it down as Claire at her desk used her spectrophotometer to measure the colouration of decades' worth of prinia eggs from the Major's collection. He had written on the title page of the *Journal*, noting that Defoe mentions 'Sir John Lawrence, Kt, Lord Mayor of London 1664–65'. He was, Claire told me, a relative of the Major's first wife.

I opened the book. It is 1665. The plague is killing London. Grass is growing in the city streets; 'death reigned in every corner . . . whole families and indeed whole streets of families were swept away together'. Against the odds, some bureaucratic niceties were maintained for a time, and details ('found dead in the streets or fields') were entered 'in the weekly bill', but soon it became impossible, almost everyone was dead, almost every thing was dead. A cart used to carry bodies to the great death pit in Finsbury Fields is later found in the pit itself, 'the driver being dead . . . and the horses running too near it, the cart fell in and drew the horses in also.' September was the worst month; between 22 August and 26 September, 38,195 died in London. The figure, Defoe is certain, is too low: 'great numbers went out of the world who were never known, or any account taken of them.'

I thought – how could I not think? – of the Major's abandoned fields where grass is rampant; of Lazaro and Claire moving eggs between nests there; I thought of grass growing through the deserted ruins of Chernobyl and Pripiat and how I heard of the catastrophe there in April 1986 on my car radio when driving to the halls of dead birds at the British Museum at Tring; I thought of the bus crash I had driven past days before, coming south from Lusaka, that had spilt people and their bags along the roadside; I thought of the young mother dying of HIV in the workers' compound the night I arrived in Zambia, and the wailing that followed; I thought of the man I saw on a bicycle riding towards the compound the next day with an empty coffin strapped crossways over his mudguard; I thought of the beautiful smoked-silver Amur falcons from eastern Siberia and northern China that winter here and that I had just seen outside above the fields, and how they reminded me of the red-footed falcons, their near relatives, that I had seen years ago catching dragonflies around the long grass at the base of a Scythian burial kurgan on the Crimean steppe, and how I had wondered whether the great mound in front of me contained buried horses as well as Scythian kings, as Herodotus said it might; I thought of the death pits of ashy soil in the forest outside Vilnius, where golden orioles sang so loud in May that I had imagined the Jews killed there being shot with that sweet sound in their ears; I thought of the Major on his sickbed and his empire of the dead, his eggs, his birds, boneyards and golgothas, and I had to stand up and walk and seek cold water for my hot face, but in the bathroom the taps didn't work.

The West Country, my neck of the woods, is important to

the Major. One of the first things he had said to me was, 'My great grandfather was the sheriff of Monmouth', and parts of his family have had long connections with Gloucestershire. Above the throne of the toilet bowl was a framed picture of some of the coats of arms of the county. I wrote some down, thinking of soft green English winter colours, of Edward Thomas and Ivor Gurney and their Cotswold poems, of a long-ago girlfriend from Guiting Power. Where were they now? And where were all the lords and ladies, Leigh of Adlestrop, Lacy of Guiting, Ligon of Arle-Court, James of Tidenham, Juxton of Compton, Lorange of Winchcomb, Kingscot of Kingscot, Keeble of East-Leech, Jermingham St Francis of Painswick, Jackson of Wartbury, Loder of Letchlade, Kemis of Wickwick?

I came out of the toilet, trying to imagine Kingscot of Kingscot and Kemis of Wickwick, and I could hear the Major talking to Claire. His conversation was swinging between the difficulties of sourcing black sealing wax in Zambia, necessary for the preparation of his will (I had brought some from Bristol for him), and some egging memories, particularly the difficulties of finding red-throated twinspot eggs, since the female 'sits like wax'. I was enjoying the pile-up or melt-down of these wax words when another came along. The talk moved on to honeyguides.

The tea things had to be cleared. Julia was called and I was enlisted to help fetch further drawers from the Major's cabinets. We brought to the dining table more dead honeyguides and blown honeyguide eggs than there are anywhere else in the world.

Honeyguides were one of my dreamt-of and hoped-for African birds. In my mind, ever since I first read about them, I have meshed them with the beginnings of humankind, with our African genesis. Poorly known, mostly nondescript, they are the size of small thrushes and related to barbets, toucans and woodpeckers. All of them (there are fifteen species in sub-Saharan

Africa) are thought to behave as cuckoos, and parasitise other birds; females puncture the host eggs and the tiny hatchling honeyguides kill any host nestlings that have survived the female's first pass. Many honeyguides eat beeswax; the greater honeyguide has even been recorded 'eating candles on the altars of Christian missions'. The greater honeyguide also – and this above all is the reason for my thrill – leads humans to bees' nests so that both may share the honey and wax.

Greater honeyguides work only with people. Having found a bees' nest, they seek someone and perch nearby and sing to them; if they are followed, the bird moves ahead, calling insistently, until in the vicinity of the nest it falls silent and 'looks on at the humans'. Think of that moment, a bird is looking at you, having shown you some sweet stuff it has found that you can both enjoy, if only you will open the bees' nest. It is saddening to discover that around African cities, such as Nairobi, the guiding phenomenon is disappearing. The *Handbook of the Birds of the World* suggests that the loss of this behaviour shows that human honey-guiding 'is not a genetically deeply embedded, very highly evolved aspect of behaviour, but that it is, rather, a relatively recent "add-on" to the wax-seeking and wax-acquiring habits of this species'. I see it more as evidence of what living in any suburb does to our relations with birds. They call to us but we don't notice.

As a child, the family story I never tired of hearing my mother tell me, the story I most wished had happened to me, was of how a pair of farmyard geese looked after her, her sister and her brother when they were small and wandered from their house near Avonmouth on the outskirts of Bristol. Chittening Farm, where they lived – now, I think, buried under a colossal aluminium smelter – was on the edge of the Severn Estuary and criss-crossed by dangerous channels and deep ditches, or rheens. The geese would herd my uncle especially – he was the youngest of the three – leading him away from the water, with agitated honks and wing flaps as if he were an incompetent gosling. I was jealous. I still am.

I've seen two honeyguide species – in Zambia and South Africa – but neither was a guiding bird. But Claire reported an occasion with Lazaro after I left Zambia when their attention was drawn by a greater honeyguide fluttering and croaking ahead of them. Lazaro followed it, whistling back to the bird so that it knew he was coming. At other times, when feeling peckish, he is able to summon honeyguides by calling them to him – happily his urban life is still some way off. When the bird stopped, Lazaro started tapping the trees. He can hear honey. Near the bees' nest the bird's calls changed, growing higher pitched and with shorter syllables. There was a final talking-down from tree to ground, from bird to man: the sweet track had been laid and the honey was found.

The Major, with the marmalade cleared away, and the egg drawer in front of us, was more interested in honeyguides as cuckoos than as honey suppliers. As he listed the clutches he had taken of various host birds with greater honeyguide eggs in them, he said, 'I am not a modest collector, as you know, I am a vast collector!' The tray of eggs was beautiful and extraordinary. Greater honeyguide eggs are white. The egg colour of their hosts varies. The Major had six clutches of African hoopoes that honeyguides had laid in; six clutches of green wood hoopoes; four clutches of scimitarbills (treasured but 'very smelly and rotten' because the female honeyguide punctured all the eggs); four clutches of striped kingfishers; eight clutches of little bee-eaters; and two very unusual hosts – a southern black tit (its brown-spotted egg half the size of the greater honeyguide's) and a capped wheatear (a clutch of two very pale blue eggs with one honeyguide's).

The Major's passion for the eggs and the lives of the honeyguides and other cuckoo-type birds is striking. He loves the British monarchy and good breeding, is hard on what he calls 'mongrel nations', and is a tough landlord, yet he is drawn to aberrations and disguises, to impostors and cheats. As we looked at his honeyguide eggs and skins, he clapped his hands to his knees and rocked with mirth telling us of John Walpole-Bond, the Sussex bird-man and egg-collector of the early twentieth century. He was especially animated by the story of 'Jock' dressed in his egging kit, looking like 'a shabby tramp', stumbling on 'a rah-rah party in the English countryside, with a parked Rolls-Royce and blankets spread and girls and a butler'; the host of the party spotted Walpole-Bond and beckoned to him, taking out five shillings from his pocket to give the tramp, 'then Jock strikes and says in his perfect Wykehamist accent, "I would rather have a glass of your excellent champagne."'

It was time to go. Claire and I returned the honeyguides to their cabinet. The power came back on. I went to put the last of the crumpets in the fridge in the kitchen. They joined a plucked and trussed chicken waiting to be eaten; an un-plucked but folded knob-billed duck waiting to be skinned for the collection; and some cockroaches happily licking at the empty egg compartment.

We drove back from the Major's farm along twenty miles of dirt road to another farm, where Claire was staying. It was dark. The last bird skins I had pulled out had been a drawer of spotted eagle owls. But for their eyeless faces, they were exquisite. Laid head to foot with their grey-barred dusty silver breasts and richly cryptic grey-brown wings and backs, they looked like silver birch logs stacked for a winter fire. Even dead they silenced the air around them. As we drove away from the farm, the first bird we saw was a spotted eagle owl stalking the sandy gutter. Its ravishing eyes, two wide plates of yellow jelly, stared and stared into our headlights, the most living thing for miles.

Then we killed something. Nightjars rest on the dirt roads. Like giant moths in a dream, they flickered up from the sand as we drove. In quick succession we saw a Mozambique nightjar with lunatic orange eyes, and a pennant-winged nightjar with weird gloved extensions to the trailing edge of its wings, and then suddenly there was another bird lifting too late from the warm track in front of the car and flying at us rather than away. We stopped and I scooped up the mess of feathers. It was a rufous-cheeked nightjar; its head rolled between my finger and thumb and I could feel its pulse faltering. Feathers fell from it like ashes from a burnt-out fire. It was dying in my hand and its warm body cooled as we drove on. Its plumage, like every nightjar's, was a fabulous mix of silver, grey, orange and brown. It looked like the complex patterning of the underside of the world, or a carpet woven with everything of the earth. Its eyes, though, like black stars, seemed to come from elsewhere.

February

Why is a raven like a writing-desk?

Lewis Carroll

Hoarse with fulfilment, I never made promises

W. S. Merwin

Dawn is long past and the day is under way. In some versions of the story it is already drawing to a close. A man, perhaps a god, stands high on a hill looking out over the world. Two large all-black birds fly at him from far apart, falling from the sky. They know him and he is expecting them. One lands on his left shoulder, the other on his right. They settle their wings and dip their beaks. He cocks his head first to one and then to the other.

The birds are ravens and they have names: Hugin and Munin. Each day they fly from the man-god who is called Odin, and later they return to perch on his shoulders and sing into his ears. We might not think of them as singers, nor what they sing as a song, but ravens, the largest of all songbirds, probably have the greatest variety of calls – sixty-four have been recorded – of any bird at all. They have much to say. Hugin and Munin tell Odin what they have seen and heard. The ravens have flown out of the past and back from the future. Munin is memory and recounts what has been, weaving the day's happenings into the dark fabric of the coming night; Hugin is thought, and projects what is to come, stitching today's dreams into the bolt of silk that is the dawn waiting beyond the night. Odin has the whole world on his shoulders.

There is another story. A man, not a god, throws a raven into the sky out over the water from the boat they have both lived on for many days. The man wants to know what will come from beyond the ocean of floodwaters and over the endless horizon. The raven flies to and fro, then far out of sight, but doesn't come back. It had nothing to say to Noah. He launches a dove. At first she finds nothing to perch on, no rest for the sole of her foot, so she flies back to Noah, who 'put forth his hand and took her and pulled her in unto him' as Genesis says, like a bird trapper. On her next flight she comes back with the beginnings of a nest, the world in her beak. White doves in this story bring better news than black crows.

Los Angeles seen south from the path to Dante's Peak at Griffith Park is an immense flat glittering plain. In the spring boil of the sun, turning cars at intersections far below flash a scarab diamante, like tiny beetles labouring in a huge dried-up field. Down there, I had watched gangs of starlings and parrots, black and green, making their way through the new world. The starlings from Europe and the parrots from Brazil: emigrants, immigrants, escapees, exotics, birds that I grew up calling 'plastics', hustling through the jungle of wires around the low buildings, the starlings clotting into evening flocks, the parrots bouncing old songs from their forest homelands off the tarmac.

Up on Dante's Peak, a still older world persists. A small aeroplane appeared, dragging a giant poster above the heating city to advertise a new burger with a meaty skywriting, the languorous flaps of the banner like the reluctant peristalsis of an overfed gut. Then six ravens arrived from all sides of the sky, upstage and down, to eclipse the city with their black plumage, darker than anything. They flew as I imagine them doing on the first day of their creation, away from Odin, or fresh off the Ark. Grave and humorous at once, they looked happy with what they had. Their deep cronked raven voice-over seemed the only commentary required on everything beneath them. More than a thousand feet above the city, one sailed on bowed wings towards the burger plane, then switched off its engine and surfed for a moment, before folding its wings away and rolling left onto its back. It drifted like this for five seconds, gliding upside down: a rectangle of black, a spy plane, a writing desk, a dark mirror of ink. With its back to the city, looking up towards space, the bird threw a single *pruk* to the upper air, before following the roll through and righting itself.

The ravens looked the oldest thing for miles and put me in mind of Borges's story 'Fauna of the United States', with its species list like no other: 'We shouldn't forget the Goofus Bird that builds its nest upside down and flies backward, not caring where it's going, only where it's been.' Perhaps my upside-down raven was looking back towards Odin Street, near the Hollywood Bowl, which I'd spotted as I drove to Griffith Park. Was it remembering the days from the beginning of the world? Or was it clocking La Brea, the tar pits below it, where raven bones have been found alongside the bones of long-extinct giant condors, fragile eagles, errant eagles, asphalt storks and a hundred thousand other bird fossils, as well as dire wolves and American mastodons and Shasta ground sloths, all trapped and then preserved – tar and feathers – by the raven-black pitch which started bubbling to the surface forty thousand years ago.

The angels of another Los Angeles, a skeleton city, assemble themselves out of the bone-hoard at La Brea. One wooden cabinet in the museum contains the feet of five hundred golden eagles that had been taken by the tar after sticky landings. As I watched the ravens at their air traffic control, I could see a staircase of aeroplanes descending to LAX stretching behind the birds far to the south. I imagined a stack of five hundred golden eagles on their approach to the dangerous riches of La Brea, backing into the distant yellow sky, the ravens bringing them down from the sierras and guiding them in.

The raven is close to being a worldwide bird. It belongs wherever it occurs. Its song remains the same, and its blackness. Crows are different. There were two American crows around the observatory at Griffith Park, bending metal as they bounced and sang across the grass their *prang* calls, black feathers flashing in the sun. To my ears, the American crow yaps; it calls like a twanged wire strung between two cans, with a sort of metallic glissando. It sounds irrefutably American. Where some sort of soil-sentimentality in me hears earth stuck in the *caw* ofour carrion crow, as it coughs its way over the fields of England, I hear a performance – look at me, listen to me – in the voice of the American crow. Ravens sing the blues wherever they are; the American crow sings Tom Waits singing the blues.

It is close to midnight now as I write in Bristol. A mile and a half from me a raven, the same species as at Dante's Peak, is sleeping on its cliff nest in the Avon Gorge. Its mate roosts in an ash tree nearby. All the corvids of Bristol, of Britain, of Europe, are sleeping their crow sleep now. They are late to bed and early to rise, but in the thick of the night they sleep.

For an hour before dusk tonight I watched six of the eight British crow species in the space of a few hundred yards of cliff top and gorge air, all of them sharp-eyed and wide awake, active and determined members of the crow nation: magpies steered by their own tail across the short turf; a jay hysterical and clowning through furring treetops; rooks skirting the city on the far side of the Gorge, moving from pasture to roost wood; carrion crows promiscuous and everywhere like dark smudges on my eyes, one five feet behind me inspecting litter, another two hundred and fifty feet below me on the tidal mud at the river's edge; then in the Gorge, making a habitat of its air, jackdaws; and last, the bird I had come to look for, ravens. These two, the jackdaws and the ravens, seem intrinsic to the character of the place. The jackdaws have never left the Gorge. When I was growing up in Bristol they alone defined it. Only since 1996 have ravens – like peregrines – returned to breed here.

In the seventeenth century, Gondar in northern Ethiopia was said to be the second-largest city in the world. I spent one Christmas there nearly twenty years ago. I walked through the town looking at its curious Italian modernist buildings, remnants of its short-lived colonial past, and its fabulous Coptic churches with their painted wooden ceilings covered in black angels. As I crossed the city, ten or sometimes twenty lammergeiers filled the air at any one time, slicing their nine-foot wings and wedged diamond tails over the city's roofs, their marrow-lusting crocodilian eyes, shaggy beards and rusting breasts coming as close as the pass of a swallow. I thought of Aeschylus killed by a tortoise a lammergeier had dropped on his head and I drew mine into my shoulders. Elsewhere in the world lammergeiers are birds of extreme landscapes. The only other one I have seen required a four-hour pre-dawn walk up to the snowline of a Turkish mountain range, and even then was miles away in iced blue skies. In Gondar they live happily among people, as once again do the ravens and peregrines of Bristol.

At the cliff edge where I watch for ravens, there is a dead tree with a dozen jackdaws perched on its branches. All face out over the Gorge; half have beakfuls of dead grass or gleaned dog fur for their new nests, making them look like beer drinkers with frothy moustaches, but their eyes hold their intelligence, their grown-up grey iris with its sober pin-dot black pupil. A ripple passes through the tree of birds and something makes them launch. They open and raise their wings and loosen their perch and allow themselves to be carried out over the void. Their legs dangle beneath them like an aeroplane's undercarriage for a few moments as they fall from the cliff and paddle at the wind, like a storm petrel on the sea, catching at an updraught that lifts them in formation, countering gravity, and throws them into the sky like black confetti, each a shadow of the other. The blast makes them talk. The *chack* of one bird immediately triggers an answering call, which in turn prompts another to speak on. They make a sound which J. A. Baker describes perfectly: 'like dominoes being rattled together on a pub table'. They are talking to themselves, and yet it is a conversation.

A second group has melted into the flock and now there are forty jackdaws flung across the air of the Gorge. They range high and far out over its gulf; black angels, I think, trying to remember my Milton as well as Gondar, angels who fall only to rise again. Their genius for riding the air seems to show its shape: pockets and waves and channels and funnels; but as I peer at them, the wind watering my eyes, I find myself marvelling at their irreducible and specific marking of the sky at that moment. If you try to empty your head and open your eyes and just watch the birds, you see they are not a metaphor for anything: they are not black angels, they are not Satan and his cohorts, or funereal ashes, or a single organism pulsing and flexing with a shared purpose. They are not metaphors (the Greek for 'porter'), they carry nothing but themselves; they are birds (a word so old we do not know where it comes from) flying (an ancient Indo-European word that has spun through all of northern Europe). Birds flying.

To be able to see jackdaws, or any crows, unburdened is particularly difficult. Because they have come close to us and lived among us, eaten us even, all the family have passed blackly into our mind. Meaning has thickened their feathers. Their shadowing of our lives has blackened their shadows. 'The raven himself is hoarse', is how Lady Macbeth puts it. He isn't, of course; she has made him so. But the raven has evolved with us perhaps more than any other bird (or wild bird, at least; the chicken has moved so far from its jungle-fowl beginnings that it has almost ceased to be a bird, at least in our mind). If we are close to any bird, it might be a raven.

Around the world and over thousands of years, human imagination has met raven reality again and again. They *cronk*, I hear a blues. They come around camps before armies clash and it seems to us a sign from the future, as if the birds have already flown through tomorrow and know that some of us will die. The ravens read us for real; they see into our future based on their knowledge of our past.

In Scotland, two ravens are overheard talking:

> Ye'll sit on his white hause-bane,
> And I'll pike out his bonny blue e'en:
> Wi ae lock o'his gowden hair
> We'll theek our nest when it grows bare.

Driving through Somerset early one morning under a drab grey sky, I turned a corner near Cheddar and disturbed a raven sipping, with the delicacy of a wine taster, from the eye of a rabbit killed by a car. A hundred yards further on was a second, this one enjoying the pink goo spreading from another rabbit's split anus.

A newspaper in January 1767 described a blacksmith from Bridgwater in Somerset – fifteen miles from Cheddar – who went shooting on Christmas Day: 'On Pallet Hill he espied a large flight of old ravens, fired and killed two, which so exasperated the rest, that they immediately descended upon him, and plied their bills and claws so dextrously about his head and face that notwithstanding all possible care was taken of him, he died last Monday. This may appear strange, but our correspondent assures us it is absolute fact.'

Gibraltar is one of the most horrible places I have ever been. But it also offers a telling juxtaposition of the sedentary and the mobile, the trapped and the free, of animals close to people and ruined by the proximity, and of animals close to people and as intact as ever. One spring day I walked up to the top of the Rock to watch drifting raptors spilling north, migrating into Europe from their winter in Africa. In the blue sky above me was a fractured chessboard of gliding black kites. They seemed not to be moving at all, but rather hanging and waiting for the turning earth to rotate beneath them. Below them was a pair of the Rock's resident ravens tirelessly working to and fro, making the outpost their own, flagging the kites on like their Californian relatives.

I looked down from the top of the Rock. On its western flank, where the town is, all is deadly, deathly, dying and dead. What do the people do here? Tourists drink lager; the shops sell booze and fags. Gibraltar's heroic past is lost somewhere in the shadow of the Rock. Down below, the street names, the buildings, the shipyards and cemeteries are all full of lives that have passed; Ezra Pound came here, Odysseus perhaps sailed by, Molly Bloom was from here and remembered its 'Moorish wall', Gilbert White knew his 'soft-billed' and 'short-winged' birds of passage came through here, but its people today and the people who come here seem broken and vague. Who are they? Spanish? English? Something else?

I had booked myself a room at the Hotel Bristol, seeking some connection that was not to be had. On the pavement outside was a dead swift, a mess of dust and feathers: the genius of escape grounded. As I looked at the dead bird, two raucous chattering parakeets flew overhead, either introduced or escaped; the bastard bird children of the Rock's human occupants.

The macaques were worse. They make you swear and gasp. Dirty brown, tail-less, tired-looking and mute – they lie around, halfway up the Rock, debauched. Stern notices in English and Spanish warn you that they bite and instruct you not to feed them; if you do, you risk a £500 fine. As I watched, one fingered his penis with his little pink hand. At first he seemed cautious, as if he were doing it for the first time, but then he sped up rapidly as if he recognised something half remembered. In ten seconds he ejaculated. He licked his fingers and then lay down as if dead like his neighbours on a wall above the town. These monkeys, the colour of dust, with bums like dried cowpats, are citizens of Gibraltar, feral, neither one thing nor the other, an old idea now forgotten, neglected and barely maintained; the living dead.

All this against the exhilarating drift of raptors high over-head, making their way across the Straits from Africa to join us for a European summer. Some are sociable: the great flotillas of gliding black kites, eighty or so in one group, making busy skies. Other migrants are on their own, battling the gulls that rise up agitated every time, wannabe keepers of the Rock, exercised by the blocky flight of an Egyptian vulture, a short-toed eagle and two griffon vultures.

This airway of life pushing north, wild and free but also long mapped and familiar, part of the great breathed exchange of spring and autumn, gives all who take part in it a past and a future. Down below, everything and everyone seems stuck, with lager to live on and rum-laced 'wobbly coffee' as a treat and revved-up cars but not enough road to get into fourth gear, and the monkeys on the twisting path to the peak, with their eyes drifting off elsewhere once they've clocked you for titbits or had their wank, glazed and dreaming of old genes back across the water in Africa, where the kites and eagles and vultures have come from.

Commuting between the flying birds of prey, the mobbing gulls, the macaques and me, were the two ravens. They flew out over the sea towards Africa, looked about – I could see them through my binoculars turning their heads – tracked back and drifted along the ridge of the Rock. At one moment they seemed impossibly distant, able to fly to Africa and to shepherd black kites into Europe, and the next one had pitched beside me and seemed to be peering deep into my eyes. Might I be carrion? Its sable throat rose and fell as it breathed. Ravens, like no other bird I know, look at you as if they really have seen you.

Ravens are hardy; they breed early in the year. Many pairs in Britain have nests and full clutches before the end of February. Every year I go to the Gorge in Bristol to look for them, but twice this February I didn't see any. Today the glare of the low sun was dazzling and I was on the point of giving up when I spotted a peregrine, a big female bird gliding up the Gorge. I cannot turn away from a peregrine. For three and a half minutes I watched her as she rode without a single wingbeat, able to pull any wind she wanted from the air. Eventually she crossed the Gorge and flew at a cliff face from where a raven – one I had failed to spot – leapt out like an angry bin-liner, a flapping dark cape. The two birds flew close and furious, twisting and tumbling, along the cliff and over the trees that cling to it. The peregrine pulled away, calling *kek kek kek kek kek*, and landed, hiding in a cage of branches and buds.

The raven flew out of view but a minute later came back, appearing high above me. Having crossed to my side of the Gorge, it had climbed and was perhaps five hundred feet up in the air. It appeared to be coasting further upwards, unflustered by the falcon's swipes. Then, at who knows what trigger, it began a triumphant tumbling sequence down into the Gorge. In two minutes I counted forty rolls. Each time the bird flapped two or three deep draughts then drew its wings to its body and rolled, always to the right, turning upside down. Its neck thickened and I could see its beak open, though it was too far away and too windy to hear what it said. The next moment it righted itself, back the way it came, except for once in the two minutes when it followed the roll all the way through. As it began to descend below the level of the cliff top into the Gorge's turbulent air, the rolling became beautifully rhythmic and almost continuous, a black slalom, a black shuttle passing through a loom. Flying is what I do, it was saying, but this flying – this rolling and righting – this is what I am.

Watching the raven in the wind at the Gorge edge, I wanted to run and flap my arms and roll through the air. My falling man was forgotten. I remembered what Konrad Lorenz wrote of his ravens, especially Roah who, only four hours after Lorenz had acquired him as a fledgling from a pet shop in Vienna in 1929, flew freely after and around his new friend: 'It was an anxious moment when my beautiful and expensive bird sailed onward after overtaking me. All I could do was to call loudly, and to start running at right angles to the direction in which the raven was flying, so that he should see me moving. (All birds respond better to a moving object than to a still one.) I saw his great curved beak turning as he looked back at me over his shoulder, and then he wheeled and came gliding back to me.' Later, Lorenz adopts a bicycle to speed up his movements. I also remembered Sir Arthur Streeb-Greebling, Peter Cook's old-buffer incarnation, detailing to an ever-corpsing Dudley Moore the complete failure of his life-long project to teach ravens to fly underwater. It seems that the raven can take it all, and as I walked from the edge of the Gorge back towards the city, I found myself making the shape of the rolling bird with my hand out in front of me and trying to synchronise my best efforts at raven-speak with it, to do some raven rock and roll. I looked back but the bird had gone.

March

The bird is dead
That we have made so much on
Shakespeare, Cymbeline

It was a fine day and K. felt like going for a walk. But
hardly had he taken a couple of steps before he was in
the cemetery.
Franz Kafka

One October, in my late twenties, I spent a week on
Bardsey Island, the detached end of the Lleyn
Peninsula in north-west Wales. My friend Greg was
a warden at the bird observatory there. It was unseasonably mild
and there weren't many migrants. High pressure brought clear
and navigable skies and the birds must have flown over invisible
to us, not needing the comforts of the ground. A wryneck did
arrive and lived like a piece of snaking bracken for a couple of
days along a stone wall near Greg's house. I spent hours watching
it, drawn into its strangeness, the brown migratory woodpecker
that twists its neck and looks like an ancient contortionist, with
feathering as complicated and as marvellous as those other go-
between birds – the nightjar and the woodcock.

Bardsey is known for its bodies. In the warm and birdless
days after the wryneck had left, I found myself sprawling in the

island's western fields where the earth dips and folds like ribs of sand on a beach. These ripples of turf are evidence either of medieval strip farming, traces of human labour, or of something even more substantially human. The island is a graveyard.

Bardsey offers outward-bound autumn birds a stopover before the sea; in a similar way thousands of human pilgrims went there at the beginnings of Celtic Christendom, pulled to the island by their sense of it as a sacred place on the edge of things that had wisdoms to offer the mainland of life. The ruins of an abbey founded by St Cadfan might date back to the sixth century, and in the fields around, where I dozed under the warm coconut-scented gorse, large numbers of human bones have been found, evidence for the truth of the legend that twenty thousand pilgrims are buried on the island. Making the journey to die, looking out towards the setting sun, sanctified these travellers. I imagined their saintly bodies laid out side by side next to where I lay and across the whole of the western half of Bardsey, as in the calm aftermath of a great battle.

Birds too have died in great numbers on the island. The image I had of human bodies began life as a photograph I had seen in the bird observatory of lines of bird corpses that had been killed when they collided with the island's lighthouse. For many years (though no longer), because of an accident of its design and position, the lighthouse fatally attracted migrants on clouded nights when the moon was new or young. One night in August 1968 nearly six hundred warblers were killed, and on an October night the same year, a similar number of redwings.

That day in my October on Bardsey, as I lay on my back straining to see migrant birds flying south overhead, I wondered whether I was being cradled by a grave. Could this local curve of the earth be a human valley? Above the Irish Sea rain clouds were building. A peregrine bolted fast overhead, a bird with a wandering name on an island of pilgrims, though this one was a resident bird. Behind it, tumbling blackly and brilliantly off the high ridge of the eastern side of Bardsey, was a gang of choughs, rarest and most buoyant of all the crows, mopping at the sky. I sat up to watch them and saw the nun walking through the bottom of the field. She lived alone on the island, tending to the however many thousand souls. She wore chough-black clothes but had armed herself against the coming squall with a plastic cape made from a cut-open fertiliser sack of translucent blue, the colour of a Tiepolo sky or a dunnock's egg.

I collected my first dead bird when I was four. We moved from Liverpool and left the flat in the big house where I was born – the house with the swallows in the shed – for a family house, a red-brick semi-detached villa in a small town in Cheshire. My sister was born in the room next to mine when I was three. I heard her first cry. I saw her jaundiced slipperiness poured into one of my father's green woollen socks to warm her first minutes. I went to a nursery just down the road and later to the local junior school a few streets further on. There were privet hedges and tarmac driveways, curved suburban avenues and parks with iron railings.

In the park I noticed blackbirds and thrushes on the lawns. They came into our back garden too. I liked the way their wide-eyed sorties across the grass were made with alternating caution and boldness. I began to learn their songs. Put to bed on bright spring evenings, I lay awake, listening to the blackbirds beyond the thin curtains. The songs always seemed sad. I felt pinned to my bed by them. The evenings when my parents went out were the worst. I willed the time to go and the birds' music to wind down to a stop. I knew there had to be silence and proper dark, and that only out of the night-quiet could come the blissful sound of my father's key in the front door, meaning everybody was at home, and all was well, and I could drift into a safe harbour of sleep.

I was a mixture of nerves and curiosity. At school I preferred to sit with the teachers in their staff room at break time rather than risk the playground. But at home I was drawn outside to the garden. Again and again, I played versions of the same games – I was a zoo keeper, and a little later an animal collector on safari. For years I had only to look up over people's heads and I could summon my imagined and desired future on the African savannah. I walked home from school as I thought I would walk through the Serengeti.

One magical birthday in the Cheshire house – my best ever, as it still seems – I was given a wooden slide, a yellow tepee and a wicker picnic basket. My would-be runaway life began. I had grown jealous of my young sister and had protested by refusing to eat anything other than fish fingers. It didn't work, so I packed a small red plastic attaché case with three pairs of underpants and ran out of the front gate, turned right down to the main road and then turned right again. There, I bumped into the father of Guy, the boy who lived next door. He scooped me up and brought me home. Another day with Guy, I dug a boat-shaped hole out of the black soil behind the garage. It looked like a grave, but we hadn't intended that. We were going to paddle our Cheshire canoe to the sea but, before we finished, Guy inadvertently split my forehead with the spade. I bled into my eyes and held my father's handkerchief pressed to my face on the back seat of the car as he drove me to the casualty department to clean the earth from my head and stitch it. I still have the scar.

Around this time, one spring day, a dunnock's tiny chalky skull appeared in front of me, seeming to come up from the earth and into my fingers. I had run from the main door of our house out across the drive and onto the lawn, where a rose bed was cut from the green baize of neat grass. A man called Mr Clare, who lodged in our house, looked after the grass and the roses. The bald oval with its twisted hands of prickly stems was his special garden. He allowed me to come onto his lawn and watch him tend it. The grass was smooth and shone and, when Mr Clare wasn't there, it was good to lie on and roll over. I loved the sensation of the sun splashing into my eyes from high above and then the cool green shoots and wet earth smells flannelling my face.

I knelt down to the grass and stretched out and began to roll around the edge of the rose bed. The soil at the base of the woody stalks was bone-meal white. On one turn, as I was rolling, I spied in front of my face the minute dome of a skull. It was one inch long and made of paper-thin bone that globed above empty eyes and tapered at the front to a needle of beak. It was so bleached and fragile it seemed more like an ancient ruined shell or a worn fossil or something even less defined, a wrapped or bandaged space. I wasn't sure whether it had sunk into the soil, or risen from it. As I remember my find now, I can still feel the trepidation with which I pulled the skull from the whitish soil, wondering how much more bird there would be beneath it. Earth had gathered in the cavity of its head and, as I eased it out, a fine tilth of dried soil empted onto my palm, like sand running through an egg-timer. Only a year or so before, I might have tasted that soil, just as my baby sister ate the bread crusts and worm casts she found on the lawn, but I was a naturalist now.

I didn't know what bird had been in that skull. It was a bird's head; that was plenty enough. I took it inside, but after that it slips from my mind and I don't know what became of it. I think it was a dunnock. I grew up calling dunnocks hedge sparrows, and around this time I noticed my first one solitarily picking through the dead leaves under the shadow of the roses or along the privet hedge. The soil at the surface where the skull came from was a dunnock's place; its beak would have needled it repeatedly, its feet minutely hoeing it over and over. Its dead skull might only be an inch from where its living head had been.

One March forty years on, my son Lucian, aged seven, walked behind me, eyes down, along the scummy surf of a sandy beach on Coll in the Inner Hebrides. The wind hammered at us blue and sweet with ozone. I watched summer-plumage great northern divers, black, silver and serious, riding the roll of the sea like well-keeled naval commanders. Lucian harvested the beach. I turned to see him draping a dead gannet around his shoulders, a wing for each of his arms, its dagger head sticking up behind his. He looked like Eagle Medicine-Man, the Crow Indian, photographed by Edward S. Curtis wearing a dead turkey vulture mounted on his head. The gannet slipped and Lucian pulled it back over his shoulders like a cloak, like King Lear at Dover, fantastically adorned and finding himself simultaneously to be made of the earth and on it and en route to being in it. A few steps further and Lucian stumbled like the Ancient Mariner, shrouded in his albatross, labouring to carry the bird he had shot, like a dead baby or a new-found twin.

Wind piled on top of wind and just offshore, above the divers, dozens of living gannets banked up, pointed their heads down to peer through the swell and tipped forward to stab the water. Two more salted and ruined gannets lay on the beach, deader than seemed possible. It was as if they had died once and then again. Dead skin looks deader than bone. Like bodies exhumed from mass graves in Bosnia, the gannets were not the old dead – the bog people cloaked in their own skins of greasy parchment or a bone-dry unwrapped pharaoh – but the recently dead, with impacted flesh and clothes mashed together, blurred feathers and muscle, the beginnings of skeleton, the body smearing off into the sandy earth. The living neatness of preened feathers had given way to mess. Grimly dishevelled, unshaved, drunk, they were both repulsive and something you could mourn.

Their eyes die first; at the moment of death the eyeball shrinks slightly and becomes scored with tiny puckers that blank any reflection. No bird collector could keep a bird's eyes. Carrion flies had arrived and were walking over the gannet's dead cornea below me, tasting it as they went. Through my binoculars from a hundred yards away, I watched my son at the edge of the sea walking towards me wrapped in his dead gannet. I waited for him and asked him what he was doing. 'I want to keep this,' he said.

Five years after collecting the dunnock's skull, I walked through a March beech wood, the bare trees hanging from a hillside of the Surrey North Downs, carrying a song thrush's nest in my outstretched hands. The scouring winter had shown me the nest the previous day, within the naked hedge that separated our garden from our neighbours. I had known about it before, but the wind and the raw March sunlight put it in front of me again like an invitation to take it up.

The previous July I had seen the breeding song thrushes going to and from the same nest; I had peered at it through the green mesh of summer leaves and branches; and had reached into it to feel its smooth mud cup. I had rolled the warm eggs, tiny pale-blue skies, into my palm for a moment; I had felt the nestlings, like shrunken water-filled leather sacks; and I had watched the fledglings – and even tried and failed to save one when it arrived bedraggled and seemingly orphaned in front of me. Now the winter had loosened the nest, unstitched it from the branches of the hedge, so that when I leaned in this time and cupped my hand around its cup, it came free like the dunnock's head. I had pulled my booty towards me: a nest curved like the sky, curved like an egg, curved like a skull.

The earthen bowl was intact, fired hard by summer sun, autumn wind and winter frost; the grass outer weave was wan, sallow and soft, the dead stems had been drenched and dried and iced and thawed in the exposed hedge. In the cup was an acorn cup, a cup within a cup, a nest within a nest. Perhaps a mouse had used the nest as a larder in the late summer, or a jay had stashed an acorn there in its buccaneering autumn days of manic collections and optimistic burials. Perhaps the mouse had eaten the jay's acorn.

As I lifted the nest from the hedge it came away easily. It seemed finished, dead even, and so I was sure I could keep it, but as I took my prize towards the nature table at school, it was as if it revived and there were still warm eggs in its cup. Through the woods I held it, crunching over beechmast on the worn path to my classroom, and my cargo began to throb in my hands. I remember the quiet under the trees. The fuse-wire-thin gold-crest calls, a single curtailed *pink* of a chaffinch, and my breath. Spring was coming, but not yet.

Above me against the harsh sky in the bare treetops I could see that there were tatty old twiggy nests and heaped squirrel dreys like footballs of leaves stretching all the way down the hill, ten dark clumps through the wood. Edward Thomas's poem 'Birds' Nests' (written towards the end of 1914 – nests prompted one of Thomas's first poems as well as John Clare's last) is about noticing these winter nests which, he says, 'hang like a mark.' This wasn't a rookery. The nests were separate and made by several species of bird: a crow, a jay perhaps, wood pigeons, maybe a mistle thrush. Yet in the wood I felt that every nest was tied to the others. Each operated on each. To see them in the twisting wires of the canopy and to discover these forces was like looking at an orrery, a model of the solar system, and my nest-star joined these others in their universe, and I could feel the suck of their atmospheres as we passed beneath them through the wood.

At the bottom of the hillside, the wood became a hedge along a playing field with a football pitch. Breaking out of the trees, I carried my nest now like a grassy trophy across the chalked white lines towards the school gate. I flushed redwings that were feeding along the muddy track below the hedge. They flew into the hawthorns, the rust-red berries and the birds' conker-chestnut flanks blurrily interchangeable in the late winter haze. As the birds landed in the hedge from the leaf-strewn track, it was as if time were running backwards, their reds and browns making autumn leaves on the trees once more, only then to fall again to the earth as I moved further away, the seasonal pull of my nest's bundle of summer weakening with every step we took towards the nature table.

Dead birds surround me as I write. Nature tables are not encouraged at schools any more: the dirt and decay of Lucian's gannet would have raised eyebrows, so it came home instead. Since that dunnock's skull, I have always lived among the remains of birds. My parents were understanding. My childhood birthday presents subsequent to the tepee and the picnic basket usually included a dead bird. A stuffed water rail looks over my shoulder; I think it died before the First World War. Next to it is the still stiffening wing of the rufous-cheeked nightjar I brought back from Zambia. I go to sleep watched over by two huge green bronzewing pigeons from Australia, glassy-eyed and awake for more than a hundred years under a beautiful Victorian dome. On my desk next to my laptop is a pot of feathers. On my mantelpiece is a line of skulls: a razorbill, a pink-footed goose, a grey heron, a fulmar, some gulls and Lucian's gannet, whose bill with a jagged lightning-strike fracture gives away its cause of death – it must have misjudged a dive. Boxes of broken eggshells open like views onto tiny glittering beaches, and there have been plastic bags of the forensic evidence of crumbling owl and raptor pellets; there was once a shed with shelves of nests like an old hat museum; and there was even, for a time, a tray of carefully gathered house-martin splatter like a dripped Jackson Pollock, and a drawer of the soft ash-ended green cigarettes of goose shit.

I learned a lot from these relics. As a child I was most able to feel the time-before-my-time not from the death of a relative, or from family photographs, or from reading books about the ancient Greeks, but from staring at the stuffed birds my parents bought for me or picking up any dead bird I found. Our pet cats brought in mouthfuls of feathers; a weasel dragged a sparrow from the bird table and hung it in a bush; a baby blackbird, fledged for only minutes, drowned in a butt of rainwater; chicks dropped from nests like uncooked scraps of meat; miles of squashed pulp matted the roads.

I peered at the green woodpecker in its glass case, stuffed and mounted in a lifelike pose, hacking for ever at a lichen-covered log, its glass eye shiny but incontrovertibly dead. In my mother's kitchen freezer, I had stowed another green woodpecker that I had found on the path through the woods. At school, a friend rolled a dead goldfinch from his palm onto my desk. He had found it in a gutter. Its frail legs and feet were folded in death as if it was still securely perched on an invisible twig or was being held by the pudgy fingers of the infant Christ in a Raphael painting. Its serenity in death emphasised what it wasn't any longer – alive, flying and nervous of men and their machines. The car that killed it must have only glanced it, as it didn't seem to have been destroyed at all; but I wondered what sort of death throes allowed it to tidy its wings away and clench its claws. And what had it wanted to do at the moment it collided with the car?

I sliced the tiny wing of a wren from its corpse, leaving specks of gristle still around the severed joint, and taped it onto an old oblong-shaped computer-programming card that my father had given me. WREN, I wrote on it, and wrapped the whole thing in sticky-backed plastic. The wing looked very dead, utterly contrary to the wren's living, hurrying whirr. I tried to imagine its life before it was hit. Another car, another dead bird. That life, which I had never known, stretching back from the bird's death with as much complexity and mystery as my own past.

'I want to keep this,' said Lucian of the dead gannet, and I gathered my bird fragments in the same spirit, against their own ruin, seeking the preservation of their specific evidence, but also to stretch the lives of the dead in my head back into their pasts. From my scrutiny of the dead I was better able to understand life. The dead birds were just feathers and dust and collecting their flightless wings to me was, I knew, as meaningless as mapping their entrails. Yet still they calmed me down by being solid and identifiable, and in death they stretched my mind, up and off, as in life they had flown.

There is a contradiction here. Birds fly away. Their dead disappear. They carry no luggage, whereas I have made birds part of my clutter. A woodcock might carry its young between its legs or on its back, and gulls and gannets must pick up seaweed and other vegetation for a few days of the year to build their nests – in March gulls fly over Bristol with beakfuls of moss looking like first-timers in a Chinese restaurant – but otherwise their lives are free of junk. To sew its nest in place, a reed warbler at Wicken Fen snips near-invisible threads of spiders' webs from the air. Above the Tamuja River in Extremadura in Spain, a swallow catches for its nest a stray breast feather of a short-toed eagle as it floats down towards the earth from the soaring bird high above. Nests are made, used and then left to disintegrate.

Young children, like birds, don't have bags. They are not weighed down with stuff. But this changes. Lucian picking up his dead gannet – like me as a child bringing dead birds home – was a way for him to join the world of the dying. To work out mortality, we gather the dead to us. Like the Major in Choma, I have become a 'vast collector' and my assembled *ornithologia*, my bird clutter, is a kind of dragging anchor of lists, notes, bulletins, books, feathers, skulls and nests. In my parents' attic, along with my soil samples, I found a box of old sandy-brown foolscap pages of Bristol bird club reports. When I took the box down, so friable and curved into itself had the pile of pages become, I wasn't sure whether it was still the bulletins, or whether it had made a wasps' nest. When I touched the outer membrane of a yellowed sheet, it gave way and my finger went through months of bird records from Chew Valley Lake in the 1970s.

I can remember days at the Lake then, but my notes, like the bird club bulletins, have mostly either disappeared or turned to dust. I wish I didn't mind – I dream of being able to birdwatch without wanting to take it down. John Buxton described looking at redstarts for the first time in his POW camp in 1940 but not writing anything then, since, as he says, 'I had no paper.' Allan Octavian Hume, the remarkable colonial administrator in India, gathered a huge collection of 63,000 bird skins and 19,000 eggs and 'had planned to write a vast book on the ornithology of India and had made voluminous notes, but in 1884, while absent from home, a servant sold the manuscript in the market for waste paper.' Hume never wrote his book, and gave away his collection. A tragedy, but perhaps a liberation too.

The Young Ornithologists' Club was the name of the youth arm of the RSPB when I was growing up. It produced a black and white magazine called *Bird Life* six times a year. I read every one many times over. Today, just by looking at a cover, I can still remember the contents of entire issues. My ability to do this stops at the point in the 1970s when *Bird Life* went to colour. By that time I was already trawling for deeper pleasures, stranger fish: the recherché field-identification papers and behaviour notes in *British Birds* ('Insectivory and kleptoparasitism by Peregrine Falcons', 'Studies of less familiar birds, Number 144 – Thick-billed Warbler', 'Turnstones feeding on human corpse'); and the bleak surveys of ordinary species, with their odd austere poetry, as detailed in *Bird Study* (my favourite of all time – 'Where have all the whitethroats gone?' – a tacit and wistful announcement that bird-men had feelings too).

Lucian, for a few years, was a member of the current incarnation of the YOC, now called 'Wildlife Explorers'. Its all-colour magazine is not the old *Bird Life*; it has no place for dead gannets, for a start. The articles are enthusiastically upbeat: one of the RSPB's slogans is 'Aren't birds brilliant!' There is nothing on birds to be collected or dissected or rooted amongst or catalogued or scrutinised on a bedside table last thing at night or kept in the kitchen fridge.

Bird Life in the 1960s and early 1970s was very different. Dead birds were all over them. 'A Collection of Birds' Feet' was among my most-read articles ('A coat of clear varnish will preserve the foot and give it an attractive appearance . . . any "swops" that you can get can be exchanged with fellow ornithologists'). Perhaps the magazine editors' anxiety about egg-collecting was behind this: an adult perception that having something of birds (in a society that didn't have very much, that still looked and felt rationed) was what would most likely draw children to them, and that egg-collecting was, though newly outlawed, a *natural* expression of wonder and curiosity. I collected feet as instructed.

Ducks' feet got me to meet Peter Scott. One teenage year I won a duck challenge run by his Wildfowl Trust. A diligent student, I was already cynical about competitions and struggled to love ducks as much as other birds, but I swotted up. On the day at Slimbridge I had to identify captive ducks in pens and photographs of ducks in flight, and duck quacks on a tape, then answer questions on duck-feeding ecology and goose migration. Finally, in a kind of far-out version of pinning the tail on the donkey, I had to match a tray of duck bills to duck feet. I won.

I went up to collect my trophy – a silver goose taking flight – from Peter Scott himself, king of the ducks and sculptor of the goose. It was a strange few moments. I had never revered Peter Scott as I had Gerald Durrell or the young David Attenborough (whose *Zoo Quest* television programmes sent me charging out into the back garden setting traps and building cages for hypothetical Surrey lemurs and tenrecs). Ducks just weren't very interesting to me. I also thought of Peter Scott as a bad man for his past as a wildfowler. I disliked his paintings; they seemed catastrophically lurid – it was always dawn or dusk with wild purple skies doing far too much – and his ducks in flight, for all his lifelong looking (and shooting), seemed no more viably airborne than my granny's ceramic trio. In addition, I knew and remembered his father's famous last letter to his wife from Antarctica ('Make the boy interested in natural history if you can; it is better than games; they encourage it at some schools. I know you will keep him in the open air.'), which kept Sir Peter, no matter how venerable, a child in my mind, and always and only the son of the great hero-failure father. To cap it all, there was his duckish-celebrity, which had put him into the great human taxonomy of the time, the Bonzo Dog Doo-Dah Band's 'The Intro and the Outro' – which featured, along with 'Adolf Hitler on vibes' and 'Princess Anne on sousaphone', 'Peter Scott on duck call . . . *mwak waak, wak, wak, wak'*. As I walked up to him, I thought he should quack my score and his approval of it. As it turned out, he shook my hand and grunted something vaguely patrician, and I thought of the touch of his father on his baby hands all those years before and realised that in my mind I thought he was already dead.

One cold early Easter holiday weekend, when my children were small, we went to Suffolk. We stayed in a bed and breakfast of nightmare chintz with a landlady to match. Lucian was a baby and Dominic a toddler. They were tired but they wouldn't sleep. I was being horrible to everyone and needed to get outside. The next day was wet and windy and my mood didn't improve. I grabbed the children, strapped them in their car seats and, willing them to sleep, drove the car like a hearse through the dripping lanes, the bare trees in the gale shying over us.

The weekend was already stuffed with bodies. On the motorway from Bristol the traffic had slowed, there was a queue, and eventually we passed the cause. A crate or more of chicken portions had slipped from the back of a truck, smearing a hundred-yard slimy mess, a pink-grey pulp with the odd drumstick still not flattened by passing vehicles. It looked horrible, dribbling across the road, and it smelled even worse, part-cooked by the heat of pummelling tyres and crudely barbecued by exhaust fumes.

As I drove the children in our holiday hearse through Suffolk, I saw more carnage. Last night's road casualties were beginning their passage into the pulped world. A carrion crow, like its raven brother in Somerset, was going in at the ripped arse-end of a rabbit, the intact fluffy scut softly stroking the bird's black head, as it dipped at the riches it found there. A wreath of cherry-blossom feathers lay on wet black tarmac, the impact scatter of a wood pigeon that must have been hit in flight and bounced onto the road before being tossed clear. A hedgehog was rolled on its side like a knocked-over table, its four legs tensed and straight. It went on and on: a badger, a giant's shaving brush; a muntjac or an abandoned coat; a moorhen with splayed and hopeless green legs; puff after puff of sparrows.

At last the children slept. I drove and counted corpses. Above the road rooks took chameleon walks along the outer branches of hedgerow trees, carefully fetching twigs to repair and rebuild their nests, intent on their spring. I thought that if the children carried on sleeping I might pull off the road and scan for marsh harriers over the seething reed beds of Walberswick, and something of the hunting birds' buoyancy might ventilate me.

I never made it. A hen pheasant stepped from the verge, turned her head for a moment towards me and disappeared under my front wheels. A ghastly *thunk* reverberated through the car. In the mirror I could see, behind my boys' sleeping heads, the crashed mess of brown on the wet road, one wing hopelessly raised in a surrender flag. I stopped and got out, keeping the engine running, wanting the children to sleep on. Feathers were still coming from under the car and were launched back into the air by my exhaust. Dark blood seeped from the pheasant's beak and eyes; her eyelids were half shut. I could hear Dominic stirring in the back seat. I knelt to the road and assembled the ruined bird in my hands and carried her to the grass and put her down. Her brown body immediately looked like the dead flowers wrapped in faded cellophane that catch your eye as you drive the roads of Britain. The pheasant's blood and some blown feathers, the impasto of our contact, was left in the middle of the wet lane.

Only once have I seen a bird simply die. In another March on my way to Chew Valley Lake, I watched a black-headed gull fall dead from the sky onto a road in south Bristol. It was part of a flock heading from their overnight roost on the reservoir back towards the city I was coming from. Its falling, flailing wings caught my eye as I drove beneath it. The flock opened slightly around it, just enough to let it fall through them as they flew on. None looked anywhere other than where they were going. Dead already, the gull spun down to the edge of the road, where it immediately looked like any other dead bird. I didn't stop.

Thomas Hardy died in 1928, aged 87. One of the last memories he spoke of to his wife, Florence, was one of his first. He remembered at the age of four or a little older 'being in the garden at Bockhampton with his father on a bitterly cold winter day. They noticed a fieldfare, half-frozen, and the father took up a stone idly and threw it at the bird, possibly not meaning to hit it. The fieldfare fell dead, and the child Thomas picked it up and it was as light as a feather, all skin and bone, practically starved. He said he had never forgotten how the body of the fieldfare felt in his hand: the memory had always haunted him.'

There are many ways to death and there are no birds there. Virgil chose the Lago d'Averno, a lake in a volcanic caldera near Naples, for his gateway to the underworld. He called it Avernus and it takes its name from the Greek word *aornos* meaning birdless. Birds flying over the lake were asphyxiated by noxious sulphuric fumes rising from the magma reservoir beneath the lake bed. They fell out of the sky.

April

Aria Spontanea . . . An Air that whizzed . . . right across the
diameter of my brain . . . exactly like a Hummel Bee, alias
Dumbledore, the gentleman with Rappee Spenser, with bands
of Red, and Orange Plush Breeches, close by my ear, at once
sharp and burry, right over the summit of Quantock at earliest
Dawn just between the Nightingale that I stopped to hear
in the Copse at the Foot of Quantock, and the first Sky-Lark
that was a Song-Fountain, dashing up and sparkling to the
Ear's eye, in full column, or ornamented Shaft of sound in
the order of Gothic Extravaganza, out of Sight, over the
Cornfields on the Descent of the Mountain on the other side
-- out of sight, tho' twice I beheld its *mute* shoot downward
in the sunshine like a falling star of silver . . .

Samuel Taylor Coleridge

. . . Nothing has stirred
Since I lay down this morning an eternity ago
But one bird. The widest open door is the least liable to
    intrusion,
Ubiquitous as the sunlight, unfrequented as the sun.
The inward gates of a bird are always open.
It does not know how to shut them.
That is the secret of its song . . .

Hugh MacDiarmid

Imagine being able to look down a giant microscope to compare two laboratory slides of cross sections of Britain, one made in Othe winter and one in the spring. Think how the edge of the section grows so extraordinarily when the spring comes. Start in February when the ravens are breeding in the Avon Gorge but all else is locked shut. Take a few square feet of the woods around their cliff nest and cut vertically down into the earth. Make a thin slice of what you have cut, your blade shearing through the twigs and branches and the trunk of a tree, and on into the earth, through roots and soil to the rock of the crust. Lay this sliver of world flat on a slide. Draw a fine line around it with a black pen.

Now prepare the same slide anywhere across the northern hemisphere in late April. The earth is stretching. The world has a new growing edge. Every twig now holds a hundred leaves, every branch a thousand more, and the drawn line must extend around each leaf as it opens. The surface of the world has ballooned. The black pen must be swapped for a green brush. Add birdsong to this cross section. Think what the shift from thin winter contact calls to the open-throated full spring song of residents and new returning summer visitors does to the volume of the world. Add the blackcap's fruit-juice song in the lime tree above the raven's nest to the biomass, and so extend the line around the world. Calculate the din.

The thought of these slices of the singing earth came to me in a mortuary in a Moscow hospital that I had visited to produce a radio feature about bodies in the Soviet world. On a stone slab I saw a corpse, a man whose purplish fingers and toes and penis looked like wild spring orchids gathered at the edge of his body. Upstairs was a pathology laboratory that reminded me of the kitchens of my junior school – the room was hot and steamy and full of dinner ladies. Large women in headscarves and white coats were talking over the grind of machinery, while aluminium pans kept stewy things simmering on hotplates. The women were preparing slides. With scalpels they cut tiny purplish slices of meat from bigger lumps and carefully poured hot cloudy fat over them. On their tables were cooling bricks of this fat, a sort of wax that became opaque when cold. Other women took the cool bricks and sliced finely at them, revealing specks of meat, tiny bloody clouds set in a sky of wax. It looked like the worst possible school meal. They sliced, and each slice became a slide, ready to be scrutinised.

Outside the wooden hospital building, a collared flycatcher sang from a tatty stand of silver birches. It was early May, old and dirty pockmarked snow, dotted with a few new green leaves, lay around the trees. The flycatcher's song was thin but strong, and his silvered notes were thrown like meltwater. The bird was just back from Africa. This was its wood and it would breed here. Glancing towards it from the pathology-kitchen cleared my head. If some accounting was going to be made, even of diseased or dead tissue, shouldn't it take notice of that little black and white bird adding itself to the fresh green leaves of the birch trees and sweetly working at the air above with its tiny song? As I left I tried to include it in the slides in my mind. The women were thinking of other things. The bubbling pans on the hotplates turned out to be their lunch.

Spring forces us to notice this effect – this extension of the world. The season arrives as a disturbance of air. New weather seems to have come from far across the sea, new music from deep within the earth. The first flying swallow seen half a mile away cutting through the March cold over Chew Valley Lake gives me hope; the first singing swallow heard adding song to the April sky confirms all that I wish to know.

*　*　*

Birdsong is inherently warm. It thickens the scene and deepens space, adding to the density of places in the lightest of ways. There is more of it in spring and it travels further than most winter calls. Song allows you to hear more distant things. The blackbird singing on the other side of the park brings the other side of the park into my head for the first time since last May. A greenfinch is singing in the next street over from mine, a street I never go down but which I can now hear.

On a late February day at a suburban crossroads in Bristol, a blackcap is calling its harsh *chack* from a eucalyptus tree. The sound bristles the leaves. The hardy and thickset warbler is here at the limit of its winter range. Much more north or any more ice and it couldn't survive. Its call seems to assert its hunched endurance. It cannot afford to say very much. Calls are cool, defensive, seeking and searching. They speak of being apart.

The next day is milder. In the same place is the same male blackcap. Today I don't see him; instead I can hear his curious inward-whispered subsong coming from deep in the eucalyptus. Subsong is one of the quiet secrets of the world. It is the soft under-the-breath singing that songbirds utter at either end of the summer. Almost everyone hears it and almost no one notices it. Blackbirds and other thrushes do it, robins and warblers. Commonly done out of sight, it is often only heard as you walk beneath the tree or past the bush in which it is being sung. It sounds like a dream song and, indeed, it is thought that birds dream and that some species 'practise new song patterns in their dreams'. This muted solitary singing is sad to me, as if it isn't meant to be heard, as if the bird is talking to itself or humming slightly self-consciously to cheer itself up, reminding itself of summer.

The day after, the sun shines. The calling and the subsong seem like ancient history; winter has turned to spring in one bird over three mornings. The blackcap is there, bouncing energetically through the crackling leaves at the edge of the eucalyptus, singing as if it has received word of the good things in life. Its song sounds like hot chocolate being poured from an old silver jug. It is last summer's music again, last summer – its fruits and its flies – made into music, the same old song but warm and new too. It opens and fills a space beyond the bird and the tree. The caution of winter is over, with its noise that can only reach as far as a breath. The bird's ambitions and energies are extended out into the air, saying here I am, this is me, and this is my place, I am staying and you should know.

At the beginning of April, I watched swallows in Shropshire, witnessing the moment they arrived back. Two birds plunged down to the River Onny to drink as if sent from the sky. They seemed desperate to sip from the river again. I stood on an old stone bridge and the two birds flashed up after their skim of the brown stream and pulled away towards the barns of the farm just up the side of the valley. Perhaps the bridge is a mark for them to turn left. Do they remember breeding or hatching here last year and do they recognise the barn? Can they feel the coordinates of the valley; know the scent of its air, the taste of its water?

Maybe this male swallow sang on its wintering grounds like the birds I heard in Zambia, maybe it hasn't sung for eight months since it was last here, maybe it hatched only a year ago and has never sung before. But something now, as it flies around the barns, is working on its beak like pliers and out comes a song to match its deep-red cut throat – a burbled song as if bubbled through blood, or a mouthful of flies, but beautiful.

The farm buildings are changed from one moment to the next as the swallows return. The birds will be here for months now, flying in and out of the barn and through the yard, filling its air with wings and singing. Their wet blue-slate back is like a roof after rain, their throat like a single red tile, their breast and under-parts the colour of pale stone, their tails streamers like a weathercock. It is no wonder we think of them as house gods.

The swallows make the place come alive. They fly around with an effortless sense of ownership and appear to be inspecting the farm, ripping and scissoring and plumbing the air between the buildings. It is as if they unpick the farmhouse, the byre and the hayloft, lifting each from their foundations, and then setting them back down again, with each given an extra dimension – an airborne configuring – making the buildings settle and sit in a new way.

To see them back – even without knowing the swallows on this farm before – is to feel jolted out of something; their returns define the emptiness of the time when they are not here; their flights make us shiver to think of the sky without them; the rippling start of their song draws attention to the silence before it.

Once I tried to fly myself, but the weather was against me. Twice I went to the airfield, on the edge of the Cotswolds, leaving my home in sunshine but arriving in cloud. On my first attempt the windsock drooped in listless air. On the second it disappeared into watery mist. With no wind and then no visibility, the glider I hoped to fly in stayed unpacked in its long chrysalis. I sat about in the old shed on the edge of the strip drinking black tea from big mugs. It's an intensely male space, a cross between a tree house and a scout hut, with old well-kept kit and a salvaged rough comfort side by side. Robinson Crusoe would be at home. The waiting was like the waiting at the ringing station or at the bird observatory on Fair Isle, outdoor men brought indoors to stir milk powder and peer through the windows hoping for a break in the weather. I had a go on the flight simulator and crashed my virtual plane, so I decided to head out.

I drove off the ridge and down the few miles to the banks of the River Severn. The cloud was higher but the rain continued. This was serious all-day professional rain. The deluge after the green burst of the weeks before made the Severn Valley almost tropically lush. All life under the rain was turned to scum. The ground was slushy with fallen things. At Slimbridge, hazy in pluvial light, low and billowing drifts of rain rolled up the Severn like a wet cloth being drawn from the river itself.

The rain had grounded a peregrine in front of me. Another failed flyer. The bedraggled falcon was like a wet cardboard box slumped on the Dumbles, the lovely cricket-pitch green fields that rise from the river's edge. It was a second-year bird, as big as an adult, but streaked and muddy, not yet slate-grey and barred.

I sheltered alone in a hide and stared at the bird down my telescope until I felt I was entering peregrine time and space. The horizon – wherever it had gone – should have been the falcon's, but in the rain it stared at the sodden grass right in front of it, its huge eyes moving. It looked sick or injured, but it was just wet and cast down. Waterlogged, its tail dragged in the wet grass, beads of rain caped its back and coursed like mercury over its head. Droplets gathered on its bare cere and rolled forward, filling the hole on its beak. Every five minutes or so it slowly turned its head and slightly raised its wings to shake off the rain.

The cloud base was at about thirty feet. The peregrine is happy at three thousand. The bird hunched into itself. I grew sleepy. At the moment I felt I could walk right up to it, it swivelled its body and seemed to be looking straight at me. How could it tell? I was hidden and there was half a mile between us, but I had been seen. Its huge dark bulbous eyes scoured over the top of its hooked beak. Even drenched and spangled by raindrops, this was death's head.

The bird turned back and resumed its vigil. The damp was thickening and it was getting dark. I had to tear myself away. The bird was still there when I left, drilling itself into the green, waiting for the rain to stop so its feathers would settle under its preen and it could restore them to the sky. Tomorrow, in a turn in the weather, it would resume its flying and would hit something up there with the force of an appalling hammer, and pigeon feathers or gull feathers would rain to the ground.

That same break in the clouds got me up into the air. I went back to the gliding club the next day and as I arrived, the planes were being wheeled onto the long strip of grass on the hilltop at Nympsfield. My palms began to sweat. Having been instructed in the use of my parachute, I clambered into the passenger seat, half sitting, half lying behind the pilot. A passenger to where, I wondered. It was like being strapped into a phone box with a stranger. The clear roof of the cabin was lowered and everything outside immediately sounded far away.

The launch was straight out of my childhood. It might have been like this to be born, and it was certainly like this at the far stretch of the back garden swing, or at the tipping moment as my go-kart went over the lip of the old bomb crater in the woods, or for the second I let go of the rope hanging from my tree house and tried to swim through the air. The scoff at gravity and its answering tug.

A winch wound in a steel rope that was tied to the plane, and pulled it fast and steeply upwards. For one second we rolled along the grass hurtling towards the winch house, for another we were pulled parallel to the grass ten feet above it, then for two seconds we were shot up from the earth, as near to vertical as seemed possible. In those four seconds we went from zero to seventy miles an hour and were tossed a thousand feet into the sky.

I thought of birds I had released back to the air, and how the feeling that followed when I opened my fingers from around them had given me an intimation of this launch, too: the kick of their feet against my palm as they spread their wings, and their rush upwards, from my hand and the shadow beneath it, away from stuff and the dark of gravity, into the air and towards the light.

Everything important and desirable seemed ahead of us. We didn't ever leave the weather, as a jet plane does, but under the glider's clear canopy I felt as if all the light of the sun was being delivered directly to my head. At this point we crested and the winch cord tightened for a moment, tugging us back, reminding us where we'd been. My ears popped and my stomach pushed at my ribcage.

The pilot released the rope and we were free and flying, gliding down the heating air of the escarpment. The noise of the launch fell back to earth with the zinging rope, like Coleridge's skylark's silvery shit, and then there was only the wind in my ears, the strange noisy silence of the sky. I felt a levelling lurch that was our weight settling, my own weight too, spreading out in the air. My eyes dropped back in their sockets. It seemed like a loosening of life, as if there was a new place to be. But simultaneously came a new sense – my flying sense – my need to stay up, to feel the air and to find a way through it. My arms were pinned to my sides, but I had a strong desire to spread them wide. I registered every bump we passed through, and found my body bending, even in the seat, wanting to take account of what the air was doing. It was an embrace, like having a lover's body surrounding mine: where it clasped I held on, where I pushed it replied, where it opened I went.

Then came a sharp tug upwards as if we had been hooked by the sky: the plane nuzzled into the air of a thermal. I looked up. Two buzzards had shown us the way. I have watched them flying from the earth for hours, but never before had I felt such companionship as the glider fell in below them and we flew together, soaring around our shared chimney of air. I felt a judder as we latched on and began to turn and rise. Around we went, following the buzzards, climbing through the creamed warm air of the thermal, sucking at its milky way. I thought of the honeyguides of Choma calling us into the sweetness of life.

The light above and the sensation of the body of the air all around had been so engrossing that I had hardly looked at what I thought I would notice most, the wind-assisted bird's-eye view of the earth from the sky; but as we came out of the thermal – the buzzards had gone on already – I began to look down. It was the place we had come from and would return to, but it had no determining power over the life of the sky. Everything below appeared beautiful but irrelevant.

Landing felt like a controlled burying of ourselves back within the local horizon. It was all sensible shoes and mirror-signal-manoeuvre. The shining map of the earth as seen from the air turned into a dull diorama and rose around our plane like a theatrical flat. Never had trees seemed so boring. I missed the birds' horizons as soon as they were out of view, the shadows, folds and upheavals of all the earthworks, the sunken ridges and furrows beneath the grass fields everywhere, the bulk of the Cotswold and Malvern hills on one side of my glider dome, the metallic flatness of the River Severn on the other and the view beyond, shared by yesterday's peregrine, across the river and into Wales. Even after a first flight it felt difficult to come back down.

As I undid my parachute, and clambered from my seat, my eye caught some swallows above the airstrip and the buzzards back up above the wood. My fellow travellers – I saw them, as I never had before, as kind-hearted acrobats who had invited a fall guy onto their stage, as generous keepers of the air, happy to let us try to raise a ladder to the sky.

I walked away from the planes and skirted the airfield. At the far end of the grass strip was a bird where it shouldn't be. A lone whimbrel set down on its migration north, its beautiful brown curves, streaked back and fine down-curved bill, like the blown brown grass it walked in. The birds normally cross Britain in the spring in parties. As they fly they call a tumbling silvery trill, musical and intimate, that seems to keep them together and makes you look up. But here was one on its own and silent. I felt drawn to the bird, but it flew nervously into the next field. I had flown for twenty minutes back and forth along the scarp; it had come from west Africa.

I helped to take the wings off the glider. Some of the planes are stored in curious custom-built hangars, adapted sheds that look as though they have been made to house a crucifix or an angel. The plane is trundled backwards off the strip, and the wings, still attached, slide into shallow but wide extensions of the shed to its left and right. The glider is wrapped up. The other storage system allows the planes to be towed from launch to launch. It's more modern but it also looks deathly; the wings are taken off and pinned along the back of the fuselage, and the folded glider is slid into a long tube on wheels like a coffin for a thin giant. Once again I thought of dead birds with their folded wings. And then I looked down and saw one. A bird grounded twice over.

At my feet under the transporter, lying on a bier of last year's dead leaves, was a female chaffinch, breast down, her wings folded neatly away. It was hard to know how she had died, but as I rolled her over onto her back, there was no question that she was dead. Her eyes had gone to nothing, the feathers of her head and wings were intact but stiff; her breast exposed by my shoe was a riot of maggots, the colour and shape of the glider transporter, which came hurrying out with their legless scuttle from a hole, like the entrance to a tunnel, in the bird's breast. She had been eaten inside out. I couldn't see anything in the cavity. For a corpse less than an inch thick it seemed to have an impossible depth, as if it opened onto another place altogether. A black hole.

An elderly man walks ahead of me down a green lane with spring oak trees shuffling in the wind above us. He stops, tilts his head and raises his left arm. His open khaki greatcoat follows him as he leans slightly, like one of the oak branches, and he points, holding his index finger up, at once shushing me and showing me and beginning to count in the music he has unpicked from the singing all around us. From the delicious warm thicket of birdsong in the trees and bushes stretching away from the lane, Mr Rimes has found a deep, fruited moan that breaks and gasps for air, then plunges again into the stream it has made of itself. I have never heard anything like it before.

All the English nightingales I have heard since this one have somehow been conjured by Mr Rimes, a short, grey-haired, schoolmasterish man who carried his sandwiches in his binocular case and wore a tie to go birdwatching. All my nightingales find their way back to him walking ahead of me and my father down Swanton Lane between Canterbury and Stodmarsh in Kent, pointing out the birds singing on either side of us. I have seen and heard far more nightingales in Europe than in England but I still identify the birds' night music as English without quite knowing why: the feel it has of old tunes being suggested and replayed, of jam in an otherwise spartan diet, of the lustre of the night sky once London is out of the way, of the phantoms of the Second World War that fill East Anglia and the Home

Counties with aerodromes and pillboxes, and concrete overrun by brambles.

I was twelve. It was 3 June 1973. I know this because a letter tells me so. Among my surviving treasures and relics, my wings and skulls, are a few letters, two from Gerald Durrell (lovingly kept as proof that I could have words with a hero), two from a girl who liked birds (proof of the possibility of such things), a couple accepting my records of a Mediterranean gull in Gower and two Cory's shearwaters off Mizen Head in Cork (proof of my status as serious bird-man), and then nineteen others, all in the same wiry but clear hand, all on the same pale blue paper, all with 3p stamps, all from Mr G. B. Rimes of Gillingham in Kent. His letters are proof, mostly, that people used to write letters and that old men shared their boyish enthusiasms willingly: his are almost entirely lists of birds he had seen on his various outings through Kent.

Mr Rimes didn't have a car. The previous spring my father and I had met him at Minsmere in Suffolk. He was staying in the same Westleton bed and breakfast as we were, run by the redoubtable Mrs Mary Macgilp (a most un-chintzy establishment much used by birdwatchers). We'd given him a lift and so began two years of occasional outings with him. My dad and I would drive to 110 Sturdee Avenue, later 47 Sunnymead Avenue, and collect him. We would go on to Sheerness, Sandwich or Stodmarsh and look for birds, have tea in a café that he had nominated, and drop him back at his lodgings. The only information Mr Rimes offered about his life in his letters – apart from lists of birds – was two references to landladies. That he lived in a boarding house in Gillingham is all I know; my father can remember no more either. Our talk, when permitted in the field, must have been entirely bird-centred.

My bird notes from this time are sparse and I cannot now

recall if we saw the shore larks we hoped to at Sheerness or the autumn migrants at Sandwich. I don't think we did. Mr Rimes did show us Cetti's and Savi's warblers (then both equally rare in Britain) at Stodmarsh. Knowing their songs as he did (they are very different, but I didn't know that then) helped him see and I marvelled at his ability to coax these birds from a reed bed by identifying them. That was amazing to me. A little old man with rheumy eyes, wearing a suit and stout footwear was calling up fabulous beasts simply by knowing them to be there.

It was the same in Swanton Lane. Mr Rimes heard the first nightingale and brought it out of the turmoil of bushes and birdsong – the full spate of warblers and thrushes and tits and finches, blackbirds and redpolls, marsh tits and robins. He siphoned its song from the stream. I heard the bird sing and then I heard it stop, but when it started up again I knew it was a nightingale. Then he managed to produce the bird itself, which he'd spotted between its song flourishes, down on the ground, shaded beneath a bramble, a little rufous thrush with a cocked tail. It paused and opened its beak and I could hear the sound and see the bird twisting its throat and turning its head and its whole body quivered and heaved as it sang.

There were maybe ten male nightingales singing along this lane that day. I have never heard so many in England since. I haven't been back, and I don't know what happened to Mr Rimes. We moved from Surrey to Bristol at the end of 1973. I never saw him again. Nor did I ever discover what his initials stood for.

Though Mr Rimes and the nightingales of Swanton Lane got there first, Keats, in his ode to the bird, did something to the nightingale – his poetic rendering of its realities and the ideas it suggests – that is hard to ignore. The poem does what the best bird poems do. Though it has plenty of 'faery' in it, it comes out of real looking and listening. We don't need to know Keats's biography or the details of the poem's making to be certain from it that he knew nightingales. The poem is full of evidence and has the smack of the real, and even – in its lines about the song apparently retreating up a hill – the ghost of a field note. It is not, though, a poem of observation put into metred lines; it wants to think about the bird too, about its reality but mostly about the thoughts that it triggers. But the bird in the poem is rescued from being just a cipher by the way the poem manages to *be* a nightingale, as well as being about a nightingale, and about what hearing a nightingale makes you think and feel. Keats is brilliantly able to mimic the bird's song and mimic the sensation of hearing the song at the same time. It is a double translation out of nature.

Because he has the nightingale's jizz right and we recognise the accuracy of his looking, we don't feel he has hijacked the bird too far from its reality. So when he puts the nightingale to work in the poem, we don't demur, because the work seems apt to us. But, we might ask, what came first: the nightingale or the ode? Was I in Swanton Lane already in thrall to the poem without knowing it? Has Keats's version of the bird lushly clogged our mind, might his poem keep us from the truth of the nightingale, or could part of the ode's success be the way it asks what the truth of a bird could be?

The poem is a lesson in the cultural construction of nature. Birds are not man-made, but all birdwatching is, whether it ends in the *Handbook of the Birds of the World*, a jar of pickled thrushes, or an 'Ode to a Nightingale'. Keats spoons a kind of sad green syrup over the nightingale, a medicine that makes you drowsy not better. An unrepentant Maltese bird-trapper and thrush-eater walks to his lime twigs with their stuck birds, glued by another green syrup. He has a different nightingale to Keats's in his mind, but nonetheless a humanly constructed one. He is thinking of his dinner.

Yet still the nightingale seems a 'poetical' bird. Think of the raven or the kingfisher or the pelican; how slow by comparison is the decay of the nightingale's romantic cultural valency. Keats got the nightingale right and no one has substantially been able to remake it for nearly two hundred years. In this the bird helps, richly complicating things. Though it sings freely in the daytime and from the tops of bushes in much of its European breeding range, including Britain, it also sings at night and hidden in thickets and scrub. Because it can skulk and because it is a fairly drab, unmarked bird – 'no oil painting' my grandmother called it when I showed her a picture of one – its song apparently compensates by being that much richer and more expressive than the song that a bright, pretty bird might need to sing. This helps the song seem like art. So does its suggestion of performance, and the way we become observers of this artfulness in a theatre – the lights go down and from some dark corner of a stage, a truth so deep that it can only be heard comes forth in tearing stabs of music. This, too – the actual progress of the song and the way it builds and moves and breaks apart and restarts – seems like poetry or music. A grasshopper warbler's song is no less heartfelt, but our hearts cannot feel it, whereas nightingale song seems to speak and we think we might be able to understand it.

Our nightingales are, in this sense, Keats's. He manoeuvred himself brilliantly between the bird and us, and brought us together beneath the same night sky. Nobody has the swallow or the blackbird or the robin as Keats has the nightingale. For a time, I thought that I minded this, thought that the nightingale was tarnished and was suffering, a gilded bird in a poetic cage. I had speeches ready to spring it from the prison of Hampstead and Highgate. I affected first to prefer other poetic accounts of the bird (John Clare's 'The Progress of Rhyme' brilliantly transcribing its song, for example), and then I unlearnt the poem and these newer favourites too. I separated my bird guides from my poetry books to prevent any wanton miscegenation. I relished science that rendered the birds' song cycles as graphs. I banished all conversational allusion to the poetic bird when in front of the real thing, attempting to record my encounters only in the department of my mind stocked with metal filing cabinets:'21st May 1977 Inglestone Common, Gloucestershire; wind: light southerly force 2–3; 2230 Nightingale: 3 H'.

The 'H' means 'heard'. The anti-poetic minimalism didn't work. It didn't need to work. The nightingale doesn't require protection from poets. I realised I was only doing what Keats said I would. All versions of the bird – poems, musical settings, scientific investigations, plumage descriptions, song transcriptions, dreams – all our nightingales are just accounts, the equivalent of a notebook entry. 3 H.

This thought also occurs in a powerful but broken-down and never-completed poem by Ivor Gurney called 'The Nightingales', written around 1925. Gurney had been certified insane in 1922 and was confined to mental hospitals from then until his death in 1937. 'The Nightingales' was written in his hand in an exercise book of poems (*The Book of Five Makings*) assembled by him, his editors say, 'without hope of publication'. The poem has now been published, with its revisions and uncertainties carefully transcribed. Like Keats's poem, it mimics the passage of nightingale song through a night, wittingly or not, and the editorial marks across its unfinished lines enhance this. It takes place not far from Inglestone Common in Gloucestershire and also describes three birds singing. Hearing them, Gurney says 'How could I think such beautiful . . . it was only bird-song.' He wants to resist quarrying nightingale music for meaning and suggestion. But to do this he has to leave the birds. They are too ready-made as poems, too veiled with the gossamer of fairyland and Keats. In order to push beyond the received nightingale, beyond Keats and even himself, Gurney takes another bird from his note-book, which stands in for a nightingale before the poets got their hands on it. A 'laughing' linnet sings and it is –

. . . As if poet or musician had never/before/true tongue
To tell out nature's magic with any truth . . .

Cleaning his poem and his ears in this way takes Gurney back, and he is able to listen to the nightingales once more. The sense at the end of his poem is not entirely clear and it isn't finished, but he returns to the specifics of the encounter. That we know now that Gurney was remembering and figuring the birds whilst he was incarcerated in a mental hospital and prone to delusions adds to the devastating effect of this. But even without this knowledge we can see him, with great care, reaching towards the singing birds and leaving them where they are at the same time, making that beautiful approach and retreat that I think is at the heart of all the best and truest bird-watching. Best and truest because it describes what birds do to us. Gurney acknowledges his own loaded entanglement with the nightingales, but is chastened by the real thing. And yet the real thing seems poetical, and the birds become poems without being made them:

Should I then lie, because at midnight one had nightingales,
Singing a mile off in the young oaks – that wake to look to
    Wales,
[And]/Dream and/watch Severn – like me, will tell no
    false/adoration in/tales?

*   *   *

In Zambia in January, in a thicket that seems to run through the whole of Africa, and just after I identify the marshmallow-frog-jumper or African broadbill, I hear a sprosser, or thrush nightingale, the nearest relative of Keats's bird. It is on its wintering grounds and has found a similar jungle to its breeding habitat in north and east Europe and Russia. It is singing – the song is similar to Keats's or Gurney's – a beautiful mud gurgle, and I am surprised. Is it practising for Europe or holding territory? I cannot see it. That doesn't surprise me.

In Moscow in May, it is hot at night and I leave open my hotel window. At three in the morning I am woken by fantastically loud birdsong. A thrush nightingale has arrived in the thin strip of roadside birches and is launching great lyrical stabs up into the city night. It is so loud that I think it is a recording. There are speakers hanging in the trees – a feature of the old communist world that was determined to make woods and parks places of instruction – and I wonder if the bird has found a microphone. A street-cleaning lorry clatters past like an embarrassed tank; the thrush nightingale is louder. I stand naked at the window looking into the dark trees with my binoculars, remembering Nabokov somehow dealing with nightingales in his autobiography by noting that he heard them from the toilet. I cannot see the bird.

In eastern Hungary in June, I walk along the banks of the River Tisza. It is hot and sticky. The air is full of willow down and savage mosquitoes, carp are burping at the surface of the water, and the aspens and willows and the scrub below are buzzing with river warblers and great warm clouds of thrush nightingale music. I am listening hard, making sure they are not regular nightingales. I cannot see them. I think I have separated the songs of the two species in my mind. I go for a drink of fresh white wine in a cool bug-free cave in Tokaj and accidentally stay for five more. When I come back out into the heat, I sit on a wooden bench at the mouth of the wine cellar and instantly fall asleep. When I wake up an hour later I cannot remember my nightingale song insights. I still can't.

On Fair Isle in September, a loose scattering wind comes up from the south-east. Fabulous birds appear. Ten steps from the Siberian lanceolated warbler in its tiny field of oats, a vagrant thrush nightingale hops on a garden wall like a robin without a red breast. Its eyes are dark. They are eyes for the dark of all the bushes of Europe and Africa and all the night skies between. But here there is no cover apart from a cabbage stalk. I can see the bird. It could be an Italian princess stranded on a northern rock. It is silent.

May

There was a tree grew in the wood
The findest tree that ever was seen
The tree grew in the wood
And the green leaves growed all around around around
And the green leaves growed all around
The limb grew on the tree
A branch grew on the limb
A nest was on the branch
An egg was in the nest
A bird was in the yolk
A wing was on the bird
A feather was on the wing
And the green leaves growed all around around around
And the green leaves growed all around

Sung by Mrs Grace Coles
at Enmore, The Quantocks, Somerset, 1906

But enough of greenwood's gossip. Birdsnests is birdsnests.

James Joyce

At eight thirty in the evening, in early May, on the Somerset Levels, the sun has gone and the day is cooling fast. It rained earlier and, though the sky is almost totally clear now, the moisture of the fallen rain is drawn back upwards and the air dampens towards dusk. Planes drive through the upper atmosphere, their wing lights blinking. Just before the black-out, two swifts, still darker than the darkening air around them, track beneath the planes. I looked up because, though it seems improbable, I felt the air being silenced. They are flying companionably, together but loose, muted and muting, and disappear into the dark after four seconds.

They are the first I have seen this year in Europe. It is like seeing a seafarer still offshore but returning from the other side of the world. What does a homecoming mean for a seafarer? Where have they been, what have they seen; where will they go, will they ever stop to tell me what they know? The news they carry from the other end of the planet and all points in between is simply themselves. They have been in another air; here they are briefly in mine; that is all. The earth passes beneath them.

The first pricks of starlight follow behind the swifts. The seafaring birds put me in mind of Coleridge, who thought about stars not far from where I am, writing for swifts too: 'everywhere the blue sky belongs to them, and is their appointed rest, and their native country and their own natural homes, which they enter unannounced, as lords that are certainly expected and yet there is silent joy at their arrival.'

Chew Valley Lake on 18 May, a few miles north of the Levels, and two months after my first swallow here. There are thousands of swifts over the water; maybe five thousand, maybe fifty thousand; it is impossible to count. Some are inches above the surface; others are perhaps a mile up. The wind dies and plump drops of rain fizz on the lake surface. Cloud smokes downwards and pushes all the swifts down with it. The air is being squeezed from above, it thickens, and the swifts, thunder-birds, thicken it some more and bring the sky down with them.

They are silent. If I shut my eyes, I wouldn't know a single one was there.

In these conditions they fly above the water in a straight line with deep powered cuts of their wings. Before they reach the lakeside, they turn and skim back to resume their passage once more across the lake. To watch their combing of the matted air is soothing. They don't seem to be feeding, they don't seem to be on their way anywhere; they are at rest in motion. They have flown from Bristol to southern Africa and back to Bristol without touching anything, carrying nothing, never perching, never landing, never tired.

Twenty minutes later the pressure eases. The rain stops, the cloud lifts and breaks. Immediately, the swifts want to escape upwards and seem to be pushing the cloud higher. They appear to be able to run uphill through the air. Some are chasing insects; others just need more height: they fly up fast and then cut from their climb with a slicing angled glide.

Those that are feeding use one of two methods. Some explicitly chase individual insects they have spotted, hawking for them like a hobby, jinking through the air. Others just fly and collect what comes to them as part of the huge black shoal of open mouths, sieving the sky like a baleen whale or a basking shark: 'from the mouth of a swift which had been shot, a table-spoonful [of insects] was extracted'.

Some swifts seem content to hang. I can see them minutely adjusting their wings to match the strength of the air they are moving through, giving them just enough forward propulsion. They are like a diagram of flight, a model of aerodynamics in a wind tunnel. 'As if the bow had flown off with the arrow', as Edward Thomas wrote. Watching them fly like this, making the best shape that works the air, it seems I can see the wind.

Some are more restive. They begin to fly using an extra-fast wingbeat that flickers quicker than my eye can follow. After these flurries they glide, some holding their wings raised stiffly in a shallow V. They are displaying. I watch as closely as I can and think I can see some turning over in the air, like ravens, and flying on their back for a beat or two of their wings. Ever more bravura flights begin, with catastrophic dives and wild slingshot accelerations, virtuoso falls and high-speed corrections. The birds – they are a crowd not a flock – are working themselves up.

I am watching this seething cloud when I notice one swift twist itself into a headlong dive, pulling hard on its wings as if it feels itself to be going too slowly. A hundred feet below where it started out, I see it pull up in the air, its wings high and flicking above its back. It is alongside another bird which it has sought out and it flies closer to this bird from behind and then, in an action I will never forget, it raises its wings still higher above its body and slides itself onto the back of the other bird, which lifts its wings too, and for two and half seconds they mate. As they do, both birds' wings beat in synchrony, extra deep to their full extent, cutting all the way down and then all the way back up. They look joined in the air, as if one bird had four wings, but it is hard to see whether the male actually rests on the female or holds himself perfectly placed fractionally above her. Then it is over, the female scoots away, apparently breaking from beneath the male, and he banks upwards after her, and I lose them in the blizzard of other swifts and in my own exhilaration at what I have just seen. All my birdwatching life seems to be contained in those two and half seconds of black magic.

On the Mediterranean coast of Spain, a sudden summer thunderstorm booms and swirls around the old barrio and the castle of Alicante. I shelter in the castle until the rain passes, climbing its dark stone stairways to its outer fortified walls. There on the ground, at the foot of a flagpole, is a pallid swift. Unlike the dead bird in Gibraltar, this one is alive, though grounded and helplessly out of its element. The storm had corralled flying insects and bashed them down towards the earth and this bird, I guessed, had followed them but had got knocked down by a surge of wind or hail. Its tiny feet and short legs are not strong enough to lift it up; it cannot take off. I think it is a young bird, hatched just a few weeks before. Its matt brown feathers are dull and dusty under the electric sky. Since it left its nest cranny, all of its life has been in the air. It has barely needed legs. If it goes back to its nest after it has fledged, it either flies straight in or scrabbles for an inch or two like an amputee using its wings to propel it. When it returns to the air it simply falls into it, tumbling casually back out into the sky, where it lives.

I bend and pick the swift up, letting its panicking wings fold and calm in my palm. It is incredibly light but its warmth and its feathery energy feel strong in my hand, as if I am holding repelling magnets made of air. Holding a bird is always a surprise like this. Between my fingers its black eyes reflect the riven clouds overhead. I extend my arm, unclench my hand, and throw the swift lightly up into the sky. For a moment it seems to falter and begin to fall then, as if reclaiming its magnificent wings from me, it flicks them, dark slivers of moon, and is gone back into its life, airborne and flying.

Every year I keep a diary of last swifts. Or I mean to. You never see them go. Every year they do their disappearing trick once more. They empty the sky of themselves. Out of the blue.

A May without an oak wood would be as bad as an autumn without migrants. In Horner Wood and East Water Valley on the northern edge of Exmoor, the trees are mostly sessile oaks. They cloak the valleys and rising land as if they have polished it over thousands of years to a series of smooth curves. The moor slopes to the sea along these valleys, and they reach towards it like limbs. Behind them, even in May, the heather on the moor is brown, as dark as dried blood. There are patches of sandy winter grass backcombed towards Dunkery Beacon. But the woods and valley floor are bright green.

Half the trees in the wood have holes up and down their trunk that look like scattered dark eyes. Almost every hole is buzzing with the begging sounds of hidden chicks. As I pick my way across the floor of the wood beneath the holes, sometimes the chicks stop, already schooled in fear; sometimes their pleading increases in volume and intensity, as if they think I have something for them.

On the moor it was windy. But as soon as I get below the tree line the wind becomes music. A timeless tonal roar modulates into something particular to the valley. A green ambush. The hanging trees are arrayed down the hillside like an orchestra, and although almost all are oaks, each sounds a different instrument.

Looking for a wood warbler that I can hear through the leaf shimmer, plying the canopy with its sewing-machine song, I peer up through the oak leaves that are still young enough to be translucent. Being beneath them all, the countless thousands of them, millions even, in just a few trees, is like being held within the skin of the wood.

I hear six singing wood warblers before I finally see one. They are the commonest bird in parts of the wood, but they are hard to spot. From below they are the same colour as the oak leaves. The birds' washed silvery-green underparts match the underside of the new leaves, and their wings shiver like quivering foliage as they sing.

The birds' colour scheme might have been invented in

Scandinavia and it is hard to think of wood warblers spending their winters in equatorial rainforests in Africa, since everything about them speaks of a cool spring day on a steep wooded slope in its first temperate green flush. I think of them as intrinsic to the anciently mild combes of western Britain, and yet their pallor and their music have been forged as much in the coppery earth of the forests of Congo and west Africa.

The males' song seems the same colour as the bird, running silver and clouded green. It is slight and thin but metallically intense. A beautiful descending thread of music, it sounds as if an invisible magician were pulling a silver wire from the bird's throat, like the thin strip of metal in a ten-pound note. The whole bird trembles with the power of its song. Released like wound-up toys, the males pour themselves into an accelerating trill that reverberates to a halt. And then they do the same again. And again. Every time I hear one I miss the fact that they are no longer trembling through the woods on the side of the Avon Gorge.

Below a singing wood warbler is the second of my oak trio. A male pied flycatcher sings from thirty feet up a tree, flitting from one side of the oak to the other. It moves all the time, except for the few seconds of its song phrase, when the muscular effort involved in singing pulls and twists at the bird's whole body so much that it has to stop doing anything else.

Between songs it makes brief flycatching sorties, but always returns to the same branch as if rhyming with itself, like its pied body. I sit at the foot of the tree the flycatcher is singing in and lean against its mossed trunk. The bird sings one phrase of song every ten seconds for minute after minute without stopping. The hunting flights, every four or five songs, do not interrupt the rhythm of his singing. He gets out and back in time. His sound is like the small flat stones on the stream-bed below him being rubbed together, *chiddit chiddit chiddit – drid drid*. As the wood warbler takes on the music of the green leaves around it, the flycatcher breaks open the stones below it, flashing a modest but glittering seam to run through the ore of wood noise. I sit and listen to the same thing for twenty-five minutes. It is beautiful.

In the tree the flycatcher is being clobbered by the wind, but it finds a high bare branch in the sun and it stays there, skimming its stony tune across the waves. I watch him through my telescope, rictal bristles quivering around his beak, his tiny dark eye like a drop of ink, the white blaze dabbed in the middle of his black forehead like a pilgrim's badge, his black back and tail, the white panel on his folded wings. The wind coming at him from behind has got into his white breast feathers, the neatness of the bird has gone. I can see every ruffled feather edge picked out like the teeth of a comb against the deep blue of the sky. Singing all the time, he turns into the wind and the feathers are smoothed instantly. That is beautiful too.

A hundred steps deeper into the wood are more pied flycatchers. The season for this pair is further advanced. Singing has become a secondary activity. The birds' few days of flirting and display are over, when the male in his crisp black and white suit spread himself on a branch, lowered his wings and shook them as he sang, the female, brown to his black, coy but beguiling, allowing herself to be chased through the fresh canopy. All this courtship has been overtaken by the reality of parenting. The male looks now as if he is wearing an old white T-shirt that could do with a wash.

The erotics of the birds' year have shifted. Pairing was musical, mobile and airy. Creation is milky, faecal, and happens in the dark. The pied flycatchers are nesting in a hole about six feet up an oak where a branch has snapped. The tree is in the hanging wood on the steep side of the East Water Valley. Moss, ferns and bracken cover the woodland floor below it, so every angle is softened as if cushions have been scattered. Dark green moss has gathered too in the furrows of the bark that rise around the hole like the sides of a diminutive volcano. The hole is dark and I cannot see inside.

For half an hour in the afternoon, I record the parents' visits. Twice in this time a nestling appears at the hole and looks out, cheeping open its orange gape. Into its tiny head sunlight presses, and so does the green fabric of the wood and the river's noise. I can't tell how many young there might be in the dark hole behind it. The adults are very busy. Between half past three and four o'clock, the male comes eleven times with food, and the female ten. At three forty-three, she comes twice in a minute. At three forty-seven, both adults arrive together and almost collide at the hole. Otherwise, little more than a minute passes without a black beetle, a green caterpillar or a brown grub being brought to the hole and its mouths. Sometimes the birds fly straight at the hole and disappear into it so fast that I am not sure whether the male or female has arrived. Seconds later they bounce out again and perch on the small branch just below the hole, as if gathering themselves, as we might pause on a landing of a staircase, before heading off again, up – always up – towards the treetops and their insects.

Whenever they pause on their branch, I can look into the eyes of the flycatchers and try to read something of their lives. They are always nervous around the nest. At first I stopped too close to it and both birds dithered in the branches above, calling until I retreated. There is always caution in their arrival and vigilance in their departure. When the male sings, as he does twice only in the half-hour, it is some way from the hole, much higher up the tree. On the branch close to the hole he calls only *tisck tisck*, and so quietly I can hardly make it out through the racket of the woods.

Just before both adults arrive at three forty-seven, the earth spins and the wind jostles the leaves above the nesting tree to allow the sun for a few seconds to fall directly on the hole. Think of it now. It is May. Picture this green oak wood in south-west England on a blue afternoon; glide over it. Come down from the warm air above the curved crowns of the trees where the buzzards go back and forth, twist through the branches thrashing with leaves to this trunk limed with moss, and fly at the dark hole in the dappled under-storey. In the time it has taken you to read this paragraph, one of the two birds, perhaps both, will have done this. If it is a May afternoon they will be doing it now. If it isn't, think of these three birds, the male and female pied flycatchers and the one chick that I could see looking out into its new world. Where are they now? Roosting in that same hole for the brief dark of a summer's night; drifting south through the combes of Devon in August; pushing north through the olive groves of coastal Portugal in March; battling rain to flycatch from an acacia in Nigeria in November; shaking the salt that has dried on their feathers from the sea spray of Biscay in April; dropping quietly from the moist night air of Exmoor back to the same trees they hatched from this May, last May, next May.

Perhaps not. Perhaps there is nothing. Carrion crows have come off the moor into the wood sensing egg yolk and chick meat. They move with exaggerated quietness and stealth through branches and leaves that are too crowded for them. Maybe moments after I stop watching, this nestling flycatcher is gobbled up or hoicked out of its hole to be stuffed down another's gape. Maybe the male flycatcher sickens and dies a day later, leaving the female unable to feed her chicks alone and the nest becomes a tomb. Maybe she will drop dead this autumn in the oven heat of the Sahara, the tiny barbs of her mild brown feathers cracking down into grains of bird sand.

I struggle to imagine beginnings and endings in the soft plenitude of a wood fully occupied with breeding birds. To say an animal has no consciousness of its coming death is surely true, but it doesn't say enough for me. The flycatchers' darkly quizzical and anxious eyes seem already to have seen it all. Auden's lines, addressed by Prospero to Ariel in *The Sea and the Mirror*, come to me as I watch the birds:

> . . . At once from your calm eyes,
> With their lucid proof of apprehension and disorder,
> All we are not stares back at what we are . . .

An hour later, after walking out of the wood towards the moor, I come off the hill and back into the trees higher up the valley, where the oaks are more scattered and open than down towards the river. This straggly edge of the wood is appealing to redstarts, the last of my trinity. The redstart, the wood warbler and the pied flycatcher – each sings; all are migrants and carry other places with them, each of them in this English wood was in Africa a month or so ago; each makes the scene without stealing it.

Sure enough, I hear a *hooeet* and catch a delicious blur of rust – a female redstart. Her red tail shimmers like the disturbed leaf-mould she is picking through on the floor of the wood. She flies and I lose her. Then a few trees away, she calls again softly. I follow her cautious movement through the branches until she heads straight at the trunk of an oak and in a single action, without stopping, she folds her wings and disappears into a small black hole in the armpit of a branch.

Within minutes I hear eight more redstarts, including two singing males. Redstart song is a dry half trill; it starts up over and over and, since it never quite finishes or resolves, it continues to shimmer like their tails. Others are calling, the wood is full of *hooeets* and the thick but quieter *tuck tuck* (like a robin's *tick* only fatter) that follow. The birds are scared and calling because crows are here too; at this edge of the trees where they can move more easily, they are bolder. Redstarts are easily agitated birds; appropriately, the verb *startle* derives from the same root as the *start* of their name. John Clare knew this. He called them fire-tails (the name is also accurate and beautiful) and his sonnet 'The Firetails Nest' ends with a couplet that Clare could have written standing next to me in Horner Wood:

> Of everything that stirs she dreameth wrong
> And pipes her 'tweet tut' fears the whole day long

I find another nest easily; if I could, surely a crow could too. In a topless birch, a trunk snapped off at about eight feet from the ground, is a large cavity shaped like a giant's keyhole or a map of Africa. The trunk is rotting and a winter woodpecker has feasted on grubs and wood pulp and hollowed it out. A redstart shows what he's inherited. Fire is the essence of the male in spring. His back and head are ashy grey, his breast like warm embers, his face black soot, and – best of all – his firetail fans flames of beckoning orange. With a beakful of the smashed wings and broken body armour of a dozen insects, the male bobs and shimmers before leaping into the air, somersaulting over himself and turning into the hole.

I creep round to look at the nest, moving further away before I stop, frightened that the crows will watch me watching the redstarts. A single chick peeps out, its downy head waving four fine feathery flags. The mother arrives; she is the more zealous parent, in my half-hour of watching I see the male visit once only. She perches with one foot on either side of the continent, and then at the broadest point of the Sahel and the Sahara she moves into their hole. If they survive the crows, it is to the open trees of this wide savannah belt of sub-Saharan Africa, south to eastern Congo and Uganda, that she, her chicks and her mate must attempt to go in just a few weeks' time.

It was getting late. I walked down through the woods to the river under more nests. A female great spotted woodpecker carrying food landed on an oak, like a spread fan of playing cards. Her claws, two to the front and two behind on each foot, scratched the trunk and made a drum of the nest, beating out some unique maternal rhythms, drawing her young up towards the disc of light that is the entrance of their hole. They fed and slid back down into the dark and immediately started begging again, panning for food with an electrical *weep weep weep weep weep weep*.

Crossing the river, I could hear a dipper singing. Through the shucking of wet stones came a weird whispered backwards song-thrush song. The bird was midstream on a rock, its feet underwater, the river rushing past it. A dipper is all head; the curves of its neck and back and its short tail are like the water-rounded boulders it stands on. They are the same dark brown too. It bobbed and sang, blinking continuously, its white eyelids flicking like a cataract over its dark eyes, just as the water of the stream broke over the rock it was standing on. I thought of the head of Orpheus', severed but singing as it floated downriver.

A little further on, in a shaded back basin away from the plunge and dive of the river's low waterfalls, a mat made from the excess of spring – leaf casings, cast-off incipient fruits and dashed-down young leaves – had carpeted the water. The home-brew scum was thick enough for a pair of grey wagtails to walk on, picking insects as they went, their clouded yellow rumps and undertail coverts giving off a dusty shimmer, their dowsing tails pumping constantly, like a grey brush stuck into a pot of yellow powder paint. Their yellow is another colour to add to the wood: a colour like all the others – the dipper's brown, the redstart's tail, the wood warbler's breast-plate pewter, the flycatcher's T-shirt white – colours already in it but which the birds manage to replenish and brighten.

I took a steep twisting path on the other side of the river up through the trees back towards the moor. Everything seemed continuous and overlapping. Honeysuckle climbed through a holly, another holly had a rowan growing from a suppurating branch, a dog rose was woven through a birch, ferns dripped from oak tops. One stretch of the path was paved with flat stones that thrushes used as anvils, and I counted thirty-eight orange snail shells smashed along it. The next stretch was an ant path and among the thousands wending their way, twelve were busy like pall-bearers shifting a comatose beetle towards their larder. Along the next, a newly fledged robin was trying out anting, opening its tail feathers and wings and squirming them into the earth to encourage ants to crawl up and squirt their formic acid, which would kill the lice on its feathers. The last stretch was a sun trap, and an eight-inch slow-worm basked so that I could stroke the dark thin pencilled line that ran the length of its malted brown back. It made me lonely and I realised that I hadn't seen or spoken to anyone all day. The last slow-worm I had seen was one caught by my sons on a Welsh path like this one. Dominic was curious but cautious; Lucian chased it through the bracken. He picked it up, holding on to it even as it severed its own tail, which continued to wriggle on the path for minutes after it was abandoned. Another Orpheus.

By seven in the evening the light had left the bottom of the valley, even in late May. I walked up the twisting track at the speed with which the deep cut below me filled with dark, keeping pace with the glare that marked the retreating line of the sun's reach, moving in and out of dazzle and shadow. As I climbed, I was walking through birdsong. There were singing song thrushes and blackbirds, first above me, then level with me, and then below me. Exquisitely counterpointed in the evening air, these voices sounded as if they were being lowered into the valley on the finest of ropes, to soften the dark for those that remained there when all others appeared to have left.

I got to the top, where the trees finish and the moor begins to rise, and turned and looked back down into the darkening green valleys. The sounds that say you are here, the daytime skyline atmosphere, the radio producer's 'wildtrack', had stilled to nothing. Caves of quiet opened to the surface of the earth. We don't often notice this muting of the day, because we are habitually more concerned with the departure of light. Our ancient night-time fire-making instincts have endured long after we have needed to gather around old embers and fresh coals. The light often makes a scene-stealing fuss over its exit as well. But today was a good day to listen rather than watch: there wasn't much to see, there was no beaten gold, no bruised clouds, the moon wasn't in the sky, and daylight simply thinned to nothing.

The sound dispersed with the light. By nine in the evening, I was able to pinpoint each singer. In the two valleys of East Water and Horner Water and the oak woods between them, I could hear six singing male blackbirds. They made a map of song that I cannot hear anywhere without thinking how right Edward Thomas's 'Adlestrop' is, and how I would send his poem into space if I could, as evidence for anyone out there of our happy entanglement with our planet. Even if you don't remember or know the lines, I defy you (or any Martian we might want to meet) not to get what Thomas is describing as soon as he says it, to feel the authenticity of his perception, the way he has noticed something that anyone might, but which he alone has brought into words, and how there he has shaped its beauty and made something proportionally beautiful.

> And for that minute a blackbird sang
> Close by, and round him, mistier,
> Farther and farther, all the birds
> Of Oxfordshire and Gloucestershire.

The last minutes of birdsong were bewitching. To listen in this way, as the birds stop singing, being able to hold on to the coordinates of the sound, allowed me to fill the dark hill and darker valley with quiet life. Because I had heard them singing, I knew they were there. It was like being at a summer party in a large garden where, as the night goes on, everyone gradually stops talking and just sits in the dark.

The birds made a beautiful concert, an ensemble piece to begin with, giving way to two soloists and their perfect cadenzas. It is very hard not to hear an elegy for the departing day in what they sang, but before the evening became even remotely hackneyed (there being no clichés in nature), there was also a magically transfiguring coda that refused to let the music finish and began it all over again, this time in the key of black.

The song thrush is a diarist and the blackbird a lullaby-singer. The song thrush's song is an account of what has gone on, a record of struggle, hardship, fear, joy and passion. The blackbird knows this – we remember its detonating alarm rattles and its dusk *chinks* and *chooks* – but its singing urge is to smooth, to take the heat out of the day and to lull it to sleep. The song thrush's song is a haw; the blackbird's is a ripe blackberry. Evening blackbird song seems to have more rubato than morning song, more complexity and liquidity. Indeed, older blackbirds are known to sing in the evening more than in the morning – dawn song is likely to be the under-developed repetitive song of younger males, whilst at the end of the day we are hearing the wisdom of years.

In this context, the third song, the nightjar's, is hardly a song at all. As I was preparing to leave for my bed, it started churring behind me and didn't stop. Night had fallen, it said. Fallen, we say, but the nightjar's song on the edge of the moor – like the grasshopper warbler's on the fen and the woodcock's grunts above it last June – seems to have come up out of the earth and brought the night with it. The sun falls and the nightjar's churring rises, like the moon, except this night there wasn't a moon, only a black vibration from deep inside a bird, like a stream of stout pouring from a tap, switched on to run at full pelt instantaneously, switched off equally abruptly. It goes like an engine, yet it is one of the most pre-industrial sounds you can imagine. Its motor is the underworld of the earth.

The nightjar's churr belongs with moth speak and bat talk. It is darkness audible. Where the grasshopper warbler's reels are too high, the nightjar's churr seems too low, surely mostly beyond our hearing. We hear the rippling burr, the hard trill – what Thomas Hardy called the scurr and John Clare the croo – and we can even imitate it. Think of the hell of a road drill. Vibrate your tongue against the roof of your mouth and top teeth. Don't stop. But though we can make the nightjar's sound in our heads, we *feel* it in our chests and register it low in our bodies. Purring inside us are the top notes from a deep shaft of furred bass, whilst somewhere down there is the full nightjar. Gilbert White felt one singing like this when it churred from the roof of a straw 'hermitage' in Selborne where he was drinking tea, it gave a 'sensible vibration to the whole building'.

The nightjar's song, its superbly cryptic feathers and its

nocturnal life remove it from us. But it is still there – singing in the dark and extraordinarily coloured. Imagine the most difficult jigsaw puzzle in the world. It is called A Sleeping Log Dies. It is made from the backs of a nightjar, a woodcock and a grasshopper warbler. The nightjar section is the hardest of all – the hardest to describe and the hardest to do.

This is how the great handbook of European birds, *The Birds of the Western Palearctic*, attempts to capture a nightjar in words – one bird sits still among all these feathers:

Forehead, crown, and nape finely vermiculated pale cream or greyish-white and grey, feathers on central forehead, crown, and nape with black pointed shaft-streaks up to 3–4 mm wide, shaft-streaks narrower towards side of crown and faint or absent on lores or above eye; shaft-streaks on central crown bordered by cinnamon-buff and grey vermiculation; top of head appears buff-brown with bold black streaks on centre, almost uniform pale grey-buff or pale grey on line from lores over eye. Patch in front of eye, sides of head, lower cheeks, and chin narrowly barred or speckled cinnamon-buff and greyish-black; a narrow streak below gape to below eye uniform cream yellow or white; black bristles bordering bill; indistinct half-collar from below and behind ear-coverts to sides of hindneck cream-buff or cream-yellow, boldly spotted black, sometimes extending across hindneck as an indistinct black-and-cinnamon-bared band.

That was a nightjar's head. *The Birds of the Western Palearctic* goes on in this vein for another 160 lines at least. The text is indicative of the whole book. It is the Great Wall of twentieth-century bird literature, eight volumes redundant before they were even finished, a neurotic encyclopedic terminus that erects a barrier in the mind. I prefer another description – one that seems no less evocative of a nightjar. My reading about the birds' diet took me once to a list of moths. Lepidopteran naming struggles as nightjar description does, but the accumulated effect of some of the several thousand marvellous attempts at moth-capture gives me at least an intimation, the *feeling*, of a nightjar. Maybe one is hiding somewhere here among these moths: the beautiful carpet moth, the green carpet moth, the water carpet, the dentated pug, Manchester treble-bar, lunar thorn, the traveller, streamer, welsh wave, dingy shell, common wave, scorched carpet, pigmy footman, magpie, feathered beauty, dotted rustic, toadflax brocade, mullein, heart and dart, uncertain, exile, scarce dagger, cameo, delicate, Hebrew character, stranger, dingy footman, ghost, common swift, goat, lobster, poplar kitten, satellite, brother, northern eggar, heart and club, flame, gothic, feathered ear, white colon, pale shoulder, double kidney, beautiful snout, Berber, Latin, figure of eight, cream wave, festoon.

The moth names are poetic and beautiful and the scientific text is accurate and as clear as it can be, but in the end neither really helps us see the nightjar. Both lists are moving monuments to human ambition – the wonder and challenge of trying to translate what you can see into something you can understand. Both fail. I love the moth names and I love *The Birds of the Western Palearctic*, for 'vermiculation' – a word I have only encountered in these and similar pages of defeat. It describes the wavy lines of colour and patterning that refuse any rigidities or edge and allow the bird to merge with its surroundings. All birds, in this way, are vermiculated; and we are not and can never be.

In July 1969, when I was eight, my father took me on my first organised bird outing: a nightjar evening on Thursley Common, run by the Surrey Bird Club. It was a bizarre and magical night. Had the participants apart from us not been head-scarved ladies and country-suited gents, it would have passed as a happening or an early piece of performance art.

The leader, an elderly man, fully tweeded, bald and with an ex-army jut to his chin, led us through the gloom and between gorse bushes out onto the sparser heath of the common. The night was moonless. We had arrived a little late and had hurried to catch up with the group and join the already moving dark cloud of scarves and shooting sticks. Silently we tagged along, not knowing what was coming.

I had never seen a nightjar, hardly knew what one was. In my *Birds of Britain and Europe* (the only field guide then: Peterson, Mountfort and Hollam, eleventh edition 1967; dedicated 'to our long suffering wives'), the nightjar was lodged at the bottom of plate 46. Above it were the roller and bee-eater and hoopoe, all fabulously Mediterranean with hot aureate colours that were not, even in the late 1960s, permitted in Britain yet, except under licence to the kingfisher. They were the birds I longed to see, but beneath them was a half-bird half-log, looking legless, dozy, drunk even, really legless, with drooping near-closed eyes. The text opposite said: 'Nightjar – "Dead leaf" camouflage above, closely barred below.' That was as much as I knew.

On the common the whispering platoon shuffled to a halt. It began to seem like an episode of *Dad's Army*. At the back, in the dark, we bumped into the stalled tweeds and scarves invisible in front of us, mouthed our apologies, but then fell into a deeper silence as all around us from nowhere and everywhere the heath began to purr. The nightjars were churring their earth song. One had set another off and the common reverberated. Our leader stepped away from the gang of listeners and took a folded hand-kerchief from his breast pocket. He flapped it open and like a surrendering major waved it through the night, a small white flag over his head. Suddenly, right above him, a nightjar was snapping its wings above its body with a feathered whiplash – a male that had been drawn to the white of the handkerchief, and flashed his rival white wing and tail spots right over the head of the bald old man. A bird conjured from the night.

Finding a nightjar's nest is very difficult. John Clare, the best nester north of Zambia, never found one. They don't really make one, simply pushing a scrape into a bare patch of heath soil. You cannot separate the sitting bird from the mess of heather stalks or bracken or pine saplings that it is concealed amongst. The eggs and the nestlings look the same as their surroundings. And in the day they all sleep.

Looking for nightjar nests to help a research project in Breckland, I went out with thirty other people and we tramped for six hours backwards and forwards, beating the ground with canes like a blind army, through heathland, bracken and foxgloves, stumpy leftovers of cropped pine woods and prickly new plantations. Though the area is a stronghold for nightjars, we managed just a single nest. A few yards from me another volunteer flushed a female off two chicks. The bird stumbled up from the ground into the air, her flopping wings feigning injury to distract us, and collapsed a hundred yards away back into some scrawny grass. I didn't see her before she flew and still have never seen the European nightjar on the ground. Because the bird is rare and protected, we weren't allowed to look at the nest, but were led away and shown a photograph of the chicks instead. Their eggshells were removed from the nest to reduce its visibility to predators. Badgers and roe deer have been caught on camera eating nightjar eggs. As a consolation I was allowed to keep a fragment of one of the shells. It is here next to me now. The day the Bastille was stormed, 14 July 1789, Gilbert White was given a clutch of two nightjar eggs, they were 'oblong, dusky, & streaked somewhat in the manner of the plumage of the parent-bird, & were equal in size at each end.' My shell is dusky and streaked too.

I was disappointed not to have seen the bird break from the ground, but something was right, oddly, about that too. Nightjars don't want to be seen in the daytime by anything. I remembered holding the dying rufous-cheeked bird on the sand road in Zambia and seeing its eyes shut against the entire world. It seems I have become a birdwatcher content not to watch birds.

But the same night, we caught a Breckland nightjar in a mist net as it hunted for moths. By torchlight I saw its living black globes for eyes, the bristles around its wide mouth, its moth-slaying moth face, the fabulous tasselled and brocaded smoking jacket it was wearing, its night mufti, the colours of tobacco juice, or a dhurrie trodden into the dusty floor of a shuttered summer house. It was a bird unearthed. And I wanted never to stop looking.

A male, it was ringed and released. For a second the white patches on its wings and tail hung in the air, like moths in a torch beam, and then drifted as if the thin half-light of the moon and night sky couldn't keep up with their brightness. It vanished. There is no keeping these birds. In August 1786 Gilbert White had a young nightjar 'for several days in a cage, & fed it with bread, & milk. It was moping, & mute by day; but, being a night bird, began to be alert as soon as it was dusk, often repeating a little piping note. [I] sent it back to the brakes among which it was first found.'

We walked back through the dark along the sandy tracks of the Brecks. The air stroked our faces. The stars were bright and clean far above us. A woodcock flew over fast, grunting through its open beak. I remembered, years before, watching red-backed shrikes a mile or so away, perhaps the last pair to breed in England. And nightjars came flying around us, calling and flashing their handkerchiefs, and glow-worms lit their 'living lamps', as they did for Andrew Marvell's mowers, along the side of the path, burning green holes in the world, ways out, ways in.

Afterword – Singing

The wild duck startles like a sudden thought

John Clare

When an individual [passenger pigeon] is seen gliding through the woods and close to the observer it passes like a thought, and on trying to see it again the eye searches in vain; the bird is gone.

John James Audubon

In November 1971, when I was ten, a girl kissed me for the first time. I couldn't kiss her back – a mistle thrush got between us.

A cold ragged day had begun without promise. The year had pulled into itself. Light came up but there was no sky, the blank space above looked as if it had been rubbed with a dirty cloth, a worn grey smear pushing over everything. It was Surrey and the weekend and I was bored. Autumn was over, Christmas a long way off.

My mother called me to the front room and pointed through the window. There was a girl standing on the road, at the bottom of our driveway, below the line of bare beech trees, looking up to the house. I knew her – it was Karen – and I knew straight away why she had come, but I wasn't ready. My mother said she had already been there for a while and that I should go out to her. I didn't want to but I did.

I opened the front door, starting down the gravel. It was about a hundred yards to Karen. As I walked I could see her lips moving, her mouth opening and closing. I couldn't hear her because a mistle thrush had started shouting its song from somewhere high up in the trees.

I heard the bird as you might *hear* a lighthouse – a voice on its own, powering away through the wind, a clean brittle shout of far-carrying pure song. It lit all quarters of the sky space with short repeated stabbing notes that made me wince as if it were cold.

Karen had come up through the hundred-acre hangar of trees – the same wood I had walked through holding my song thrush's nest – from where she lived, near our school. She was like a mistle thrush herself – lean, leggy, a little severe, with a short haircut and spectacles – and as I stepped closer, though I still couldn't hear her, her lips moved and she seemed to be singing the thrush's song, as a troubadour might recruit an 'auzel'. Love had brought her here, love of a kind, like the thrush. She and it were working against the season – it was November, the days were still shrinking back, but the bird was lighting the way to spring and Karen wanted to do the same.

I couldn't answer her. I was not even eleven, she was six inches taller than me, and it was all too soon. The thrush had stopped my ears. Karen smiled and tried again. She looked down sweetly to me, her head falling to her chest as if she'd been hung from a hanging tree. She steeled herself and said that she would go if I would let her kiss me.

She leant in and kissed me on the lips. The mistle thrush was directly above us, high up in the broom head of the bare trees. I felt it was singing into my skull, annealing my whole body with its bright white music, heating me up and cooling me down. I followed Karen's eyes as she looked up, and replied with a peck on her cheek; it was all I knew. She turned and as I watched her cross the road and start down the path through the wood, the mistle thrush was still banging on, shouting after her.

The same afternoon my mother, father, sister and I visited a travelling funfair that had stopped on a playing field in a village south of where we lived. At one stall my dad and I tried to throw ping-pong balls into glass bowls. One of his shots went in and we won a goldfish, an inch of orange peel in a clear plastic bag of water. Somehow, at another stall I won a beautiful globed balloon, silver and round like the full moon, and filled with helium. In the car, on the way back, I was happy; Karen and the thrush were somewhere in my mind, but not at the front of it. I played with the balloon, loving its buoyancy, its tug away from me towards the roof of the car, its urge to go, like a dog on a lead. I held the fish in my other hand, turning the bag around it while it stayed still, facing me, unmoving and hanging in its pint of water.

At home, I hurried towards the back door to take my two prizes inside, but as I ran under the washing line in the garden, the string snagged and I instinctively let go to free myself, and in an instant the balloon was released and lifting, the string lurching up, too high already to catch, and worse – I don't remember doing it, but at some point on our journey I had tied the string to the handles of the plastic bag – it took the fish with it. The balloon and fish lifted fast, up over the lawn and the roof of the house, where the wind took possession of them and bumped them across the opening sky, back towards the road, getting higher, not just above our garden any more, but over our neighbours' as well, and higher still, clearing the beech trees where the thrush had sung, the balloon's silver and the swinging gold-fish tiny like a toy, like a cut-out in a paper theatre against the twilight, so small and going, but going on and strongly, away from me.

The palm at the end of the mind,
Beyond the last thought, rises
In the bronze décor.

A gold-feathered bird
Sings in the palm, without human meaning,
Without human feeling, a foreign song.

You know then that it is not the reason
That makes us happy or unhappy.
The bird sings. Its feathers shine.

The palm stands on the edge of space.
The wind moves slowly in the branches.
The bird's fire-fangled feathers dangle down.

Wallace Stevens

Notes and References

Place of publication London unless otherwise stated.

ix   *this running sky* – Philip Larkin, 'If hands could free you, heart', *Collected Poems*, ed. Anthony Thwaite, Marvell Press and Faber and Faber, 1989, p. 294. Hereafter Larkin.

Introduction

1   *these were the first words* – Louis MacNeice, 'All Over Again', *Collected Poems*, ed. Peter McDonald, Faber, 2007, p. 572. Hereafter MacNeice.

5   *Here at the fountain's sliding foot* – Andrew Marvell, 'The Garden', *Andrew Marvell*, ed. Frank Kermode and Keith Walker, Oxford: Oxford University Press, 1990, p. 49. Hereafter Marvell.

June

6   *I will sing of the white birds* – Ezra Pound, 'Cino', *Selected Poems 1908–1969*, Faber, 1977, p. 16.

6   *The seagull has no English* – David Thomson, *The People of the Sea: Celtic Tales of the Seal-Folk*, Edinburgh: Canongate, 2001, p. 81. Hereafter Thomson.

17   *a moribund black-capped petrel* – William Yarrell, *A History of British Birds*, 4th edn, rev. Alfred Newton and Howard Saunders, 1871–4, vol. 4, pp. 8–9. Hereafter Yarrell.

17   *storm petrels caught up in vile weather* – Norman Elkins, *Weather and Bird Behaviour*, T. & A. D. Poyser, 3rd edn, 2004, pp. 216–17.

18   *storm petrels were funnelled into Bridgwater Bay* – E. M. Palmer and D. K. Ballance, *The Birds of Somerset*, Longmans, 1968, p. 46.

July

22   *The full moon glided on* – Samuel Taylor Coleridge, notebook entry, Cumberland, 31 October 1803. Geoffrey Grigson, ed., *The English Year*, Oxford: Oxford University Press, 1984, p. 145.

22   *Rusham Road, 6–7.15 a.m. one thrush hammering away* – Edward Thomas, notebook entry, Balham, London, 8 July 1913. Quoted in Edward Thomas, *Collected Poems*, ed. R. George Thomas, Faber, 2004, p. 213. Hereafter Thomas: *Collected*.

23   *big humming ewer* – Gerard Manley Hopkins, journal entry, Lancashire, 16 June 1873, ed. Gerald Roberts, *Selected Prose*, Oxford: Oxford University Press, 1980, p. 57.

25   *'Reelin' in the Years'* – the first song on side two of Steely Dan's debut album, *Can't Buy A Thrill*, released in 1972.

25   *the poetry of earth* – the opening line from Keats's poem 'On the Grasshopper and Cricket', *John Keats*, ed. Elizabeth Cook, Oxford: Oxford University Press, 1990, p. 53. Hereafter Keats. The poem was written on 30 December 1816.

26   *cockeroades* – see J. H. Gurney, *Early Annals of Ornithology*, H. F. & G. Witherby, 1921, p. 192. Gurney quotes George Owen writing in 1603 on woodcocks in Pembrokeshire: 'Their chief taking is in cockeroades in woods, with nets erected up between two trees, where in cock shoote time (as it is termed) which is the twilight, a little after the breaking of the day, and before the closing of the night, they are taken, sometimes two, three or four at a fall [of the net]. I have myself oftentimes taken six at one fall, and in one roade at an evening taken eighteen...' Hereafter Gurney.

26   *quorr quorr-quoro*PIETZ – Stanley Cramp et al., eds., *Handbook of the Birds of Europe, the Middle East, and North Africa: the Birds of the Western Palearctic*, Oxford: Oxford University Press, 1977–94, vol. 3, p. 454. Hereafter *BWP*.

26   *The woodcock with her long nose* – John Skelton, 'Philip Sparrow', *Selected Poems*, ed. Gerald Hammond, Manchester: Carcanet, 1980, p. 51, l. 459. Hereafter Skelton.

26   *rhynchokinetic* – J. del Hoyo, A. Elliott and J. Sargatal, eds., *Handbook of the Birds of the World*, Barcelona: Lynx Edicions, 1996, vol. 3, p. 466. Hereafter *HBW*.

26   *the writhings of a worm* – Yarrell, vol. 3, p. 329.

26   *eating almost its own body weight* – BWP, vol. 3, p. 449.

27   *entry for woodcock* – *Larousse Gastronomique* (English edn translated from 1984 French edn), Paul Hamlyn, 1997, pp. 1160–1.

28   *a banquet for a new Archbishop of York* – Gurney, p. 87.

28   *Stephyn Percy was paid tuppence* – Gurney, p. 127.

28   *Mr. Richardson of Bramshot shot a woodcock* – Walter Johnson, ed., *Journals of Gilbert White*, George Routledge & Sons, 1931, reprint Cambridge, Mass.: The MIT Press, 1971, pp. 143–4. Hereafter White: *Journals*.

28   *the Flying Scotsman* – Lord Home, *Border Reflections*, Collins, 1979, p. 62. Hereafter Home.

29   *the Reverend J. T. Pine Coffin* – Yarrell, vol. 3, p. 334.

29   *Fair seed-time had my soul* – William Wordsworth, *The Prelude*, the 1805 text, ed. Ernest de Selincourt and rev. Stephen Gill, Oxford: Oxford University Press, 1978, book 1, pp. 9–10, ll. 313–24.

30   *woodcocks settled in the street of St Mary's* – White: *Journals*, pp. 269–70.

30   *impaled on the weathercock* – Yarrell, vol. 3, p. 325.

30   *struggling to prop young between feet* – BWP, vol. 3, p. 453.

31   *woodcock as porter* – Home, p. 58, and Yarrell, vol. 3, pp. 326–8.

37   *edge of the orison* – *John Clare by Himself*, ed. Eric Robinson and David Powell, Manchester: Carcanet, 2002, p. 40.

38   *knot coming and going* – HBW, vol. 3, p. 477.

43   *King John flew his goshawks at cranes* – Gurney, p. 49.

August

44   *We were all day hunting the wren* – quoted in Edward A. Armstrong, *The Wren*, Collins, 1955, p. 5.

44   *now he must hold his hand* – Seamus Heaney, 'St Kevin and the Blackbird', *The Spirit Level*, Faber, 1996, p. 20.

50   *light silver threads* – John James Audubon, 'The Pewee Flycatcher', *The Audubon Reader*, ed. Richard Rhodes, Everyman's Library, 2006, p. 8. Hereafter *Audubon Reader*.

51   *the sweet fruits of poetical despondence* – Jane Austen, *Persuasion*, ed. James Kinsley, Oxford: Oxford University Press, 2004 (first published 1818), p. 72.

September

53   *Herds of reindeer* – the last stanza of W. H. Auden's 'The Fall of Rome', *Collected Poems*, ed. Edward Mendelson, Faber, revised edn, 2007, p. 331. Hereafter Auden. The poem is dated January 1947.

59   *Tracing a memory* – W. S. Merwin, 'Shore Birds', *Selected Poems*, Tarset: Bloodaxe, 2007, p. 159. The poem was first published in 1999.

66   *gyndagooster* – quoted by Hugh MacDiarmid, *The Islands of Scotland*, Batsford, 1939, p. 89.

67   *a hollow place in the rock like a Coffin* – from Coleridge's notebooks, quoted in Richard Holmes, *Coleridge: Early Visions*, Hodder and Stoughton, 1989, p. 304.

69   *wind thrush* – so called in Christopher Merrett's list of British birds, published in 1666, Peter Bircham, *A History of Ornithology*, Collins, 2007, p. 53. Hereafter Bircham.

71   *a favourite with me* – William Eagle Clarke, *Studies in Bird Migration*, London: Gurney and Jackson and Edinburgh: Oliver and Boyd, 1912, vol. 2, p. 133. Hereafter Eagle Clarke.

71   *as it rose from some rough grass* – Eagle Clarke, vol. 2, p. 136.

73   *Poseidon sat at his desk* – Franz Kafka, 'Poseidon', *Descriptions of a Struggle and Other Stories*, trans. Malcolm Pasley, Penguin, 1982, p. 118.

October

75   *Hope, Joy, Youth* – Miss Flite's ('the little crazy old lady' – p. 204) caged birds, Charles Dickens, *Bleak House*, Oxford: Oxford University Press, 1996, p. 217.

75   *No, no, no, no!* – Shakespeare, *King Lear*, V.iii.9–10.

77   *Aristotle thought that the summer redstarts* – see John Buxton, *The Redstart*, Collins, 1950, p. 112. Hereafter Buxton.

78   *In the summer of 1940* – Buxton, p. 1.

78   *the best handwriting* – Peter Marren, *The New Naturalists*, Collins, 2nd edn, 2005, p. 283.

79   *These redstarts . . . I loved* – Buxton, p. 4.

79   *I must be understood* – Buxton, pp. 3–4.

80   *I wish that some naturalist* – Buxton, p. 107.

80   *There is scarcely any point* – Buxton, p. 140.

80   *The notebooks and papers of Buxton* – some of these are held in the Alexander Library at the Edward Grey Institute in Oxford. The letters are in a box file labelled Buxton 5. The letter from Huxley to Buxton is dated 13 January 1948, the one from Fisher to Buxton 11 June 1948.

82   *since it is by this that they recognise* – Buxton, p. 112.

82   *The action is performed so often* – Buxton, pp. 72–3.

83   *The displaying male* – Buxton, p. 30.

83   *Perhaps it would have been better* – Buxton, p. 140.

84   *Fisher approves of John Clare* – James Fisher, *The Shell Bird Book*, Ebury Press and Michael Joseph, 1966, p. 193.

84   *Hullo birds* – Geoffrey Willans and Ronald Searle, *Back in the Jug Agane*, 1959. In the collection *Molesworth*, Penguin, 2000, p. 313.

85   *Nor would I change* – Buxton, p. 140.

85   *Yet even now* – Buxton, p. 139.

86   *negative capability* – John Keats, letter to George and Tom Keats, 21 and 27 December 1817, *Letters, A Selection*, ed. Robert Gittings, Oxford: Oxford University Press, 1977, p. 43. Hereafter Keats: *Letters*.

87   *scientific people and their followers* – Edward Thomas, letter
        to George Bottomley, quoted by Edna Longley in notes
        to Thomas's poem 'The Unknown Bird' in Edward
        Thomas, *The Annotated Collected Poems*, ed. Edna Longley,
        Tarset: Bloodaxe, 2008, p. 183. Hereafter Thomas:
        Annotated.

87   *collection of stuffd birds* – John Clare, Natural History
        Letter III, quoted in *John Clare's Birds*, ed. Eric Robinson
        and Richard Fitter, Oxford: Oxford University Press,
        1982, p. 14. Hereafter *Clare's Birds*.

88   *He clasps the crag* – Alfred Tennyson, 'The Eagle',
        Christopher Ricks, ed., *The New Oxford Book of Victorian
        Verse*, Oxford: Oxford University Press, 1990, p. 19.

90   *poem on a yellowhammer's nest* – John Clare, 'The
        Yellowhammer', *John Clare*, ed. Eric Robinson and David
        Powell, Oxford: Oxford University Press, 1984, p. 417.
        Hereafter Clare.

91   *built of stalks* – H. F. Witherby, F. C. R. Jourdain, N. F.
        Ticehurst and B. W. Tucker, *The Handbook of British Birds*,
        H. F. and G. Witherby, second impression 1943–4, vol.
        1, p. 114.

91   *yellowhammer's eggs* – *Clare's Birds*, p. 14.

91   *out hunting* – Walter Scott described in 'Finding', Guy
        Davenport, *The Geography of the Imagination: Forty Essays*,
        Picador, 1984, p. 365.

92   *letter from D. H. Lawrence* – to Lady Cynthia Asquith
        from Garsington Manor, Oxford, 9(?) November 1915,
        The Collected Letters of D. H. Lawrence, ed. Harry T. Moore,
        Heinemann, 1977, vol. 1, p. 378. 'When I drive across
        this country, with autumn falling and rustling to pieces,
        I am so sad, for my country, for this great wave of civil-
        isation, 2000 years, which is now collapsing, that it is

hard to live. So much beauty and pathos of old things passing away and no new things coming: this house [Garsington Manor] – it is England – my god, it breaks my soul – their England, these shafted windows, the elm trees, the blue distance – the past, the great past, crumbling down, breaking down, not under the force of the coming birds, but under the weight of many exhausted lovely yellow leaves, that drift over the lawn, and over the pond, like the soldiers passing away, into winter and the darkness of winter – no I can't bear it. For the winter stretches ahead, where all vision is lost and all memory dies out.'

92   *Bruno Schulz's* – see 'Birds', a story in the collection *The Street of Crocodiles*, in *The Collected Works of Bruno Schulz*, ed. Jerzy Ficowski, trans. Celina Wieniewska, Picador, 1998.

92   *Ted Hughes's crow poems* – From the Life and Songs of the Crow, Faber, 1974. See also Leonard Baskin's accompanying artwork of testicular corvids.

92   *Joseph Cornell's box constructions* – see Deborah Solomon, *Utopia Parkway: The Life and Work of Joseph Cornell*, Boston: MFA, 1997.

92   *Peter Szöke* – The Unknown Music of Birds/Az Ismeretlen Madárzene, Hungaroton LPX 19347, 1987.

92   *Ian Dury* – 'Billericay Dickie' is the final track on side one of *New Boots and Panties!!*, released in 1977.

92   *Rimbaud kept a list of pigeon names* – see Graham Robb, *Rimbaud*, Picador, 2000, pp. 258–9.

93   *Feather-footed through the plashy fen* – Evelyn Waugh, *Scoop*, Penguin, 1943 (first published 1938), p. 16.

93   *Pisan cantos* – Ezra Pound, *The Pisan Cantos*, ed. Richard Sieburth, New York: New Directions, 2003.

95   *experiments on swallows* – John J. Videler, *Avian Flight*, Oxford: Oxford University Press, 2005, p. 182.

97   *Song thruhes and robins predominated* – R. M. Lockley, *I Know an Island*, George G. Harrap, 1938, pp. 168. Hereafter Lockley.

98   *goose-stepping* and *Dr Shildmacher*– Lockley, p. 176 and p. 172.

98   *Zugunruhe* – Ian Newton, *The Migration Ecology of Birds*, Academic Press, 2008, p. 338. Hereafter Newton.

98   *inkpads* – Newton, p. 37.

99   *letters in code* – John Clare, *Selected Letters*, ed. Mark Storey, Oxford: Oxford University Press, 1990, p. 220.

100   *his son found a nightingale's nest* – *Clare's Birds*, p. 45.

November

102   *Look through my eyes up* – W. S. Graham, 'Enter a Cloud', *New Collected Poems*, ed. Matthew Francis, Faber, 2004, p. 216.

102   *A huge and birdless silence* – 'Next, Please', Larkin, p. 52.

105   *At eleven o'clock* – J. A. Baker, *The Peregrine*, New York: New York Review Books, 2005 (first published 1967), pp. 106–07. Hereafter Baker.

106   *but it is too far* – Baker, p. 120.

106   *crow catchers* – Baker, p. 27.

106   *tramps and gypsies* – Baker, p. 28.

106   *unusual concentration of such nests* – Baker, p. 28.

106   *inhibited by a code of behaviour* – Baker, p. 26.

107   *The odd are always singled out* – Baker, p. 32.

107   *I found myself crouching over the kill* – Baker, p. 95.

107   *a man descending through the trap-door of a loft* – Baker, p. 112.

107   *Imprisoned by horizons* – Baker, p. 170.

111   *extremely abundant* – Herbert C. Playne, *Some Common Birds of the Neighbourhood of Clifton*, J. Baker (Clifton) & Simpkin Marshall (London), 1907. The redstart is described as 'fairly common in the oak trees of Nightingale Valley' of Leigh Woods. I have never seen one there.

December

120   *An Airy Crowd came rushing where he stood* – Virgil's *Aeneid*, translated by John Dryden, ed. Frederick M. Keener, Penguin, 1997, first published 1697, Book 6, p. 159, ll. 422–32.

120   *an alternation of flights and perchings* – William James, *The Principles of Psychology*, New York: Dover, 1950, vol. 1, pp. 243–4.

122   *the Sweet Track* – Oliver Rackham, *Trees and Woodland in the British Landscape*, J. M. Dent, 1983 (1st edn), p. 48, and Phoenix, 1996 (revised edn), p. 37.

122   *thousands, even millions, of starlings* – David K. Ballance, *A History of the Birds of Somerset*, Penryn: Isabelline Books, 2006, p. 310.

128   *myre dromble* – Gurney, p. 183: 'literally it means the sluggish bird of the marshes, but corrupted as it soon became into the shorter name of miredrum, it signifies the bird which drums or booms.'

129   *Shoo aller birds* – *The Idiom of the People*, ed. James Reeves, Mercury House, 1962, p. 76. Hereafter *Idiom*.

129   *Nero's starling* – Pliny the Elder, *Natural History: A Selection*, trans. John F. Healy, Penguin, 2004, p. 147. Pliny also reports a Roman raven, the pet of a shoemaker, that could talk too, but which was killed by another cobbler

for shitting on his shoe, but was then given a funeral of great pomp, 'the draped bier carried on the shoulders of two Ethiopians' (p. 148).

129   *Bobby Tulloch's scientific note on starlings* – see Ian Wallace, *Birdwatching in the Seventies*, Macmillan, 1981, p. 34, and Bobby Tulloch, *Migrations: Travels of a Naturalist*, Kyle Cathie, 1991, p. 3.

130   *Bertolt Brecht* – 'Song of the Flocks of Starlings', *Brecht Poems, Part two 1929–1938*, eds. John Willett and Ralph Manheim, Methuen, 1976, pp. 204–05. The final verse: 'Now we are flying over the plain/In the province of Hunan/We see great nets beneath us and know/Where we have flown to, taking five days:/The plains have waited/The warmth increases and/Our death is certain.'

130   *Rosa Luxemburg* – see John Berger, *Here is Where we Meet*, Bloomsbury, 2005, p. 227: 'Rosa loved birds – particularly the urban starlings who fly en masse above the streets and over the roofs.'

130   *starlings in Dante* – *The Inferno of Dante Alighieri*, trans. Ciaran Carson, Granta, 2002, p. 32, ll. 40–43.

130   *Edward Thomas in France* – Edward Thomas, 'War Diary' in Thomas: *Collected*, p. 165.

130   *starlings flying across Columbus Circle* – Christopher Lever, *Naturalised Birds of the World*, T. & A. D. Poyser, 2005, p. 195.

130   *Rachel Carson* – see *Lost Woods: The Discovered Writing of Rachel Carson*, ed. Linda Lear, Boston: Beacon Press, 1998, p. 24.

130   *starlings detected on a radar screen* – Bircham, p. 308.

131   *abundant excrement* – Gurney, p. 232.

131   *Sterne's caged starling* – Laurence Sterne, *A Sentimental*

Journey and other Writings, ed. Tom Keymer, J. M. Dent, 1994, p. 60.

131 'Starlings!' shouted derisively – Thomson, p. 139.

131 Coleridge keeping starlings in mind – letter to William Godwin, 1802, Samuel Taylor Coleridge: Selected Letters, ed. H. J. Jackson, Oxford: Oxford University Press, 1988, p. 101.

131 watching winter starlings from a coach – Coleridge's Notebooks: A Selection, ed. Seamus Perry, Oxford: Oxford University Press, 2002, p. 39.

132 endorsing summer – Louis MacNeice, 'Nature Notes – Corncrakes', MacNeice, p. 549.

132 sourdine in their throat – Andrew Marvell, 'Upon Appleton House', Marvell, p. 66.

132 the 'brabbling' starling – Skelton, p. 51, l. 461.

133 W. B. Yeats's 'stare' – W. B. Yeats, 'The Stare's Nest by My Window', poem VI of 'Meditations in Time of Civil War', Collected Poems, Macmillan, 1978 (first published 1928), p. 230.

133 John Clare's 'starnels' – 'Autumn evening', Clare, p. 241.

134 a green thought in a green shade – Marvell, p. 48.

135 made me think of Bede – Bede's sparrow is in his Ecclesiastical History of the English People. Wordsworth adapts the idea in his 'Ecclesiastical Sonnet' (XVI) 'Man's life is like a Sparrow ... /Fluttering,/Here did it enter; there, on hasty wing,/Flies out ...' William Wordsworth, The Poems, ed. John O. Hayden, Penguin, 1977, vol. 2, p. 453.

136 if a Sparrow come before my Window – John Keats, letter to Benjamin Bailey, 22 November 1817, Keats: Letters, p. 38.

137 *You acid-blue metallic bird* – D. H. Lawrence, 'The Blue Jay', *The Complete Poems*, eds. Vivian de Solo Pinto and Warren Roberts, Harmondsworth: Penguin, 1980, p. 375.

137 *What birds were they?* – James Joyce, *A Portrait of the Artist as a Young Man*, ed. Seamus Deane, Penguin, 1992 (first published 1914–15), p. 245.

140 *three orange trees* – Antoine de Saint-Exupéry, *Wind, Sand and Stars*, trans. William Rees, Penguin, 2000 (first published 1939), p. 8.

140 *willow warbler* – Newton, pp. 149–50.

141 *290,000 ringed in Britain* – see *The Migration Atlas*, eds. Chris Wernham, Mike Toms, John Marchant, Jacquie Clarke, Gavin Siriwardena & Stephen Baillie, T. & A. D. Poyser, 2002, pp. 465–7.

141 *pendent bed and procreant cradle* – Shakespeare, *Macbeth*, I.vi.9.

145 *birds would like them ready made* – John Clare, 'Childhood', *Selected Poems*, ed. Jonathan Bate, Faber, 2004, p. 108.

145 *birds like to 'nestle'* – 'Autumn Birds', Clare, p. 267.

146 *Tis spring* – 'Birds Nests', Clare, p. 427.

150 *death reigned in every corner* – Daniel Defoe, *A Journal of the Plague Year*, Penguin, 1966 (first published 1722), p. 118. Hereafter Defoe.

150 *drew the horses in* – Defoe, p. 192.

151 *great numbers went out of the world* – Defoe, p. 116.

153 *eating candles* – Frank B. Gill, *Ornithology*, New York: W. H. Freeman, 3rd edn, 2007, p. 171. Hereafter Gill.

153 *looks on at the humans* – HBW, vol. 7, p. 279.

153 *not a genetically deeply embedded* – HBW, vol. 7, p. 280.

157   *writing-desk* – Lewis Carroll, *Alice's Adventures in Wonderland* and *Through the Looking-Glass*, Penguin, 1998, p. 60.

157   *Hoarse with fulfilment* – W. S. Merwin, 'Noah's Raven', *Migration: New and Selected Poems*, Port Townsend: Copper Canyon Press, 2005, p. 84.

157   *sixty-four have been recorded* – Derek Ratcliffe, *The Raven*, T. & A. D. Poyser, 1997, p. 265. 'The oft-repeated statement that the species utters no less than 64 recognisably different calls appears to date from the days of the Roman augurs, to whom they had immense significance.' The raven's name comes from the Old English *hraefn*, from its cry – Gurney, p. 31 and *SOED*.

159   *Goofus Bird* – Jorge Luis Borges, *The Book of Imaginary Beings*, trans. Norman Thomas di Giovanni, Penguin, 1974, p. 69.

162   *like dominoes* – Baker, p. 88.

163   *The raven himself* – Shakespeare, *Macbeth*, I.v.36.

163   *Ye'll sit on his white hause-bane* – 'The Twa Corbies', *The Oxford Book of English Verse*, ed. Christopher Ricks, Oxford: Oxford University Press, 1999, p. 295.

164   *This may appear strange* – Clifford Morsley, *News from the English Countryside*, Harrap, 1979 p. 58.

164   *Molly Bloom was from here* – see James Joyce, *Ulysses* (e.g. Penguin edn, 1992, pp. 932–3). Her memories of the Rock come right at the end of her monologue.

164   *Gilbert White* – like Molly Bloom, White was put in mind of Africa when thinking of Gibraltar – see his Letter XXXIII 1770, *The Natural History of Selborne*, ed. James Fisher, The Cresset Press, 1966, pp. 75–6. Hereafter White.

167   *Roah* – Konrad Lorenz, from an article in *The Countryman*, in *The Bird-Lover's Bedside Book*, ed. R. M. Lockley, The Country Book Club, 1960, p. 26.

168   *Sir Arthur Streeb-Greebling* – aka Peter Cook, 'We're knee-deep in feathers off that part of the coast . . . not a single success in forty years of training.' The internet widely publishes these scripts.

March

169   *The bird is dead* – Shakespeare, *Cymbeline*, IV.ii.247–8.

169   *It was a fine day and K. felt like going for a walk* – Franz Kafka – 'A Dream', *A Country Doctor*, in *The Transformation and Other Stories*, trans. Malcolm Pasley, Penguin, 1992, p. 185.

170   *Birds too have died in great numbers* – see *Bird Observatories in Britain and Ireland*, ed. Roger Durman, Berkhamsted: T. & A. D. Poyser, 1976, p. 38.

174   *Eagle Medicine-Man* – see Edward S. Curtis, *The North American Indian: The Complete Portfolios*, Cologne: Taschen, 1997, p. 185.

176   *Edward Thomas's poem* – 'Birds' Nests', Thomas: *Annotated*, p. 43.

180   *ornithologia* – Bircham, p. 98.

180   *I had no paper* – Buxton, p. 1.

180   *Allan Octavian Hume* – see Michael Walters, *A Concise History of Ornithology*, Christopher Helm, 2003, p. 157. The photograph of Hume on the same page shows a balding man in a wing collar with bushy grey eyebrows and a drooping bird's-nest moustache. It is hard to read the catastrophe anywhere but in his half-closed eyes.

181   'A Collection of Birds' Feet' – Bruce Taggart ('Y.O.C. member'), *Bird Life*, vol. 6, number 4, October–December 1970, p. 117.

182   *Make the boy interested in natural history* – Robert Falcon Scott, *Journals*, ed. Max Jones, Oxford: Oxford University Press, 2005, p. 419.

182   'The Intro and the Outro' – with words by Vivian Stanshall, the first song on side two of *Gorilla* by the Bonzo Dog Doo-Dah Band, released in 1967.

185   *being in the garden at Bockhampton* – Florence Hardy, *The Life of Thomas Hardy*, Studio Editions, 1994. A single volume reprinting both *The Early Life* and *The Later Years*. *The Later Years*, p. 263.

April

186   *An Air that whizzed* – Samuel Taylor Coleridge, 'Aria Spontanea', *Selected Poems*, ed. Richard Holmes, HarperCollins, 1996, p. 257. Hereafter Coleridge. The odd word, *mute*, means bird shit. It comes from the French *émeut* and is first recorded in English in 1575 (*SOED*). Richard Holmes showed me this poem.

186   *Nothing has stirred* – Hugh MacDiarmid, 'On a Raised Beach', *Selected Poems*, eds. Alan Riach and Michael Grieve, Penguin, 1994, p. 178.

189   *new song patterns in their dreams* – Gill, p. 207.

199   *Keats, in his ode to the bird* – 'Ode to a Nightingale', see Keats, pp. 285–8.

201   *John Clare's 'The Progress of Rhyme'* – Clare, pp. 158–9. Lines in this poem are remarkably accurate field notes or transcriptions: 'Wew-wew wew-wew chur-chur chur-chur/Woo-it woo-it – could this be her/Tee-rew Tee-rew

tee-rew- tee-rew/Chew-rit chew-rit – and ever new/Will-will will-will grig-grig grig-grig'.

202   'The Nightingales' – Ivor Gurney, Best Poems and The Book of Five Makings, ed. R. K. R. Thornton and George Walter, Ashington: Mid Northumberland Arts Group and Manchester: Carcanet, 1995, pp. 135–6.

204   he heard them from the toilet – Vladimir Nabokov, Speak, Memory, Penguin, 2000, p. 67.

May

206   There was a tree – sung by Mrs Grace Coles at Enmore, West Somerset, 1906, collected by Cecil Sharp, Idiom, p. 211. The village of Enmore is the site of the first free school in England, founded by John Poole in 1810; perhaps Grace Coles studied there. Poole was the nephew of Thomas Poole of Nether Stowey, the friend of Coleridge and Wordsworth. They might have known the song.

206   Birdsnests is birdsnests – James Joyce, Finnegans Wake, Penguin, 1992, p. 450.

207   everywhere the blue sky belongs to them – S. T. Coleridge, gloss to The Rime of the Ancient Mariner, part IV, l. 263. Coleridge, p. 89.

208   from the mouth of a swift – The Rev. F. O. Morris, British Birds: A Selection from the Original Work, ed. Tony Soper, Spring Books, 1987, p. 78.

208   As if the bow had flown off with the arrow – 'Haymaking', Thomas: Annotated, p. 95.

216   At once from your calm eyes – W. H. Auden, The Sea and the Mirror, Auden, p. 405.

217   the verb startle – see Francesca Greenoak, All the Birds

of the Air: The Names, Lore and Literature of British Birds, Harmondsworth: Penguin, 1981, p. 239.

217   'The Firetails Nest' – Clare, p. 212.

220   *Edward Thomas* – 'Adlestrop', Thomas: *Annotated*, p. 51.

222   *older blackbirds are known to sing in the evening* – David Snow, *A Study of Blackbirds*, British Museum (Natural History), 1958, revised edn 1988, pp. 191–2.

222   *Scurr* – Thomas Hardy in *A Pair of Blue Eyes*. See Joanna Cullen Brown, *Let Me Enjoy the Earth: Thomas Hardy and Nature*, Allison and Busby, 1990, p. 100.

222   *Croo* – *Clare's Birds*, p. 64.

222   *Gilbert White felt one singing* – Letter XXII 1769, White, p. 55.

223   *Forehead, crown, and nape finely vermiculated* – BWP, vol. 4, pp. 633–4.

225   *the nightjar was lodged at the bottom of plate 46* – Roger Peterson, Guy Mountfort and P. A. D. Hollom, *A Field Guide to the Birds of Britain and Europe*, Collins, 11th edn, 1967, p. 181.

227   *two nightjar eggs* – White, *Journals*, p. 338.

227   *a young nightjar* – White, *Journals*, pp. 281–2.

228   *living lamps* – Andrew Marvell, 'The Mower to the Glow-worms', Marvell, p. 43.

Afterword – Singing

229   *The wild duck startles like a sudden thought* – John Clare, 'Autumn Birds', Clare, p. 267.

229   *When an individual is seen gliding through the woods* – *Audubon Reader*, p. 65.

233   *The palm at the end of the mind* – Wallace Stevens, 'Of Mere Being', *Opus Posthumous*, Faber, 1959, pp. 117–18.

Acknowledgements

My deepest thanks are for my father. I couldn't have had a more fortunate beginning as a birdwatcher. My parents gave me my first pair of binoculars when I was seven, and my dad took me birdwatching countless times through my childhood, long after his own interest was exhausted. His patience and enthusiasm were matchless. He bought me most of the books I have cited here, often years before I realised their value, and his tolerance of my requests – taking me and my earnest birdwatching friends out on day trips in atrocious weather, covering my paper round for me for months so I could chase rarities, and driving me across the country many times looking for avocets and nightingales, a black vulture, and a scops owl – made him a perfect dad. That is still the case. My mother was lovingly tolerant of my obsession and my calls upon my father. My sister put up with regular and savage attacks – rabbit punches and Chinese burns – on her back and arms, when she failed my impromptu bird-identification tests. I am sorry, Jenny, though I am sure you are better now on your finches than you would have been.

My own children have been more than kind. A birdwatching dad is dire, but they have sweetly accepted my absences and my erratic driving (frequent stops, reversals and muddy tracks) and bizarre holiday plans (hot Spanish plains, Scottish islands without toilets, birdwatching in Los Angeles). Dominic's comically wilful ornithological ignorance is a regular and happy corrective to my enthusiastic excesses. Lucian is, whether he wants to be one or not, a born naturalist (at Christmas aged six he asked for 'a wolverine, if possible'), and has been great company on many trips, as well as an ace finder of dead things and grabber of the living. Their mother, Stephanie Parker, has been incredibly accommodating to all sorts of my demands, and much else besides; she has helped this book happen more than anyone, without her generosity and support through several hectic years I couldn't have done it. The words here began in many places – one such was a walk with her across Exmoor in early summer more than fifteen years ago, when redstarts, wood warblers and pied flycatchers retook possession of my imagination. In the middle of her (briefly) difficult pregnancy, we walked the Doone Valley as if we were both carrying a glass of water filled to its brim. I won't forget it. She also introduced me to Thomas Tallis. I won't forget that.

Many others have helped me. My writing began thanks to Marybeth Hamilton, who asked me to contribute to the *History Workshop Journal*, and Redmond O'Hanlon, who did the same for the *TLS*. Lavinia Greenlaw and Claire Armitstead helped me on my way in the UK and Eliot Weinberger and Bradford Morrow in the USA. Andrew McNeillie of *Archipelago* has kept me going as I have been writing. Some of the words here first appeared in various forms in the *HWJ*, *Conjunctions* and *Archipelago*. I thank all on those journals.

Mark Cocker, as well as being a superb birder with the sharpest ears around, and a writer of great bird-words, is also brilliant company for dirt tracks in Morocco, dawn treks in Turkey and drenchings on Rum. He is the best possible bird friend. Greg Poole keeps me on my bird toes in Bristol; as well as being the finest bird artist of our time, he is the funniest man to go birdwatching with. Adam Nicolson is the kindest of men, as well as wonderfully stimulating company, and the owner of the most marvellously abandoned laugh on these islands, including his own. A long time ago, through the autumns of the 1970s, Tom Nichols and Antony Merritt let me accompany them on their endless circumnavigations of Chew Valley Lake as they counted ruffs. In part, this book is for them – in those days I couldn't have explained it, but much was being laid down. Tom is a perfect cousin too, and though our designs, also from the 1970s, for the animal-collecting vehicle to be called The Deenick 2000 never left the drawing board ('packaway cages that packaway' etc), I hope he finds some of those dreams in these pages. I also thank Nigel Collar and Martin Jenkins, two one-time colleagues from my short-lived career in the early 1980s as a professional conservationist. Both are more literate and literary than me, but both, in their different deep antipathies to nature writing, kept me from starting this book. Since I couldn't have done it before, I thank them for the drunken arguments that kept me going through the lost years. Paul Dodgson and Ken Arnold have made fun of my birds and me in the friend-liest way imaginable, in Ken's case for nearly thirty years; I love them for it.

At the BBC a friendly and supportive team of colleagues have made it possible to be a radio producer who wants to write. My particular thanks go to Clare McGinn, Kate Chaney and Ali Serle, and to Iain Hunter and Mike Burgess – 'let money and work be as casual in human life as they are in a bird's life – damn it all' was how D. H. Lawrence put it.

Specific thanks go to the following: on the Wash, Peter and Anne Welberry Smith, Richard Coles, and the crew of the Eastern Sea Fisheries *Protector III* patrol boat; at Chew Valley Ringing Group, my trainer Robin Prytherch and the other ringers; on Fair Isle, the skipper of the *Good Shepherd*, Neil

Thompson, the observatory wardens Iain Robertson and Deryk Shaw and their expert teams, and Mark Ward and Adrian Cooper who enlivened my second stay; in Zambia, Ian Bruce-Miller and Emma Bruce-Miller, Lazaro Hamusikili, Kiverness Moto and Collins Moya, Ailsa Green, and the late Major John Colebrook-Robjent and his wife Royce (the Major died as the book was going to press – it was a privilege to have met him); at the Bristol and Gloucestershire Gliding Club, Tim Allen; in the Brecks, Paul Dolman; Helen Macdonald shared her work on John Buxton and her brilliance on all bird things.

Much of the birdwatching in the book was done on my own, some was done in company, all of it was informed by talking to others. For multiple stimulations, on the page and on location, I thank Fraser Harrison, Richard Holmes, Zinovy Zinik, Robert Macfarlane, Jonathan Davidson, Harry Cory Wright and Richard Mabey. Simon Armitage and Paul Farley both came out as birders in the time that I have known them with characteristic and inspirational brilliance and much comedy. Michael Longley and Peter Reading already were great bird poets and remain lodestars. More than anyone, Kathleen Jamie challenged me brilliantly by writing the most original poetry on how we all live in nature; she was also excellent company on various saturated Scottish islands and the tossing boats between them. That the names on this list are not mentioned within my chapters only means I am terrified that all I say has been said before and better by them.

Some people read the entire book or part of it as it came in to land. For their readings, suggestions and encouragements I am deeply grateful to Susannah Clapp, Tessa Hadley, Jeremy Harding, Andrew Motion and Robin Robertson. To have such writers as friends and friendly editors has made me very happy as well as improving my prose beyond measure.

Pat Kavanagh, my agent until her death, was my first reader and without her encouragement and acumen the book wouldn't exist. It is awful and sad that she didn't see the end of what she had started and read only part of the finished work. I will treasure, though, her enthusiasm for what she had read and a shared evening of hopeless birdwatching on Hampstead Heath with shrieking parakeets and screaming swifts and almost nothing else until some exquisite Banyuls rosé came into view. Sarah Ballard, who worked alongside Pat, has taken the book on with wonderful enthusiasm and was exceptionally helpful. Zoë Pagnamenta has guided me brilliantly in this regard into the New World.

Much of this book was assembled and rewritten in a beautiful room at the top of a stone tower at the Santa Maddalena Foundation in the Tuscan countryside. Wild boar hunters in the woods kept me indoors and every morning a green woodpecker stapled my head into place, furiously tapping around the eaves outside. Without them, the instant friendship there of Nayla El Amin and the amazing trusting openness of Beatrice Monti della Corte I would have foundered.

The teams at the Free Press and Jonathan Cape have been extremely good to me. I thank Donna Loffredo and Tim Waller for their patient brilliance with my timetable, my words and me. I met my American editor, Leslie Meredith, for the first time when we had lunch in a smart Manhattan restaurant. I knew everything was going to go well when we skipped coffee, she pulled out her binoculars from her handbag and we headed out into Central Park. She has been enormously helpful and encouraging. Dan Franklin, in the UK, manages to be both everything you want and nothing that you expect in an editor. He has a unique way of being exacting by being generous, so getting the words right for him becomes the most important thing. I hope I have.

I didn't think it was possible to fall in love with a birdwatcher, and I hadn't when I started this book. I began it writing about the impossibility of a shared life. Claire Spottiswoode has changed my mind, my heart, my bird-list, and my world.